Nightwork

Nightwork

Sexuality,
Pleasure, and
Corporate Masculinity
in a Tokyo
Hostess
Club

Anne Allison

The University of Chicago Press
Chicago and London

The University of Chicago Press, Chicago 60637
The University of Chicago Press, Ltd., London
© 1994 by The University of Chicago
All rights reserved. Published 1994
Printed in the United States of America

03 02 01 00 99 98 97 96   4 5

ISBN: 0-226-01485-1 (cloth)
0-226-01487-8 (paper)

Library of Congress Cataloging-in-Publication Data

Allison, Anne, 1950–
    Nightwork : sexuality, pleasure, and corporate masculinity
in a Tokyo hostess club / Anne Allison.
        p.   cm.
Includes bibliographical references and index.
    1. Bars (Drinking establishments)—Japan—Tokyo.   2.
Entertaining—Japan—Tokyo.   3. Male friendship—Japan—
Tokyo.   4. Corporate culture—Japan—Tokyo.   5. Cocktail
servers—Japan—Tokyo.   6. Tokyo (Japan)—Social life and
customs.   I. Title.
GT3415.J3A45   1994
394.1′2′0952135—dc20   93-34877
                                                                CIP

For Adam and David

Contents

Acknowledgments

During the long years I have spent conceiving, executing, and writing up this project, its subject—corporate fraternizing in a Tokyo hostess club—has been often greeted with reactions of bewilderment, bemusement, or even out-and-out rejection. Not quite standard for the field of "Japanology," somewhat unusual in the discipline of anthropology, curiously male-oriented for feminist scholarship, and uncomfortably sexual for serious or easy discussion (for many, I found, both in Japan and the United States, in both academic and nonacademic settings), this study has been frequently treated as controversial at best, and "weird," as my children fear, at worst.

That there have been other reactions to this work I am most grateful, and to those persons who have given me support and encouragement at various stages of the project I would like to give thanks. At the beginning, when I was entertaining the so-called antiwar clause in the Japanese constitution as a subject for doctoral research as a graduate student in anthropology at the University of Chicago, it was Harry Harootunian who dissuaded me and suggested an area in gendered relations instead. When I decided on the topic of corporate entertainment in the nightlife, it was Harry, as a member of my dissertation committee, who guided, supported, and helped shape this study and my ability to carry it through more than any other single person. He has been my mentor, critic, supporter, and friend during this long journey, and my debt to him, in true Japanese fashion, can never be repaid.

Bernie Cohn challenged and sharpened the issues I was pursuing, and to him and the other member of my committee, David Schneider, whose interest and support in my project has been unceasing, I am deeply grateful. Other faculty members and graduate students in the Department of Anthropology were also supportive; in particular, I thank Jean Comaroff, Joyce Canaan, and John Comaroff for their input at various stages of the project. I am also appreciative of the support I received from faculty of the Department of Far Eastern Languages and Civilizations over the years—Bill Sibley, Bernie Silberman, Norma Field, and Tetsuo Najita.

While conducting research in Tokyo, I was greatly assisted by a number of Japanese who were willing to talk to me about issues that others were not and to accept me in the roles of hostess/anthropologist/inquiring foreigner I variously assumed. To the Mama of "Bijo," the hostess club I studied, I am especially indebted. She was gracious and gentle in handling her foreign charge, and because of this acceptance the other Bijo staff—the waiters, piano player, cook, manager, and hostesses—treated me with an openness that enabled my work. To all of them, and to the customers who willingly conversed with me about the very behavior they were engaging in as we spoke, I am thankful. The manager of Bijo was particularly helpful: he guided me as both practitioner and theoretician of hostessing while I was employed at Bijo, and he gave me fifteen hours of intense interviews six years later (1987–88), when I returned to Tokyo for a postdoctoral fellowship. His insights and observations about the *mizu shōbai* and its interconnections of sexuality, maleness, and corporate interest have been invaluable in helping me understand the behaviors I write about in this book. I thank him deeply for his willingness to share this world with me and to speak about it with such forthrightness and clarity.

There were many others in Japan who spoke with me formally and informally, in interview or casual conversation, about various behaviors I touch upon in these pages. To all these people I give my thanks, and particularly to Tomita Kōichi of JASE (The Japanese Association for Sex Education), Narabayashi Yoshi, and Wagatsuma Takeshi. To friends and colleagues I am also indebted. Miriam Silverberg was in Tokyo while I conducted fieldwork, and her humor, friendship, and intellectual support are as valuable to me today as they were then. Steven Platzer was a great resource in helping me think through this project at different stages, make connections—personal and intellectual—to carry it through, and find the wherewithal to enter a hostess club and stay for four months. At the University of Colorado, where I wrote this manuscript, colleagues and students were enthusiastic and indulgent as I rehashed my work during numerous presentations, seminars, class lectures, and dinner conversations. For their patience and support I would like to thank particularly Dennis McGilvray, Paul Shankman, Payson Sheets, Darna Dufour, Margaret Eisenhart, Linda White, Susan Erikson, Sawa Becker, Kate Hartzell, Sarah Makarechian, Nancy Ehrenreich, and Steve Snyder. In day-to-day coping, Mark Balas helped me to rediscover humor and hope at times that were stressful and hard. At all times, Charlie Piot acted as friend, colleague, and support system par excellence. To these two, my gratitude is deep.

In the stages of submission to and copyediting by the University of Chicago Press, I would like to thank Debbie Otterstrom for the weeks she spent typing the manuscript with far greater proficiency than I could have managed. I was much helped by the comments of two anonymous reviewers; one of these read the manuscript particularly closely and suggested its title, and for this attention and the suggestions it generated I am very grateful. I appreciate as well the work of two copyeditors, Michelle Asakawa and Wilma Ebbitt, which has benefited the manuscript's style.

I would like to thank the Japan Foundation for a postdoctoral fellowship that made it possible for me to conduct some of the interviews used in this book. The Department of Far Eastern Languages and Civilizations at the University of Chicago was continuously generous at different points in my graduate studies, providing funds for language study in Japan and for dissertation write-up; granting a postdoctoral fellowship to teach about Japan; and nominating me for the Rikkyō University–University of Chicago joint fellowship that partially supported my fieldwork. I am also grateful to Rikkyō University for the associate student status and scholarship it gave me, which further facilitated my fieldwork.

To my family, I give final thanks. My parents and siblings have always been proud of my work and supportive of its direction, despite the unconventionality of its subject. My children, David and Adam, are unsure of what this book is actually about but have endured with me the years of its production. I express my love for them with this dedication.

Prelude

Four *sarariiman* (white-collar workers) in a large corporation in Tokyo have been asked by their boss to go out drinking after work. Leaving the office about eight o'clock, they first have a light dinner, then head for a place where they can further unwind.[1] As soon as they are seated at a table in the small, dimly lit room, a waiter brings a bottle of scotch, kept at the club in the company's name, and within five minutes of their arrival drinks are poured. Nakajima, the boss, offers a toast, calling on the men to forget their worries and enjoy a well-earned evening of relaxation.

The men sit back and drink up. Looking around, they recognize the marks of an expensive club: imposing furniture, fresh flowers, conspicuous art, a gold phone. And they know that they can expect service as polished as the decor and the accoutrements. The waiters, dressed impeccably in tails, stand ready to attend to their needs—pouring drinks, lighting cigarettes, replenishing bottles of water and buckets of ice, almost without being asked. The provision of a baby-grand piano and a piano player to accompany those who will break out in song when sufficiently drunk is a further sign that the club belongs to a class above clubs which offer only taped music.

The men's attention shifts to the surrounding tables. They see men much like themselves: middle- or higher-level executives, officials, and white-collar workers dressed in dark suits. Most of the groups consist of boss and employees; a few include clients or friends who may bring in some business. In this intimate room, as in a Japanese business office, all can see and be seen, but rarely does communication with other tables exceed the few words of a joke or a brief aside. Instead, members of a group concentrate on each other, maintaining the business connection that circumscribes their relationship.

---

1. The description here is culled from the fieldwork I conducted in 1981 at one hostess club in the Roppongi district of Tokyo. I introduce and describe this club at length in part 1 and call it "Bijo," a pseudonymous name.

1

Now the men try to relax. To cast off the worries and responsibilities stemming from their office roles is their common goal. In the company of coworkers and perhaps clients, the propriety that governs relationships during the workday must be replaced with genial camaraderie. Fidgeting, each man silently downs his first drink, aware that shoptalk is to be avoided and that any mention of his private life—home and marriage—would be inappropriate. Unsure of what to say to achieve common ground, they view the approach of a hostess with relief. With her, they know, there will be conversation in which they can participate simply as men.

The woman, asking politely if she may join them, takes a seat next to the boss, whom she has previously met at the club. Though Nakajima has forgotten her name, she remembers his; and she tells the others that the story about bean stalks that Nakajima told the last time he was here kept her laughing for days. Giggling at the thought of their poker-faced boss telling a joke, the younger men ask the hostess to repeat it. She declines, saying that Nakajima has been remiss about visiting the club of late and that, as punishment, he must repeat the joke. The employees clap their hands in hearty agreement, and Nakajima, reluctantly acceding, repeats the story. The listeners applaud; Nakajima wipes his brow; and the hostess, who orchestrated the whole scene, pours everyone another drink.

Now the atmosphere has warmed up, and the men begin to talk. They ask the hostess her name; she spells out *Emiko* and asks each man how his name is spelled. She tells Yamamoto that she used to have a boyfriend by the same name; the other men suggest that this Yamamoto could charm her as well. Nakajima asks how many boyfriends the hostess currently has; Emiko answers none, because she has been waiting for Nakajima to ask her out. At this last remark, the men advise Emiko to look elsewhere. Their boss is already aging and gray, he demands that everything be done exactly his way, and he is too serious for a free spirit like her. Cuddling up to Nakajima and placing her hand confidently in his, Emiko disagrees: he is distinguished, not old; sure of himself, not selfish; not stuffy, just quiet. Nakajima, in short, would make the perfect lover for a woman like herself, and she can only envy the one he must surely have hidden away in some luxurious apartment. Quiet until now, Nakajima laughs out loud, denying that a man as straight as himself would even know how to go about finding a mistress on his own. At this, however, another in the party declares that such a comment is itself evidence that Nakajima is intimately involved.

All the while, Emiko has been adding ice to the drinks, lighting cigarettes, and refilling the glasses after each swallow of scotch. Sipping a drink that's mostly water, she is the first to notice the Mama's entry into the room and points her out to the four men who are seeing her for the first time. A slender woman of about thirty, the Mama wears her hair in traditional fashion and is robed in a spectacular kimono with perfectly matched accessories. Smiling serenely, she greets the men at a nearby table. Emiko remarks that tonight the Mama looks particularly stunning, and the men reply that the Mama is indeed a *bijin* (beautiful woman), attractive in a traditional Japanese way. Nakajima, looking pleased, admits that the Mama is the reason he brought them all here tonight. Besides being a beauty, she maintains a level of service in her establishment rarely found in clubs today. For example, the Mama sees all guests off personally when they leave the club, sends Nakajima a gift on his birthday, and forbids her hostesses to smoke or eat in front of the customers. This attention is taken to be a measure of the club's elegance as well as the high status of those who entertain or are entertained here.

At this point, the Mama approaches the table, and Emiko relays the compliments of Nakajima and the others. Smiling, she takes Emiko's place beside Nakajima and asks him if he has recovered from the stomach ailment he was complaining of the last time he was here. Nakajima can't even remember having a stomach problem, but the Mama says, admonishing him lightly, that's because he hasn't been here for so long—three months, to be exact. Now that she has seen his healthy face, she adds, she's much relieved. Nakajima appears embarrassed. Emiko, however, gaily summarizes the discussion they've had about Nakajima and passes on the group's conclusion that he undoubtedly has procured a mistress. Smiling enigmatically, the Mama says, "Of course," and, leaning close to him, goes on to say that Nakajima is an attractive man, one with much appeal for a woman such as herself.

After learning the other men's names and asking whether they find her club a nice one, the Mama engages Nakajima in private conversation. Emiko talks nonstop to the others, telling them how much she likes Chinese food, asking for the names of good restaurants, wondering if the guest named Minami eats a lot, and inviting herself out with them one night to a place across town that serves great noodles. Yamamoto suggests that maybe she could go into the food business, since it seems to him she's getting too old for this type of work. Emiko, pulling her blouse out a couple of inches and looking down, retorts that if firm breasts are a measure of a woman's age, she is quite young. The men, laughing loudly, shout that they must be the judge of Emiko's breasts. When one man tries to take a look, Emiko grabs his hand, allows a brief touch, and then demands judgment. "Beautifully firm, right?" Emiko urges. "So firm, you can't be more than ten," comes the reply.

The Mama has been chatting with Nakajima for five or ten minutes. Her hand in his, they have been laughing softly, like lovers on a date. She now turns to the other men at the table and asks who will join her in singing a duet. Nakajima resists, claiming he can't carry a tune. He suggests Tanaka, who sang in a chorus during his high-school years and has even gone abroad on a concert tour. Tanaka tries to pass the task on to Minami, Minami to Yamamoto, Yamamoto to Tsuda, and Tsuda back to Nakajima; but in the end the Mama prevails on Tanaka to get up and sing a song she has selected. The room hushes as the two stand next to the piano, Mama looking coquettishly in her partner's direction but plainly serious and concerned with singing well. When the song is finished, everyone applauds. Those at other tables comment on how well the two have done, and the men of Tanaka's party go on at great length about his brilliant performance. A waiter who snapped a picture of Tanaka and the Mama brings it to the table, along with a flashlight so that Tanaka can see it in the dark room. The photo is passed around, commented on, and lavishly praised until Tanaka finally slips it into his wallet, from which it will be retrieved from time to time throughout the evening.

The Mama sweeps over to praise Tanaka for his fine job and encourages the others to sing too. Each does so by taking a turn at singing alone, and though none has Tanaka's flair, all experience both a sense of relief at having made the effort and a closeness with the others who have also exposed themselves.

An hour has passed since the group first entered the club, and the men have become relaxed and fairly drunk. They exchange stories they all laugh at. Their topics of conversation—brands of liquor, dirty jokes, insults to the boss, Sunday golf—change rapidly and are unlikely to be remembered the next day. For tonight, however, this random talk identifies the participants less as workers than as men who, when enjoying such pleasures as women and drink, behave as equals.

Emiko has been replaced by Yumiko, a gregarious hostess in her early twenties, wearing a low-cut vermilion dress. The men have noticed the size of her breasts and have told her she's a bit pudgy and could stand to lose some weight. A second hostess, Mieko, has been brought over, and while Yumiko holds Tsuda's hand, she cuddles against Nakajima. He tells his hostess that she's pretty and feminine, a woman he'd like to see again. Yumiko flirts with the others, noting that while they are all cute, Tsuda is good-looking enough to be an actor.

Suddenly Nakajima announces to the party that they're leaving. He signals to a waiter for the bill and signs nonchalantly for an amount his company will pay on their monthly account. The Mama, informed of their departure, hurries over, and Yumiko, who's been directed to another table by a gesture from her boss, comes to say good-bye. The guests walk out quickly and are thanked obsequiously by the waiters at the door. Mieko, who had been telling Nakajima that she loves him madly, accompanies them down in the elevator and kisses him on the cheek. The Mama waits with the party until a cab pulls up. She cautions Nakajima to be more careful with his stomach in the future so it won't be another three months before he comes again.

For an hour and twenty minutes at this one club the company has paid approximately 13,000 yen ($65) per man.[2] The price includes a plate of cold bean pods for each man, several bottles of mineral water, a few buckets of ice. No new bottle of scotch has been purchased this evening, so the price of the liquor is not included in the bill. The men go to two more clubs. At one they have some food, at the other only liquor. All the costs, including those for the taxis and the light meal they had eaten before going to the first club, are borne by the company, through Nakajima.

The Mama will call up Nakajima the next day and thank him for his patronage the previous night. If and when their customers return, Yumiko, Emiko, and Mieko will try to greet them by name. The men will pat each other on the back at work the following morning and exclaim about the fine time they had the night before. The wives of these men won't know where their husbands were until past midnight, nor will they ask. The company will pay the club's bill at the end of the month.

This nightlife, this after-work activity, is a fixture of life in Tokyo, particularly among corporate, middle-class men. The question is, What kind of fixture is it? And what does it fix, to what end, and for whom?

2. Monetary equivalents throughout are consistent with the exchange rate at the time I conducted fieldwork; 200¥ = $1. Since that time, prices in Japan have escalated, with the rate as of this writing (August 1992) at about 122Y to the dollar—so the price of the visit described would be about $106.

Introduction

Hostess clubs differ from the other clubs, bars, restaurants, and sex joints in the *mizu shōbai* (literally "water business," the nightlife of urban Japan) by providing hostesses for their customers. While most of the businesses in the *mizu shōbai* have staffs that consist exclusively of women, the role of hostess is distinguishable from that of the others: the singer in jazz or chanson clubs; the singer who sings naked (*no-pun karaoke*); the waitress in bars, pubs, "snacks," restaurants; the waitress who waits tables without underpants on (*no-pan kissa*); the "soap girl," who soaps up men and performs sex acts (*so-pu* = soap or soaplands); the "girl" who gives "assisted masturbation" and oral sex (*pinku saron*); the model who poses half-naked (*nozoki* = Peeping Tom clubs); and the Mama, who manages and often owns her own "snacks," bar, or hostess club.[1]

Precisely what kind of service is given at a hostess club and by what kind of woman depends somewhat on the individual club, particularly on its prices and its degree of classiness. Four factors, however, are universal: the hostess must be, or must act like, a woman;[2] the hostess must treat the

---

1. *No-pan* means literally "no panties." *Karaoke* (literally "empty orchestra") refers to a cassette system that provides accompaniment for customers who sing their favorite songs into a microphone. Many bars and clubs have *karaoke; no-pan karaoke* are clubs that provide the service of women wearing no underpants, who will sing duets with customers at the front of the room. *Kissa* is the abbreviation of *kissaten,* "coffeehouses." *No-pan kissa* are *kissaten* that offer a limited menu, served by waitresses wearing no underpants. Customers are generally forbidden either to touch or to talk with these women. Soaplands are probably the most common place for prostitution in Japan. Once called *toruko,* their name was changed when the Turkish Embassy protested the reference. Several services are usually offered by *pinku saron:* fellatio, "assisted masturbation," and other sex acts. For a recent account of a *pinku saron* and profiles of women who work in them, see Kakinuma 1992.

2. What it is to be or act like a woman is one of the main subjects of this book. Here, using Butler's notion of gender as performance (1990), I am simply pointing out that a hostess must be willing to assume a type of public and performative stance that is gendered as "female." Far less important is the anatomy of the hostess or even her sexual preference as acted on outside the club.

customer as a superior and tend to his various desires; the service, while alluding to sex, cannot proceed to genital penetration or oral sex; and the service is conducted primarily at the level of conversation. In short, what characterizes the hostess and differentiates her service from that offered by others in the *mizu shōbai* is that her medium of service is primarily talk. The job of the hostess, as both speaker and listener, is to make customers feel special, at ease, and indulged. Or, as one Japanese man told me, the role of the hostess is to make a man "feel like a man."

In practice, how a hostess serves customers comes down to something like this. The club is ranked high—an exclusive club in Akasaka or the Ginza—and the room is small, seating only thirty customers. The Mama, who owns and runs the club, is an elegant older woman. She has five hostesses working for her, all under the age of twenty-three, all beautiful, refined, well educated, and exquisitely dressed. When men come in, they are seated at a table by a waiter and then joined by one or two hostesses, perhaps those they have requested. The women light their cigarettes and keep their glasses filled, meanwhile maintaining a conversation that engages the men and flatters their egos. The hostesses are witty and charming, yet also worldly and not beyond the suggestiveness of flirtation, sexual innuendo, and erotic foreplay. They smile and touch the men's hands or arms, but while sexual intimacy may be implied, both their comments and their actions remain guarded and indirect. When the men leave, the hostesses may give them a good-bye kiss on the cheek and ask them to return soon. For this service, the cost per man per hour runs from $300 to $500.

At a club of lesser rank the scenario will differ. The club may be either small or much larger—the huge open room seating hundreds close to the station at Shibuya, for example. The decor is glitzy, the furnishings chosen more for utility than for chic. The atmosphere may be cozy if the club is small, the Mama friendly, and the hostesses familiar to the customer. The service will be personal and the talk suggestive. In a big club the mood will be less intimate and the service more regimented. Once a party sits down, hostesses will immediately appear at the table, lighting the men's cigarettes, serving them drinks, encouraging everyone to sing,[3] and starting a conversation that veers repeatedly into sexual terrain. Periodically, men are allowed to touch or grab at the hostesses' bodies, and a hostess may return a touch

---

3. This system of participatory singing is very common in Japan today and occurs in a variety of establishments in the *mizu shōbai*. At certain places, usually the higher-priced ones, a piano may substitute for the more common *karaoke,* and a piano player will accompany singers.

in kind. The profiles of hostesses who work in lower-ranked clubs are far more varied than those in upper-level clubs. They are more likely to be older, plumper, less educated, less sophisticated, less well dressed, less conventionally beautiful, and certainly more brash. For service in such hostess clubs the price range is from $80 to $120 per customer per hour.

The activity, generically referred to as *settai* when entertaining clients and *tsukiai* when socializing with colleagues, became popular in the period of postwar economic growth, particularly in the years following Japan's astounding spurt of growth in the late 1960s. Within most large companies, there is a specific budget category for entertainment expenses, which are referred to as *settaihi, kōsaihi,* or *settai kōsaihi (hi* means expenses, and *kōsai* is another word for socializing that is only used in business in relation to expenses). The principle of *settai* is to entertain workers and clients at some place away from work—golf course, restaurant, bar, hostess club—as a means of strengthening work or business relations.[4] Big business perceives that corporate entertainment is a means of making itself stronger and more competitive, and therefore corporate expenditures for recreation increase even in years when the economy is depressed or when the real economic growth is lower than expected, as in 1986 (Tabe 1986:1). Belief in its economic value led the Japanese government to endorse the practice with a corporate tax law that, between the years 1954 and 1982, allowed most corporate entertainment to be written off as tax-deductible.

The economic slump of the early 1990s is affecting *settai* even more severely than in the 1980s. It is now most widely used by medium-to-large companies that are financially stable or growing, in businesses relying on trade, investment, or big sales.[5] For these firms, corporate entertainment can consume as much as 5 percent of annual operating expenses, and is considered an "indispensable expense of industrial operations" (Tabe 1986: 204). The biggest spenders are those with the highest national and transnational prestige, such as Mitsuibussan, the trade company that ranks as the top or one of the top *kōsaihi* spenders annually (197). Similarly, those workers who are most frequently entertained on *kōsaihi* are the elite of the corpo-

---

4. There are two kinds of such relationships, those between workers at the same company (a boss taking out his employees, for example) and those between members of one company entertaining a client or potential client from another company. The principle of corporate entertainment is basically the same for both these relationships, I was told, though companies spend more money on intercompany than on intracompany entertaining.

5. According to a ranking of the two hundred top-spending companies of *kōsaihi* issued since 1979 by the magazine *Shūkan Daiyamondo,* the ten biggest spenders are invariably trading companies. Other top spenders are brokerage firms, construction firms, and pharmaceutical businesses (Tabe 1986).

rate working world: the *sarariiman* (literally "salaried man"), who is a male white-collar worker in a prestigious firm. He has achieved such a position by passing the competitive entrance examinations to a top-ranked university and gaining access to an "elite course" open only to those who can succeed in the rigors of "exam hell."[6] For an employee of this caliber, companies will pay as much as $6,000 a year on corporate entertainment. The rationale is double. First, as a perquisite to the work of a *sarariiman,* outings to fancy places are a way of augmenting and glamorizing jobs that, despite their prestige, are often boring and underpaid. Second, as a business ploy, the aim is to bond the worker to his company or the company soliciting his business.

In this book, I will examine a particular arena for company outings—a high-class hostess club that is considered by many to be a highly desirable or even the most desirable site for corporate entertainment. I will describe events of *settai* at a hostess club, link the specifics of these outings to the stated objectives of corporate entertainment, and analyze why, how, and with what various effects this practice of Japanese business is structured through rituals of masculine privilege serviced by women in the role of hostess. My focus is on precisely what takes place in outings doubly marked as work and play, business and entertainment, worker and male, and how these doubled categories—in the context of a corporate practice observed in the early 1980s, and intended for one group of male white-collar workers—construct and condition one another.

The Subject of the Book

In this study, I am motivated by a number of issues in anthropology, gender studies, and feminism as well as by a number of gaps in the study of Japa-

---

6. The Japanese term for the connection between career and educational record is *gakureki shakai* (literally "society of academic record"). What university one attends is the single most important determinant of one's adult career, particularly for a male. Acceptance into a university depends on a single criterion: results on entrance examinations, which are nationally standardized and given once a year. (For a critique of this sytem, see Horio 1988). Those admitted to top-ranked universities are virtually guaranteed graduation and thus prestigious positions afterwards. The positions with most social status are in medicine, law, education, high-ranking departments in the government, and executive posts in big companies. The attraction of becoming a *sarariiman* in a major company is security, for, in practice, only fulltime, white-collar workers in medium to large companies are assured of what, in principle, is a Japanese labor policy—lifetime employment (*nenkō joretsu*). Well-placed *sarariiman* can count on steady promotions, salary increases, and respectable work.

nese culture. The latter is what initiated my research, for as I entered this field as a graduate student in anthropology in the late 1970s, I was struck by the scant attention given three subjects in the literature—sexuality, women, cities. The inclination at the time was to focus on the more traditional, rural, and so-called normative aspects of the culture, those behaviors that could be traced back in time and were thought to define Japanese as culturally distinct. John Embree's village study *Suye Mura* (1939), and Ruth Benedict's totalizing culture study *The Chrysanthemum and the Sword* (1946), were, though outdated, not yet displaced as paradigms for researching Japan. Influenced by moves in anthropology to give our studies of culture a historical dimension and to locate the behaviors of people within relations of power, economics, and institutional policy that are neither static nor reducible to customs adopted by all members of a population, I sought to examine some aspect of Japan that was urban, modern, and an effect of cultural, political, and economic relations. The scholarship on Japan, I might add, has increasingly turned in this direction over the past fifteen years.

Motivated as well to develop the still nascent interest in issues of women and gender in the Japan field, I encountered coincidentally, the subject of the *mizu shōbai*.[7] Japanese, I found, reacted curiously to this topic. On the one hand, their openness about bars, clubs, and sex joints extends to laxness in zoning even explicit sex clubs, frank advertising by call girls in newsmagazines, acceptance on the part of many wives of their husbands' visits to soaplands, and a general cultural indulgence of drinking and drunkenness, particularly for men. Japanese are not prudes or puritans when it comes to matters of sex, drink, and varied kinds of sexual entertainment, all of which are considered "natural" desires for a man. Yet almost no Japanese I mentioned it to thought the *mizu shōbai* was an appropriate topic for anthropological research. Other foci would, they implied, convey a "truer," "better" side of their culture. The *mizu shōbai,* they insisted, was a trivial, insignificant part of the urban landscape. When I would point out that thousands of bars and clubs existed in Japan's cities and that an incredible amount of business was conducted there every night, except perhaps on Sunday, they would still insist that "culturally" the *mizu shōbai* was not a factor at all in the "essence" of Japanese behavior.

Emerging was a very limited concept of culture, one in which Japa-

---

7. Gender, too, has been increasingly addressed by other scholars in recent years; for example, Bernstein 1983; Robertson 1991, 1992; Tamanoi 1991; Imamura 1987; Rosenberger 1991, 1992; Kondo 1990.

neseness—what Japanese do because they are Japanese—was confined to certain institutions, behaviors, and traditions. In this view, the *nihonjinron,* the debate about who and what the Japanese people are, seemed to the Japanese to be reasonably consistent with what constituted the study of Japan in this country. Sexuality fell outside of both and, as such, constituted a type of cultural "other."[8] Indeed, as Japanese scholars either suggested or stated, anything that deals with sex or sexuality (unless the angle is physiology or reproduction) is not suitable for serious scholarship. The *mizu shōbai,* by association, is verboten, and little about it has been studied by Japanese academics. Because of its marginality both in the literature on Japan and in a dominant model of "culture," I decided to pursue some aspect of the *mizu shōbai.* To do so would fill in, at a descriptive, ethnographic level, domains of Japanese life relatively unrecorded. And examining a behavior indulged in by Japanese people, though dismissed ideologically as of no cultural significance, would provide an approach for understanding culture different from that usually taken: not only what people say it is, but also what they say it is not, and how both of these attitudes affect behavior at an everyday level.[9] To borrow a concept from Lacan, I surmised that what is culturally "not" gives form, meaning, and substance to that which culturally "is."[10]

Work

Within the broad parameters of the *mizu shōbai,* I became increasingly interested in two specific behaviors: the use of *mizu shōbai* by big business, and the activity in the class of *mizu shōbai* establishments whose service includes sexual talk—hostess clubs. I learned quickly that these two dimensions of the *mizu shōbai* are intertwined. How deep that intertwinement is, what it

8. This blind spot, like that concerning gender and women, has also begun to be corrected. English scholarship on these subjects includes Smith 1982; Robertson 1991, 1992; Silverberg 1991, 1992; Buckley 1991; and Tamanoi 1991.

9. Again, I'm not alone in approaching cultural issues by way of behavior that some deem to be deviant, subaltern, or marginal. Others whose work on Japan has been similarly directed include Sato 1991; Silverberg 1991, 1992; and Buckley 1991.

10. Lacan speaks, for example, of the relationship between what he calls the Real—"the hard, impenetrable kernel resisting symbolization" (Zizek 1989:169)—and the symbolic—the processes of linguistic and social forms. While the Real is structured in terms of a lack that seemingly opposes and resists society's symbolic, Lacan argues, according to Zizek, that this opposition is illusory. The Real doesn't precede or stand outside the symbolic, but rather is produced by the symbolic *as* its antithesis. As Zizek puts it, "The real is simultaneously presupposed and supposed by the symbolic" (169).

consists of, and how it affects a variety of behaviors (that is, constructions of worker, family, gender, sexuality, national identity) far beyond the narrow borders of the *mizu shōbai* itself became the questions that I devoted my research to and that form the central issues of this book.

Of particular interest to me was the nexus between play and work. Why did businessmen convene at a place like a hostess club, what precisely was it they hoped to accomplish, how were these objectives met by being entertained in the company of a hostess, and were these outings a mere extension of work or a form of pleasure made possible only by work? I investigated these issues by a number of means: (1) I worked in a hostess club for four months. (2) I interviewed a number of Japanese: married men and women; unmarried men and women; *sarariiman* who frequent hostess clubs at company expense and wives of these men; new company employees; managers of various *mizu shōbai* establishments; the Mama and the manager of my club plus many of its customers; researchers of family issues, gender issues, and sex; journalists; a sex counselor; gynecologists—all these I interviewed about issues pertaining to the *mizu shōbai*, its endorsement by big business, and the impact of corporate entertainment on other realms of social life. (3) I gathered, read, and analyzed various materials and the scholarship of Japanese on the above issues. (4) I engaged various works and concepts in analyzing my data, such as Horkheimer and Adorno's essay on the leisure industry (1991), Marcuse's theory of alienated sexuality in societies of late capitalism (1966), Butler's thesis of gender as performative (1990), Silverman's concept of fantasy as dominant fiction (1992), Lacan's essay on the mirror stage (1977), the Comaroffs' model of ideology, culture, and hegemony (1991), and Barthes's concept of the alibi (1972).

What emerged from these various investigations was a recognition of how vague the conception of corporate entertainment is, compared with the actual practice, and how limited the practice, restricted as it is to elite companies and elite male workers. When I asked Japanese to state the objectives of business *settai*, for example, the responses were typically imprecise. The most common answer was that it is important to relax, unwind, let off steam, have a good time, be oneself, become friendly, and to pursue these activities in the company of fellow workers, one's boss (or one's employees, depending on the position of the speaker), and business associates. But precisely for whom and for what these opportunities for "opening up" (*uchitokeru*) and "relieving tension" (*kinchō o yurumeru*) are important were matters avoided or addressed only in oblique fashion. One attitude was that the subject is so obvious it "goes without saying" (Barthes 1972:143). A realm of the commonsensical—this is what Barthes calls "myth" (1972:142–45) and the Comaroffs (1991) call "hegemony," referring to aspects of behavior considered so "natural" that their envelopment in or by relations of power and economics is invisible and, in this sense, naturalized. What is a policy of big business as corporate entertainment, in other words, is accepted as a tradition of Japanese culture: a custom of sharing entertainment as a group that is common among groups of all kinds of people in Japan.[11] That it is only certain members of certain groups that entertain at company expense in places such as hostess clubs, however, was a factor of corporate entertainment left unstated or understated by many respondents.

Those who accepted *settai* as only natural tended to frame it in terms of *ningenkankei*—the sets of human relationships which form and weave the Japaneseness of business in Japan. It is *ningenkankei*, I was told, that differentiates work patterns in Japan from those in other societies at a comparable stage of industrialism. Japanese work hard, are loyal to their company, and structure their work relations on a model of family. Workers must consequently feel, or be made to feel, strongly attached to their workplace, and the attachment must be based not on a rational calculation of self-interest but on a warm, "human" connection that is shared with fellow workers. To kindle and rekindle this "humanness" (*ningenmi*) of work relations is the principal aim of corporate entertainment. And the payoff, by this logic, is to worker as well as company: the worker is made to feel more human, and these feelings of humanness build the ties needed between those who work or do business together.

Play

In practice, what is needed in order to realize the objectives of company outings is an environment in which workers can "play" (*asobi*). The word is commonly used to reprimand or encourage anyone appearing to be stiff or serious. Delivered as an imperative (*Asobō!*), it is a directive to engage more enthusiastically in drinking (and behaving as if drunk), singing (in front of the room, at a mike, and to the accompaniment of a piano), talking (of inessential, unimportant, noncontroversial, or ridiculous things), joking (preferably about bawdy or sexual matters), kidding (sizing up, discussing, propositioning the hostess) and flirting (acting as if smitten with her). I was

11. For discussion of group membership in Japan, see Nakane 1970; Benedict 1946; Rohlen 1974, 1989; Aida 1972; Minami 1978; and Tada 1974.

told that it was important for all members of a business party to participate equally in such play at a hostess club and thus to be similarly involved and exposed. All this leads to the opening up and releasing of tension sought for in such an outing and to the trust that is thus established between men who work together or are negotiating a transaction. It is this scene of camaraderie, rather than a discussion of actual business, that can lead to the signing of a contract the next day when months of haggling in an office might not produce that result. It is also this convivial companionship that breaks down the hierarchy of employer-employee relations operative at the office and allows accumulated strain a periodic release.[12]

What role does the hostess play in corporate outings? She is functionally useful: she is what facilitates and expedites the night's event. As phrased by one Japanese woman, the wife of a man who frequented hostess clubs at corporate expense, the hostess provides a useful "service" for the business encounters between men. When asked precisely why or how, she answered vaguely. She had never been to a hostess club herself and didn't know the details, but she assumed that it had something to do with a hostess fixing the drinks and managing the table so that the business between men could proceed unobstructed. Male respondents were more specific. A hostess's skill in keeping men involved in conversation was mentioned most often, and next was her ability to give men a good time. When entertaining, my interviewees said, the host wants and needs his guests to be entertained. But this can be a burdensome task, one that a host is only too happy to transfer to a competent hostess.

Money

Given a functionalistic explanation for corporate entertainment, the hostess's role within it, while desirable, seems hardly necessary.[13] After all, couldn't men relax and open up to one another in a vast range of other

12. It is accepted that when bosses are out drinking with their employees, the latter can treat them with a disrespect and impudence never tolerated at work. This joking can lead to insults and even physical violence, but a good boss is one who will "forget" such slights the next day when back at the office.

13. I use the word *functionalistic* to mean explanations which assume there is a function to a behavior and describe and analyze the behavior in terms of the assumed function. Almost all Japanese that I know of regard corporate entertainment as a practice that fulfills a useful function (and thereby disregard other questions about it, such as whom it benefits, whom it does not benefit, and what other effects it has on, for example, family life, gender constructions, sexual relations, and class).

settings? In principle, high-ranked *sarariiman* in big companies would agree that they could: a cheap *yakitoriya* (a restaurant that sells skewers of meat, fish, and vegetables) or *akachōchin* (a "red lantern pub"—that is, an inexpensive drinking place) could serve just as well as a high-class hostess club or expensive golf course. Yet in practice, the men admitted, *settai* in big companies are held almost exclusively in one of the latter. The reasons, when given, were the cost and (in the case of a hostess club) the women. As related to me by a man who had recently been entertained by a company soliciting his business, clubs are chosen that are not only pricey but that conspicuously display their priciness. In his case, this meant an evening of being taken to three opulent clubs, at each of which the party remained for one hour. For him, a rare critic of the system, the night was unpleasant because just as he was becoming comfortable with a hostess, his host would rush him off to the next club. It was by the expenditure of money alone that his hosts aimed to accomplish their objective—to project their own status as a prestigious firm and to project their esteem for him as a desired client. These intentions were, in fact, accomplished, for the man signed the deal despite the fact that he was less than entertained during his night of entertainment.

In Japan, utilizing money as a symbolic currency in social relations is a practice hardly limited to corporate entertainment. One sees it in the gift of exorbitantly priced fruit—for example, perfect melons that cost as much as $200—and in the presents given during gift-exchange seasons that are chosen almost entirely by a calibration of price (Creighton 1992). Yet the principle—that lavish expenditure at a hostess club underlines the importance of both giver (the company) and receiver (the individual)—seems to contradict that other principle of *settai:* developing human relationships. The latter promises something that is lasting, full, Japanese, and "human"—the fomenting of *ningenkankei,* which members of all groups in Japan depend upon and ritually ignite or reignite in outings. Yet the former is a commodity that is evanescent, an empty form, not uniquely Japanese, and hardly human—a transaction between people through money.

What is the relation between these two facets of corporate entertainment, both mentioned (though rarely at the same time by the same speaker) as critical to its operation? Is money a shorthand for "humanness," or does money displace something human? Is money what purchases the fullness of being human? Is money the sign of the Japanese human—the more money, the more human, the more Japanese the person? The eliteness of *settai* as a practice, of course, undercuts its advertisement of itself as indistinguishable from behavior that is culturally standard for any Japanese group. Corporate entertainment is increasingly a privileged activity for a privileged class of men. Yet exactly what does this privilege purchase? Is it something that is valuable in its exclusivity (which gives its participants greater access to some "essence" of Japaneseness, for example) or something that is symbolically empty and transparent, as experienced by the prospective client who criticized the system?

Marx, of course, has written about the transformation of all "natural relationships into money relationships" (1978:185) during the course of industrialization into capitalism. More recently scholars such as Lukács (1971), Harvey (1989), and Haug (1986) have described the dominance of the commodity form (money being only one of its manifestations) in economies of late capitalism, under which all aspects of life become organized into objects that can be bought and sold on the market. As Haug says, the commodity form encodes a contradiction: the seller is only interested in its exchange-value (price), the buyer in its use-value (its uses). To enhance one's profits, the seller promotes the commodity as if it were full of uses. Increasingly what results are commodities that promise more than they can deliver (the gap between use and exchange value coming down on the side of the exchange)—thus depending on an illusion of benefit which will never fully or even approximately be realized.

> Right from the start, therefore, because of its economic function, the emphasis is on what the use-value *appears* to be—which, in terms of a single sales-act, is liable to be no more than mere illusion. The aesthetics of the commodity in its widest meaning—the sensual appearance and the conception of its use-value—become detached from the object itself. Appearance becomes just as important—and practically more so—than the commodity's being itself. Something that is simply useful but does not appear to be so, will not sell, while something that seems to be useful, will sell. Within the system of buying and selling, the aesthetic illusion—the commodity's promise of use-value—enters the arena as an independent function in selling. (Haug 1986:16–17)

The sites most preferred for *settai*—exclusive golf courses, top-ranked hostess clubs, expensive restaurants—all have two characteristics in common: a high price and an aesthetic perfection that is encoded in the word *service* (*sa-bisu*). In the case of the hostess club where I worked, for example, the furnishings were all exquisite, the maintenance was flawless, the ice buckets were crystal, the waiters wore tuxedos and the Mama expensive kimonos. Like any exclusive spot for leisure and entertainment in Japan, this club sells what Haug refers to as a "sensual appearance"—a beautiful surface and excellent service. Does this sensual appearance, as he suggests, take on a life of its own and come to constitute the primary value of hostess clubs—a commodity of superficial beauty from which any utility, including "human bonding," has been displaced? Certainly there is a contradiction between these two services of the hostess club, and it is one that some customers at Bijo alluded to—a contradiction, to use Barthesian terminology (1972), between a form that is empty (money, image, surface) and a meaning that is full (humanness, Japaneseness, work relations).[14] In my experience at Bijo, I found that customers would often speak for and from both of these positions (though rarely at the same moment)—that nights at hostess clubs were meaningless and empty and that they were engaging and fun (tanoshii).

Sex

At another level, there is a contradiction between the role of money in hostess clubs and the service it advertises—masculine pleasure. The nexus of this contradiction comes in the importance of women to a club's rank. While ranking of hostess clubs is affected by other factors—decor, location, price, level of service—the ultimate determinant is the class of women serving as hostesses.[15] For a club to be top-ranked, the women need to be beautiful, slender, young (no older than in the early twenties), sophisticated (preferably well educated), worldly, and well dressed. As these characteristics are conventionalized in Japan, such women are sexually desirable, yet this very class of desirability makes them, almost by definition, off limits for sex to all but the most wealthy or most powerful men. But despite the limited

14. Customers occasionally spoke of this contradiction in terms of the emptiness of the endless ritual of going out every night to hostess clubs that ultimately had no personal connection with them. In this context, a few men said they longed to be at home with wives and children. A few others said they longed to be doing something else, like pursuing a hobby that would be more fulfilling. By implication, both these alternatives (hobbies, family time) are inhibited by the obligations of work, which include long nights at hostess clubs.

15. For example, the club where I worked—Bijo in the Roppongi district of Tokyo—was considered in every factor except one to be in a top-ranked class. The caliber of the hostesses was such as to bring the rank down, according to Bijo's manager and most of the customers I questioned, to a second tier. But since the ranking system includes about eight ranks, Bijo was rated high-class if not of the highest class.

availability of the hostesses, the people who discussed hostess clubs with me said that the clubs' greatest appeal is the women, because, as it was explained, it's "in a man's nature" to be sexual. In this context, the word used to denote male sexuality was, almost without exception, *sukebei*—one that translates as "lewd, bawdy, lustful, lascivious" (Kenkyusha: 1227) and is a crude rather than refined terminology. It is also a word heard often in the milieu of hostess club talk itself: a man will speak of the breasts of the hostess and refer to himself as a *sukebei*, men will discuss among themselves who in their party is the biggest *sukebei*, and a customer will proposition a hostess while announcing that he is, after all, a *sukebei*.

To a hostess club whose class depends on the refinement of its hostesses come men who describe their sexuality in terms that are basic and crude. What precisely do they gain from interchanges that allude to sexual intercourse, that circle around discussion of body parts and desires, and that simulate an intimacy which promises realization, yet are all confined to the space of the hostess club and the dimension of talk? Some have suggested that this confinement does not register as absolute in the minds of the men. They hope that a woman will actually fall for them and that she will fall for love and not just money. This, of course, is how the hostess behaves, and the higher the class of the club, the more crafted the hostess's performance and the more tailored it is to the particulars of her individual customers. Her aim is to be convincing, covering any signs of relations with other men, invoking various signals to convey that her interest in a customer is special, and telling him that he is extraordinary and unique.

The hostess acts *as if* she were sexually and romantically interested in the man, and since there are always stories of hostesses becoming involved with customers, a man may assume he has a chance. Yet there is a fundamental hitch in this assumption, one that forms a contradiction in the system of hostess clubs itself. This is that as a club increases in rank, the more desirable the women become and the more convincing and personalized their performance as hostess, yet the less likely are they to form sexual liaisons with their customers outside the club. High-ranked hostess clubs may even forbid such alliances and threaten to fire any hostess who is so inclined (as did my hostess club). More to the point, perhaps, is the issue of money. A high-class hostess is an expensive commodity, and corporate entertainment rarely covers the cost of such liaisons.[16] The man himself must foot the bill.

16. In the early 1980s, I was told, the going rate for a classy hostess was 10,000 yen, then about $50. This would be for a sexual encounter in a love hotel, but if a man wanted to pursue

Hostess clubs provide what is commonly recognized and valued as a genderized and (hetero)sexualized service—the company of women who flatter men and imply a possible sexual or romantic intimacy with them. Yet the service stops at the implication—at the foreplay, so to speak, rather than the climax.[17] What precisely is the commodity here? Is it deceptive advertising—a category of what Haug has referred to as "aesthetic illusion"? Do men actually believe the promise suggested by hostesses? Do they not? Does it matter? How does this aspect of hostess clubs connect to those other needs and desires dictated by corporate entertainment—to the building of human relatedness and the display of pecuniary importance?

What seems apparent in terms of this last question is that the utility of the hostess club provided by sexual promise does not depend on fulfillment of that promise—in fact, quite the opposite. Acts culminating in sexual release would seriously disturb the other two agendas of *settai*. The first, achieving collective bonding, is much better served by keeping the woman sexually interesting—so that there is something and someone around to which all the men can bond—yet ultimately out of bounds to any one of them; thus the focus of the evening is kept on the relations the men share rather than on a pairing relationship that would remove a man from the group. The second agenda, displaying conspicuous consumption, is also better met by the service of a high-class woman who, by definition, is off limits or exorbitantly expensive for sex. A more sexually accessible woman would be cheaper in status as well as price, so the hostess capitalizes on her class by stressing her inaccessibility. In doing so, she hopes, of course, to

---

a more extended relationship with such a woman, he'd be required to take her on expensive dates, buy her extravagant gifts, and set her up eventually in a luxurious apartment or condominium.

17. Defining sex or sexuality in terms of acts that culminate in sexual release is, of course, only one of many possible constructions. It is the one Freud adopted for the definition of what he called "normal" adult sexuality: acts of genital intercourse with a gendered other that end in climax (1962:107–8). By this model, which has been dominant and hegemonic, according to such theorists as Foucault (1980) and Marcuse (1966), in Western societies, any sexual form or act that is not heterosexual or does not reach climax is either subsidiary or deviant. It is by this model that "foreplay" acquires its name and status: as an activity that leads up to an act of genital contact and release. In the hostess club, customers would seemingly adopt this model in words and statements indicating their desire to realize sexual contact with a hostess. And it is this desire that is frustrated by sexually provocative talk that will rarely, if ever, end in a genital act. That Japanese men abide this structure of hostess club sexuality so willingly raises the question of whether it is so frustrating after all and, if not, whether hostess club talk isn't "sexual" or whether its "sexuality" is constructed, in fact, along a different model. These issues are explored in part 3.

increase her desirability—desire being that which, as Lacan has argued, is unrealizable.

The sexual service of hostesses operates as a fetish.[18] It is both a presence (the implied promise of sexual access) and an absence (the denial of access), and the simultaneity of these two operations is what makes it a valuable commodity. When either aspect diminishes, the commodity loses its value both to corporations, which purchase it as a business tool, and to the marketers of hostess clubs, who sell it as their product. To quote Haug:

> Sensuality in this context becomes the vehicle of an economic function, the subject and object of an economically functional fascination. Whoever controls the product's appearance can control the fascinated public by appealing to them sensually. (1986:17)

What of that public, however? Are its members such passive dupes of a "functional fascination," or have they, in the case of the hostess club, assessed its operation and clearly seen it for what it is: the come-on without follow-through that suits a business outing? Certainly the latter is what some men suggested. So far as genital release is concerned, hostess clubs are sexless. When a man wants such release, he goes to places that explicitly offer it.[19] As one man explained, there is always the forty-minute set at a *pinku saron*, where a man can stop on the way home after hours spent in hostess-club talk. Why not just go home, one might ask, or has the commodity form so deeply insinuated itself into sex that not exchanging money for it impoverishes the act? This is the case, some men implied—not surprisingly perhaps, for the class of men whose jobs must require that they spend even their evenings where every intimacy is mediated in terms of both money and work. Yet how such men experience the relationship with a paid woman must be understood as well. In the accounts I heard and read, one element was repeated, no matter what type of woman it was or what the nature of her sexual service—narcissistic control. Men said that, by paying, they were relieved of the responsibility of having to be accountable (in whatever sense). This they experienced as a relief and often a pleasure.

In paying money for sex, men are not only buying a commodity but putting themselves into the commodity too. That is, there is a fetishization of subject (man) as much as of object (woman), and the customer is not

18. For his definition of fetish, see Freud 1962:42–43.

19. Kakinuma (1992:68) has called this the ejaculation industry (*shasei sangyō*), referring specifically to *pinku saron;* 150 of such establishments, he says, now operate in Tokyo.

only purchasing one thing or an *other* but is also paying to become one other as well. He seeks to be relieved of his everyday persona—the one to which various expectations are attached—and given a new script in which he plays a different role. In the case of the *pinku saron,* this may be just a man who can sit back and do nothing; in the case of a soapland, it is a man who is the master of a head-to-foot body "massage"; and in the case of the hostess club, it is a man whose every word will be listened to, accepted, and praised. Hostess club service, men said, is a known commodity, a reception that is guaranteed and guaranteed to be only flattering. So while the hostess may not deliver an act of sex, something most of them admitted they still desired, she *will* project an image of the man that is pleasing and potent. The service that is purchased, then, is an eroticization less of the woman than of the man—his projection as a powerful, desirable male.

In the language of Kaja Silverman (1992), this hostess-bred image of men is a fantasy, encouraged and conditioned by the money and power of elite institutions. She argues, following Lacan, that all social existence entails a loss, and fantasy is what we use to compensate for the real "lacks" in our lives. Accordingly, fantasies are "scenarios" or "tableaux" that imagine, as completed, what in reality can only remain fragmented and partial. Fantasy gives form to desire, and imagination to reality, but is itself an impossibility. That is, fantasy posits objects that are "capable of restoring lost wholeness to the subject," and it gives "psychical reality" to these objects which, while not real in a phenomenal sense, "stand in metaphorically for what is sacrificed to meaning—the subject's very 'life'" (Silverman 1992:20).

Certain fantasies, Silverman points out, are politically or economically expedient. These "dominant fictions" are collectivized and institutionalized to suture over the losses subjects have incurred by their membership in certain domains or relations of power. Principally, the image projected is that of a phantasmagorically complete and ideal subject, one that compensates for and thus conceals the demands and expectations placed on real persons as they assume the subjectivity of a social role. It is a dominant fiction of masculine privilege, superiority, and perfection that big business in Japan is purchasing with its endorsement of corporate entertainment for one class and gender of its workers—well-placed *sarariiman.* Only this stratum of employees is so compensated; and as a "perk" to their jobs, company-paid outings to exclusive places become a sign of elitism, indicating what kind of worker doing what kind of work is worthy of ideological and phantasmagorical completion. Other positions and categories of labor—the blue-collar worker or the mother laboring at home, for example—

are not given such institutionalized fictions, paid for as compensatory benefits of their employment. On the other hand, such workers consequently avoid being seduced into mistaking themselves as artificially complete—a fantasy that, managed by big business through the practice of *settai*, not only flatters *sarariiman* but bonds workers ever more closely, completely, and inescapably to their work.

Ideological Convergences

So is corporate entertainment, in the end, more privilege or manipulation? Is it a benefit, exclusive to one class, rank, and gender of worker, that confirms his work status by projecting his phallic desirability, or is it a manipulation that extracts an almost totalizing work commitment by masturbating the ego? Certainly the answer is complicated, and it should not be reduced to an either-or alternative. Indeed, there are Japanese who would take great exception to the very posing of these questions. Scholars such as Tada Michitaro (1974), Aida Yuji (1972), and Minami Hiroshi (1978) have argued that the convergence of play and work, player and worker, exhibited in the corporate behavior of spending evenings and weekends entertaining in the interest of work relations, is unproblematic because it is culturally "Japanese." As Aida has written, this is what a Japanese worker does because he is Japanese and is operating according to a traditional worldview in which the categories of work and play are not rigidly demarcated.

Members of the Frankfurt School, by contrast, have argued that the convergence of play and work and player and worker, supposed and presupposed by the institution of company-paid entertainment, is a feature of any society progressing through the late stages of capitalism. The boundaries between such spheres as private and public, home and work, culture and industry disappear as the result of economic rather than cultural conditions and do so inevitably no matter what culture is involved (Horkheimer and Adorno 1991; Marcuse 1966; Habermas 1989). In the case of Japan there are certainly both economic and cultural factors shaping the conflations at work in corporate entertainment. And these conflations are further complicated by being crosscut and differentially affected by relations of gender, class, race, and power. Because Koreans and *burakumin* are discriminated against in staffing executive positions, for example, they rarely, if ever, participate in exclusive *settai*.

Hostess clubs and golf courses have become so exorbitantly priced in recent years, as a result, in large part, of their use for company entertainment, that individuals can no longer afford them. Nada Inada has observed that the leisure industry (*reja- sangyō*) is the big beneficiary because it can target its fees to the budgets of big companies rather than those of private individuals. He writes further that all individuals are losers in this process because work becomes inextricably linked to the play activities of golf and high-priced drinking (Nada 1992:24). Yet even by this calculation, not everyone "loses" in the same way: while certain workers are denied access to the most desirable forms of commodified play, others have access but must play in a manner that is legitimated or endorsed by their work.

Still, in a society so thoroughly organized by relations of money and work, isn't it the *sarariiman* who is in a position of privilege, a privilege exhibited in the corporate policy of entertaining only this one class and gender of worker in places increasingly off limits to anyone else? It is they, after all, who become the recipients of a high-priced ego massage, a service that other men whose jobs do not include it speak of with envy and lust. A hostess satisfies what is a desire of every man, I was told, a desire for what Yoda (1981) has called *jikokenjiyoku,* which translates awkwardly as the wish to expose oneself and have this self-exposure well received. This is the service a good hostess can give a man by listening to him, encouraging him to express himself, and building him up. These behaviors replace something in the man, Yoda implies, that becomes depleted in the other spheres of his life—mainly home and work, where the weight and obligations of his various roles (husband, father, worker) take their toll. So when what is partly taken away by and at work is partly replaced by a practice endorsed by work, it is a privilege, according to many Japanese men whose own jobs do not include such a regular benefit.

That women are less likely than men to hold this view is hardly surprising. For those who are themselves in the working world, the practice of corporate entertainment is often seen as the sexist policy that it is, one that fosters an attitude of chauvinism in the workplace and excludes women from the activity of networking and status building so important to business. As a gender-based practice, *settai* in places like hostess clubs is a reflection and construction of work as a gender-based role. Women can work but only men can have careers. The assessment of women whose husbands participate routinely in company entertainment is framed in similarly pragmatic and sober terms. Outings may be essential to and for a man's job, but the sacrifices called for from family, wife, and marriage are considerable. Because some husbands are rarely seen at home, domestic life is centered on the mother-child bond. Further, when men whose jobs keep them away at night assume little in the way of responsibilities for children and home, and when women's own career aspirations are obstructed, marriage has little opportunity to be anything but a relationship of expediency.

Finally, what of the men themselves, for whom hostess clubbing is both a legitimate and an expected part of their jobs? How do they relate to, conceptualize, and experience a practice overdetermined by multiple and contradictory meanings: play/work, human-relatedness/ego building, flashy display/friendly relating, duty/privilege, heterosexuality/homosociality, sexual flirtation/sexual frustration? Do they actually believe that hostesses are sincere in their affectionate treatment of customers, that they are motivated to display affection and approval by anything but money and the requirements of their job? The answer seems obvious. The performances of hostesses are too repetitive and formulaic to be anything but a contrivance to insure good business for them, for the hostess club, and for the companies paying so much for their services. Yet, as I came to understand, the principle of hostess club business (in the double sense of a business itself and as a site for the business of big corporations) is neither dependent on a belief in its sincerity nor defeated by recognition of its impersonal basis. Men would "see through" the ploys of hostesses, telling me how boring or artificial they were and how much an encumbrance rather than a pleasure it was to spend nights in the company of such women as a part of one's job. But even these men would readily turn to a hostess only minutes later, laughing, talking, and flirting with them as is customary.

Men "play," in other words, even if they don't believe. Or, to restate this, "play" is not dependent on belief, partly because play is not just play but also work.[20] And it was my impression that as time goes on, as men grow older and as the nights at hostess clubs turn into years, words of protest about hostesses and the artificiality of their performances tend to disappear. The *mizu shōbai* scene then becomes, for better or worse, *the* scene of desire and fantasy—what Abe, the manager at my club, called the *sarariiman's* "bad habit" (*warui kuse*). What men are given, get used to, and eventually come to expect are women who massage their ego and assure them of their masculine worth.

It is also what becomes the site for a desired and imagined subjectivity as men come to recognize themselves in the images created for them by paid hostesses. A system used to extend and accommodate business, in

20. According to Zizek, belief is no longer necessary to sustain an ideological operation in what he calls our "post-ideological" age (1989:33–43).

other words, becomes internalized into the structures of male desire and self-recognition. And it is from both sides of this relationship that a man must disengage at the time of retirement. He stops working and stops the company-paid jaunts to hostess clubs. Two identities, in their interconnectedness, are also stopped: one as *sarariiman* and the other as glorified male— the phallicized self-image bred by hostesses that will be a commodity too expensive for most men to continue to afford. So divested, a man returns to his home, a space in which he has probably been more an absence than a presence during his working years. And it is here, as a retiree, that he must resume or assume a subjectivity, so often satirized in the popular press, as "just" a man.

The Work of the Book

The first half of this book is what anthropologists refer to as ethnography, a description of a particular phenomenon based on various anthropological methods for gathering data. In my case, I decided to conduct research in only one hostess club rather than many, in order to gain an in-depth understanding of the interpersonal dynamics constituting *settai*. In 1981, as a participant as well as an observer, I worked as a hostess for four months at Bijo, a high-class club in the Roppongi section of Tokyo. During that time, all the staff knew of my intentions, as did many of the customers; and most of my material comes from talking with the staff, talking with customers, observing interactions, and interacting myself. My focus was on the relationship(s) between the stated aims of company outings (opening up, relaxing with one another, bonding as fellow workers) and what actually takes place at a site for corporate entertainment—a hostess club.

As I have said, descriptions of real events in a hostess club are almost totally absent in the scholarly literature on Japan, whether in the English language or in Japanese. While more is written on the principles that are assumed or presumed by this corporate practice (male pleasure, *ningenkankei*, belonging to a group), little of it addresses how these principles operate in the sites and behaviors chosen for *settai*. Concentrating at this micro level, my ethnography is divided into three chapters. In chapter 1 I discuss Bijo through the dimensions of space and place—where it is located physically and socially, how it fits in with other spaces (of home and work, for example), how its interior is arranged, and what its visual aesthetics are.

In chapter 2 I describe what men actually do at Bijo, by way of hostess club activities that are highly but not entirely formulaic and standardized:

drinking, singing, joking with each other, speaking to and about the hostesses in a specific *mizu-shōbai* language, and "revealing" themselves through various kinds of anecdotes. In chapter 3 I examine the role and service of Bijo's female attendants (the Mama and the hostesses) in light of the fact that the women are often said to be the reason that men, or the companies they work for, will pay such exorbitant prices to drink their own alcohol in places such as hostess clubs. These services vary both in content and structure and address the men, both collectively and individually. I ask what, descriptively, these behaviors are and how, structurally, they situate men in relationships conducive to business.

A word about my ethnographic style in part 1: I have attempted to make this section as readable and accessible as possible, assuming that many readers who are interested in the phenomenon of company-paid entertainment at hostess clubs will be uninterested in certain debates, theories, and discourses within the discipline of anthropology. For these readers I have tried to give a precise structural outline of what is most crucial in the relationship between hostess clubs and business *settai*. Both the structure and the account I give of the intersection of club and business have been conditioned by a number of factors. These factors are not always explicitly delineated in the text, however. The theoretical issues guiding my description, for example, I lay out in this introduction and in parts 2 and 3. Also, the specific interchanges, conversations, and customers on which descriptions are based are not always as fully documented here as they are in the rest of the book.

In Part 1 my aim was to present certain dimensions of the hostess clubs in as fluid, graphic, and comprehensive a manner as possible. I use stylistic devices—the third person, the present tense, and unidentified persons— that have been challenged in recent critiques of ethnography, for example, Clifford and Marcus (1986). It is for reasons of style and presentation, however, that I adopt these devices in the first part and, for reasons of ethnographic politics (to make visible the ethnographic process and my role as ethnographer), largely abandon them later.

Part 2 addresses a different set of concerns. Standing back from the ethnographic site of a particular hostess club, I ask how Japanese speak about, make sense of, and contextualize the specific practice of corporate entertainment in the *mizu shōbai*. Using three sources of data—interviews with participants in the practice, spouses of participants, managers of hostess clubs and other establishments in the *mizu shōbai*, researchers of related issues; statements or comments by Bijo staff members or clientele made in the course of conversation; and written material by Japanese scholars, journalists, and specialists that focuses on or touches on this practice—I explore the dominant view of *settai* as both legitimate and comprehensible in cultural terms—indeed, as an effect and reflection of the culture. Discursively, this represents an apparent contradiction. While explicit discussion of company-paid jaunts into the *mizu shōbai* is avoided because the content of these events (or their association with the commodified sexuality of the *mizu shōbai*) is regarded as culturally insignificant, the practice is spoken of indirectly and generally by reference to cultural behaviors that ground it as only "natural." It lacks "culture," yet is culturally based.

How Japanese speak of company outings in the *mizu shōbai* in terms of Japaneseness is formulated through a number of overlapping yet distinct cultural categories. Again, none of these specifically addresses the corporate behavior of *settai* (which becomes a de-centered subject as a result); yet each becomes a frame for contextualizing and legitimating this corporate practice. Each of the five chapters in part 2 focuses on one of these categories: Japanese notions of place and identity (chapter 4), Japanese work patterns (chapter 5), the Japanese family and a gendered division of labor rooted in the family (chapter 5), Japanese concepts of play (chapter 6), and the Japanese domain of and for male sexual license (chapter 7). These frames of intersecting, overdetermined Japaneseness are what give cultural meaning to *settai* (for both participants and nonparticipants) and what sanction not only its business operation but also the relations of power, money, desire, gender, and work by which this business operation is organized. Cultural categories, in other words, are the guises and disguises of an economic policy—the props of an ideology. They are discussed in part 2 as a means for understanding the languages by which the ideologization of *settai* can be carried out.

In part 3 I consider the implications of corporate entertainment *as* an ideology. To address the question of what the ideology is, for whom, and with what implications on various subjectivities, relations, and social domains, I return to the ethnographic "thick" of Bijo, and analyze first (chapter 8) how specific interchanges and behaviors structure what is consciously recognized and articulated to be the objectives of company *settai* (bonding, opening up, relaxing, humanizing business relations). I argue that it is the hostess as woman, with a particular construction of *mizu shōbai* femininity, that makes the selection of a hostess club for corporate entertainment so desirable. It is she who through her service, position, and discursive strategies masculinizes the customers, and it is the collectively realized and ritualized masculinity that serves the needs of business *settai*.

Next I consider (chapter 9) how the masculinization assumed and constructed or reconstructed by corporate entertainment operates at a level less conscious or harder to verbalize than that typically used to discuss this practice. By these features, constructs of masculinity that the *mizu shōbai* encodes and business adopts are hegemonic rather than ideological, using the Comaroffs' distinction between ideology as that which can be formulated into conscious language and hegemony as that so "taken for granted" it evades the consciousness of articulation (1991). Questioning this masculine hegemonic in terms of where the sexual and gendered constructs implied in the hostess club come from, I challenge the common argument (as put forth by Ian Buruma [1984] and a number of Japanese scholars) that *mizu shōbai* women serve as mother substitutes for men who find the eroticization of maternality both satisfying and comfortable. I argue that this thesis is too simple and essentialist, reducing the heterosexual and homosocial relations expressed (as well as formed) in the *mizu shōbai* to dynamics of only the family rather than those of work, money, and business at work as well. I suggest instead that what is desirable is not a mother-like woman but a woman who acts maternal yet is not a mother herself. By encoding a split, the *mizu shōbai* woman is a fetish of both presence (motherly indulgence and ego support) and absence (lacking the emotional pull and interminability of real mother-child relationships) on which, I argue, the gendered and heterosexual pleasures of the hostess club rest.

Finally, in chapter 10 I ask what effects the system of playing with fetishized women in hostess clubs at company expense has on both those who are directly involved with the system and those who are not. First, as a material practice, corporate entertainment acts both to exclude certain categories of persons from assuming elite jobs as *sarariiman* and to include *sarariiman* so totally in their jobs that their involvement with home, marriage, and family is restricted. Second, as a practice with symbolic effects, I take an image of impotence commonly used to represent *sarariiman* in the popular press as a commentary on the white-collar worker's relationship to the work/corporate entertainment connection: while enticed by the flatteries of that connection, men are also reduced by a system that pumps them up as super-phallic and sutures this phallicism to their jobs. Corporate life depends on a commensurability between penis (real) and phallus (symbolic) which, as Silverman writes, "calls upon the male subject to see himself, and the female subject to recognize and desire him, only through the mediation of images of an unimpaired masculinity" (1992:42). That this commensurability is artificial is revealed on the body of the *sarariiman himself* (satirized as impotent) at the point of losing or retiring from his job.

I would like to add a brief note about my conducting fieldwork in a hostess club. Some have questioned how the fact that I was different (at the time, I was the only foreign hostess working at Bijo) affected my reception as a hostess. There were many differences about me that were noted: my being an American; an academic, as many knew; an academic interested in hostess clubs, as was known by about a third of the customers. And certainly some men treated me with attitudes quite different from the way they treated the other hostesses, that is, with more apparent curiosity, interest, impersonality, reserve, hesitation, respect, fascination. I have attempted to factor these effects of my own position as ethnographer/hostess into my observations and analyses of Bijo and also to observe and report on as many encounters as possible between customers and other hostesses. Whether my account is nevertheless biased, I must leave to others to judge.

I would like also to comment on how fieldwork affected me as a woman and a feminist. Parts of hostessing were difficult and stressful, mainly because I had to accept the subordinate and sometimes servile position of servicer. Being a novice hostess, I was spared the touching accorded veteran hostesses, yet there were other behaviors I had to accept—constant references to my body, particularly my breasts; sometimes rude or deprecatory remarks; questions about my private life and references to personal matters; and the continual expectation that I would flatter and compliment even insulting men and never counter or protest what they said. Though many of the customers and the interchanges I had with them were pleasant, respectful, and refined, the element of crudity was ever present.

I cannot say that the disagreeableness of some hostess club behavior from the perspective of a woman working in this world has not affected my presentation and analysis of this activity. Yet my aim has not been to write a polemic on the chauvinistic or sexist attitudes of Japanese men in the nightlife or to reduce these behaviors to some essential attribute that is biologically male or universally patriarchal. Rather, in the tradition of such feminists as Linda Williams, who has written on Western pornography (1989), and Kaja Silverman, who examines phallic imagery (and its disruption) in Western film (1992), my objective has been the analysis of a masculinist behavior in terms of its historical, institutional, and ideological background. Consistent with this agenda, too, my aim has been to consider the implications of a phallocentric practice in terms not only of the privileges it accords men but also of the price it extracts from them.

Part One

Ethnography
of a Hostess
Club

1

A Type of Place

The nightlife is defined by Japanese more by what it does than by where it exists. Accordingly, it is not geographically specific and does not occur in only one region of Japan or one section of a particular town. Rather, men recognize the nightlife by the pleasure it promises to deliver. Here customers can escape from the responsibilities that burden them elsewhere—so runs the advertisement, and the message is encoded in the decor, atmosphere, and service offered by bars and clubs.[1]

This sense of distance from the social spheres of one's normal habits is the mark of the *mizu shōbai*, the broadly based service and entertainment industry within which the more specifically male-oriented establishments of the nightlife are set. Literally "the water business," *mizu shōbai* connotes fluidity—an occupation that one can float into and out of without the rigidity required by other forms of employment, and a service that one can enjoy while being freed from duties and responsibilities that matter elsewhere.[2] As in the ubiquitous *kissaten,* the often intimate and luxurious coffee shops where the price of coffee is exorbitant but the service is exquisite, being a customer in the *mizu shōbai* allows not only the taste of a particular luxury but momentary displacement from the mundane world outside.[3]

1. While the nightlife is often associated with definite neighborhoods, and different neighborhoods may be known by their different types and classes of nightlife entertainment (in Tokyo, for example, Kanazawa has the Turkish baths; Asakusa, the prostitutes; Shinjuku, the seedier sex establishments), nightlife per se is not confined to one area even in a city. Though the more pedestrian local establishments tend to be congregated around train stations, even here they are in full view of local residents.

2. Donald Richie (1987) refers to this other form of more rigid life as *katai,* meaning "stiff," to which he finds the *mizu shōbai* operates in contrast.

3. *Kissaten,* as with the regional terrain that is recognized for its distinguishing features, often have a specialty by which they are known. This could be anything such as the use of Limoges china for the coffee cups, tables made out of bottle caps or coasters from around the

It is these distinctions of service that situate the *mizu shōbai* in the broader landscape of Japanese society. They are critical to the operation and meaning of the nightlife, service in this context being symbolized by one gender of servicer—female—and one gender of serviced—male. This is not to say that no women enter the nightlife as customers or that no men enter the nightlife as servicers, but the operative of the nightlife is that of a woman who serves.[4]

The kind of woman who gives the service and the quality of service a woman gives, however, vary greatly. The two extremes are the expensive, refined, and mildly provocative format of the *geisha* or high-class hostess club and the moderately priced, seedy, and overtly sexual enticements of the *pinku saron* or touchy-feely bar. The reasons men choose one type of female service over another also vary: one man only has enough money for a *pinku saron*, another desires the sexual guarantee of a "soapland," a third prefers the voyeuristic distance of a strip show. Those who choose the hostess club, in contrast, do so less out of financial or sexual considerations than for the club's convenient double life as an arena for (male) work and (male) play.

Play and Work for the Businessman

Men go to a hostess club to relax; they also go there on business. Such was the commonest explanation I was given for the existence and popularity of hostess clubs in Japan. Yet the one purpose seems to oppose the other. Work is escaped when one relaxes, for example, and play is defined as being "not work." It is a floating reference (or floating signifier, in Barthes's sense [1972]) between, around, and within these two concepts that ultimately produces and makes meaningful the institution of the hostess club. When relaxation is the essential spoken, work is the essential unspoken of its motivation.

Men will go alone to the hostess club, but much more commonly they go in groups, either as coworkers, or in some way socially related, or in an existing or potential business relation. No matter what the relationship,

---

world, an extensive selection of African or South American coffees, or theme motifs in interior decoration such as Western, South Sea Island, or England.

4. So-called host clubs, where those who service the customers are male and the customers are female, have opened in urban centers such as Tokyo in recent years. Though well-publicized, such clubs remain few because the women who can afford their services are generally limited to the *mizu shōbai* women or wives of extremely wealthy men.

however, most men, when asked, would tell me that they were friends (*to-modachi*). The friendly atmosphere—masculine, egalitarian, and liberating—appears to be the motivation for choosing the hostess club over other forms of nightlife. Here, coworkers can associate on a basis different from that of the hierarchy that operates during the day. And in this setting, men approaching one another for a business deal can learn to trust one another simply as men.

Work thus provides the guise, rationale, and impulse for the hostess club. Employers will take their employees out periodically for a night of drinking and making the rounds of various hostess clubs. The expense is exorbitant and the pleasure for the host perhaps nonexistent, but the social interchange is considered crucial to the sustenance of so-called healthy relations. Why this is so is commonly articulated by Japanese in terms of structure and *communitas*, as these concepts are used by Victor Turner (1969). During the day, work relations are structured by hierarchy and by the accompanying control of expectations and responsibilities. At night, men can obscure and displace this hierarchy by drinking together. At night, in other words, men can become buddies.

When a group of men from the same company come into a hostess club, the highest ranking among them is likely to set the tone with "*Bureikō de ikimashōka?*" (Shall we *bureikō*?). *Bureiko* means a breaking of regimen, courtesy, and demeanor—a release from status and tensions. When status is suspended, the employees are allowed to tell their bosses what they think of them, and the bosses are expected to "forget" everything once back at work. In a similar vein, the employees may be asked for personal or business advice by their supervisors. The relationships, in short, are pseudoegalitarian. And through such relationships, business is sustained in Japan.

It is typically accepted that men working together should go out to a place like the hostess club every so often. It is also acknowledged that business deals must be initiated and cemented within the relaxed atmosphere of such an establishment. Women as well as men explained to me that hostess clubs are "only business"—business in different surroundings, conducted at night, but business all the same.

The Japanese I talked to always coupled the concept of work with the seemingly opposing concept of relaxation. Some Japanese would claim that relaxation was the real purpose of the hostess club. Men work hard, men are always responsible, men must be dutiful both at work and at home, and the nightlife provides the only setting in which they can relax. Here their *honne* (their "true" feelings, intentions, motives, self) can come out, they do not have to worry about anything, they can be whatever or whoever they wish, and they can "rest up" psychologically for the ordeal of living and working.

Choosing the Hostess Club from among Other Places

Answering the need for a space away from work that will encourage both a release *from* work and an extension of the commitment *to* work, the hostess club is theoretically only one of several possibilities. Individual homes, inexpensive pubs, hostessless bars—all are used by groups of workers to "have a good time." What distinguishes the hostess club, and particularly Bijo,[5] is revealed primarily by Bijo's clientele: middle- to high-level white-collar workers, most of them middle-aged (between the ages of forty and sixty-five), with tabs being paid by their companies. Approximately 70 percent arrive in the company of coworkers, usually with an employer or superior as host, and approximately 25 percent more come in a business relationship, with the host entertaining actual or potential clients or customers. Roughly 5 percent come with friends. The business affiliations that predominate are brokerage firms, followed by trading companies and construction firms. Rarely seen at Bijo are professionals, scholars, government employees (unless they are present as guests), and men working in small- to medium-size companies, banks, and blue-collar jobs. Men who are young, alone, or dressed in anything but a suit are infrequent customers. Women are less common still.

Beyond providing a relaxing and convivial atmosphere for its customers, the hostess club offers *a space that is not home.* For a number of reasons, a Japanese home is impractical, inappropriate, or even hostile to either work or social gatherings. First, most homes in Tokyo are located far from business centers and require a lengthy commute. Second, most of the men have wives involved in raising children or, if beyond that stage, unaccustomed to entertaining their husbands' business colleagues at night. Some Japanese men do bring friends or coworkers home after work, but this happens least often when the men have white-collar jobs in large companies and their wives are taking care of children; from the perspective of both the mother and the family, such wives must concentrate their energies on child rearing.

Third, for many Japanese *sarariiman,* home is not the space where they

5. Discussion of the hostess club is based on fieldwork conducted at one hostess club in the area of Roppongi, Tokyo, between the months of June and October of 1981.

can or want to relax. There they are constantly reminded of the problems and responsibilities of being a husband and father. And the demands of work may keep men away from home so much that home lacks the familiar, comfortable appeal that Bijo and other hostess clubs hold for regular cus tomers.

Another appeal is the club's luxury and status. As virtually everyone who enters Bijo does so on a company expense account and for reasons that are at least ostensibly business- or work-related, a connection is made between the money spent, the class of the establishment, and the importance of the client or employee. Bijo has the air of a first-class club. The Mama is gracious, the furnishings are beautiful, and the cost is about $105 (15,000 yen) per person, compared to perhaps three times that at a club on the Ginza or in Akasaka. Despite the fact that the top clubs are much more costly, Bijo has strong appeal.

Finally, the hostess club offers its customers excellent service by concentrating on the people who are doing the entertaining. Bijo is very much a club where the host (in many cases the boss) is the main concern. The piano and piano player will accompany guests as they sing, the hostesses and the Mama will stimulate conversation around the table, and so the "host"—here used in the loosest sense—is free to relax. The men who entertain at Bijo know their party will be satisfied, but they will themselves be spared the responsibility for making the outing a success.

The Spatial Order and Appeal of Bijo

Bijo is located on the top floor of a modern high-rise in the Roppongi area of Tokyo. Situated close to the kōsaten (a crosswalk by which the geography of Roppongi is calculated), it comprises a neighborhood of shops, coffee houses (kissaten), restaurants, discos, bars, and hostess clubs. Roppongi offers, in atmosphere, a mix of the sleaziness of Kabuki-chō (in Shinjuku), the youth of Harajuku, the funkiness of Asakusa, and the expense and elegance of Ginza and Akasaka. Its signs of middle age and respectability are counterbalanced by the glitter and excitement of its many discos.

Bijo, at the time I worked there, was a relatively new club, established about the beginning of 1980. Consisting of two main rooms, a small kitchen, a bathroom, a hallway, and a small receiving closet area, it is of average size for a hostess club. Very large clubs seat two to three hundred people, but most are small, even minuscule, seating a handful of customers and offering a cozy, intimate environment. Bijo is neither so small as to be homey nor so large as to seem strictly commercial. It can accommodate up to forty-five or fifty customers but manages about twenty-five or thirty most comfortably.

A little glitzy by Western standards, Bijo has floors covered in deep carpet, walls hung with Parisian paintings, and a glass wall, etched with butterflies, separating the hallway from the main room. The front door opens into a hallway, with the bathroom and receiving closet off to the right. Straight ahead is the closed door to "A" *shitsu*, the more private area of the club, which contains a velvet booth against the back wall, three small tables, chairs, plants, a painting, a mirrored wall, and the pièce de resistance, a tiered, locked glass table displaying expensive bottles of liquor. Off to the left of the hallway is the main room, "B" *shitsu*, into which most customers are immediately ushered. Approaching, one first sees the red of the baby-grand piano filtered through the glass wall. Obviously the focal point of the club's furnishings, the piano is fitted out with a polished wooden counter and five expensive bar stools. A mirrored wall to the right of the piano reflects the keyboard and the bar's occupants.

Plain, heavy drapes along the left wall of the room cover the club's only window and conceal the outside world. High plush booths, separated by potted plants, line each of the three unmirrored walls. Nearby are small glass tables for individual parties. Facing each booth are several high-backed chairs, stately if not also somewhat cumbersome.

The same heaviness characterizes the room itself, despite its modest size. Even the painting of a young girl is hung so as to command rather than to adorn its surroundings. And even the fresh flowers are intentionally luxurious and are displayed in thick glass vases. Viewed together, the furnishings and decorations of Bijo create a nighttime sanctuary.

The spatial arrangements of Bijo produce a sense of luxury and order that is appreciated by most Japanese. The obviously costly objects themselves—the chairs, tables, vases, and artwork—are chosen with great care and kept in prime condition. The mirrored lavatory is cleaned after each use, the shining gold-plated phone and sparkling glass wall continually polished, the velvet chairs pushed in if they seem to project a few centimeters too far, and the lacquered piano never allowed to retain a single smudge.

Furnishings are not solely responsible for the sense of aesthetic well-being. Also contributing are the service provided by the manager and male waiters; the snacks, drinks, and ice at each table; and, most important, the Mama, owner and ultimate manager of Bijo. Her given name is Tamae-san. When I met her in 1981, she was thirty-three years old and a longtime veteran of the *mizu shōbai*. Trained as a *geisha* (a woman trained to entertain and serve men who is highly skilled in a number of Japanese arts such as dance, singing, and the playing of Japanese instruments), she initially entered the mizu shōbai when she was nineteen and came to manage her first club when still in her early twenties. Her father, a sumō wrestler, and her mother, a woman of the mizu shōbai, apparently never married. For many years the owner of a club in Nagoya, Tamae-san's mother now teaches the samisen (a traditional stringed instrument), adhering to the old association of "night women" as keepers of the arts.

Like her mother, Tamae-san has adopted the self-image of a refined lady of the traditional nightlife. She is always impeccably dressed in beautiful, extremely expensive kimonos; her outfits are subdued but perfectly coordinated, her accessories few but exquisite. She has her hair coiffed daily in the traditional upswept style, and makeup, though heavy, is never extreme. She is often described as a bijin—a beauty of the traditional type—in reference not only to her figure (which is delicate) and her attractive features, but her attitude, style, choice of fashion, and even her singing voice. For Tamae-san, the description serves as recognition of her success as a mizu-shōbai woman. Her "beauty" is that of both refined taste and seductiveness; she keeps her pinky raised and her mouth modestly hidden behind a hand, yet smiles mischievously in a way few wives ever would. Called "Mama" by all the employees and by most of the customers, she is Bijo's principal attraction.

The waiters are in their mid-twenties, slender, handsome, and faultlessly groomed. Like the manager, who is in his late thirties, they always dress in black tuxedo, white shirt, black bow tie, and black shoes—models of elegant correctness.

The manner in which food and drinks are served at Bijo follows a similar style. The care given to the presentation may even overshadow the food, often no more than an insignificant snack—three bean pods, a small mound of peanuts, five or six grapes—elegantly arranged on a beautiful small plate and ritualistically served. The snack often remains untouched by the customer, for to actually consume this dish as if it were intended as food runs counter to the purpose for which it is presented.

Drinks are a somewhat different matter, for imbibing alcohol is the basic activity of the club, and men will drink their liquor no matter how it is served. Still, service as a formal display is important at Bijo: bottles, usually purchased in advance by the company and kept on the premises, are brought out immediately by a waiter and set before the customers with an air of ceremony. The hostess will add ice from crystal buckets to the glasses of guests and fill them with mineral water poured from freshly chilled bottles. Thus, the mundane act of drinking is given a touch of elegance. The bottles of mineral water, silver ice tongs, and cut-glass ice bucket remain on the table, their presence a reminder of the status of the customer and of the faultless service provided by the club.

The customers who frequent Bijo are by no means unique in their appreciation of how things look and how one is served. What is significant, however, is the pattern and logic of a certain visual style, one selected by the club's management and found pleasing by this particular clientele. This logic requires, first of all, a setting that is meant to be seen. A person who walks into Bijo for the first time will be struck by the sumptuous materials and arrangements. The setting itself demands attention.

Another element in the stylistic logic of Bijo's space is the focus on concrete objects: the piano, the painting, the glass partition, the Mama. Of course, there is a general landscape as well—one carried through to the waiters' tuxedos and the three bean pods on a plate; yet articles in and of themselves are central here. The piano is a conspicuous example: its unusual color, its size (large for Japan), its newness, and its glistening sheen make it stand out and take over, particularly in a room where it occupies about one-fourth of the total space. Not selected to blend in with its surroundings, this piano conveys a style and posture all its own.

Actually, for the customers at Bijo, the setting offered by the club's limited space may be simply an exaggerated version of their own homes. These are moneyed men in a country where, since even large amounts of money buy little in terms of land and housing, a person's money is often, more visibly, converted into possessions. As has often been said, the Japanese are devout consumers, and high price can be an attraction to purchase rather than a deterrent. Modern Japanese fill their living space with objects that convey a sense of comfort and well-being. In the case of Bijo, what is to someone from the West a small space crowded with too many physically large things—a piano too massive, chairs too big, a painting too wide—is to most Japanese an area that accommodates a luxurious number of luxurious things. Bijo lacks the boxes of tissues, the stacked newspapers, and the hanging laundry found in Japan's residences. Instead, its objects have been selected for reasons that refer only to the objects themselves—their beauty and their costliness. Testifying to an aesthetics of consumption, the furnishings at Bijo are enjoyed by a class of men whose members include some of the biggest capitalists and consumers in Japan.

The size of Bijo's furnishings give an effect of overstatement. Everything is in a sense overdone, as though intended to parody something else. Like bars in London with Old West decors or ice-cream parlors that advertise an "old-fashioned" atmosphere, Bijo gives the impression of being a caricature of a style that is immediately recognizable.

Stepping into Bijo, one feels an instantaneous and definite sense of presence. The customers call this a sign of a first-class club—the flourishes of classiness that may not be specified but are nonetheless perceived. Not only does Bijo seem classy but its classiness belongs to a certain category, that of the *mizu shōbai*. This means that while some of the material objects at Bijo may not differ from those customers have or would like to have in their homes, the total effect would be inappropriate there.

On the one hand, Bijo's *mizu shōbai* decor could be called simply ostentatious, a high-priced version of the tinsel, glitter, and bright colors one finds in the lower and seedier echelons of *mizu shōbai* bars and clubs. On the other hand, in its showiness, it is as if this club is making clear precisely what it is: a place where atmosphere and service are added to the price of what one drinks. In this sense one could say Bijo is dressed for the occasion. And in a society where dress is very important and people in general tend to overdress (hikers in the mountains donning mountain-climbing gear, for instance, and golfers appearing in golf outfits), Bijo signals what it is by dressing, and overdressing, the part.

Bijo not only seems to be engaged in self-reflection; it also encourages self-reflection on the part of its customers. A guest, for instance, sees in the piano an expensive *mizu shōbai* artifact, yet also the instrument that will accompany him as he sings; in the mirrors, a beautiful and visually orienting fixture, yet also a surface that reflects his image; in the Mama, an attractive and fashionable proprietress, yet also a woman whose attentions flatter him; and in the luxury of the club's surroundings, a scene pretty to look at and also a sign of his status and potential wealth.

2

A Type of Routine

When men enter the hostess club in the company of other men, what they do there reflects their two objectives: to get away from work and to have a good time together. The first objective stems from what is generally said to be the great stress and strain of being a working man in Japan. Hours are long, demands are rigorous, and one is discouraged from complaining. When a man walks into a bar or club at the end of the day, he does so to release and let go, position himself in a place that looks different from the workplace, and participate in activities that are self-indulgent and carefree.

Achieving the second objective, enjoying oneself in the company of co-workers or business relations, requires that the relaxation promote business and strengthen work ties. Most Japanese believe that how men relate to one another outside the office foretells how they will behave inside. The hostess club provides customers with a common, more egalitarian ground than is possible at the office.

The activities of a hostess club—the drinking, talking, joking, flirting, singing—serve to both break down and build up; they dissolve the structure that operates outside and create a new one. The first is the more apparent. The customers drink, loosen up, and talk about things that will be forgotten or seem unimportant the next day. As simple and undirected as these activities appear, however, there is also the agenda of uniting the men. Talk should rarely be divisive, and drinking should lead men not to solitary contemplation but to an effusiveness rarely displayed elsewhere. For the evening to be considered successful this double platform must be maintained; the men get away from work, and they get together in ways essential for work.

Membership

The person heading for Bijo will be first greeted by a man in a tuxedo who opens doors and parks cars for the entire building. To the guest's right is an elegant *kissaten* (coffee shop) on the first floor; to his left, a fancy Western disco down a mirrored flight of stairs to the basement; and on the vertical roster a list of all the bars and clubs in the building. As he enters the open foyer, the customer encounters his own image reflected in the mirror covering the whole back wall. As he rides up in a small elevator encased in mirrored door, walls, and ceiling, his gaze is inevitably directed toward himself.

Having been presented immediately with three motifs of the *mizu shōbai* domain—service (from the attendant), glitter (from the ambience of the building), and self-reflection (from real mirrors), the customer alights on the sixth floor with only two doors to choose between: one to Bijo and the other to a bar specializing in bourbon. The door to Bijo is open, and one of the three male employees (the manager and waiters) monitors it to keep out men who are not members and to greet those who are. Addressed by name, unless he is a newcomer, the customer is immediately welcomed into a familiar setting, shown into the club, and quickly seated, most likely in "B" room. He is greeted by all the employees in a position to do so with an "*Irasshaimase*" ("Please enter"), a standard greeting to private visitors and to customers in general in Japan, in restaurants, stores, small businesses. The Mama and other hostesses may also greet the customer with a nod, although their attention will be focused on their charge of the moment.

Typical of hostess clubs, Bijo services a "members-only" clientele. Potential members, introduced and recommended to the club by a member, undergo an informal interview with the Mama. The Mama exchanges *meishi* (business cards) with the prospective member and calls him the next day to make the offer definite. If he is interested, she will then turn over any subsequent practical and financial aspects of membership to the manager, thus fostering the pleasant, though hardly realistic, impression that a member's relationship with the Mama is personal rather than financial.

Another standard practice of hostess clubs is the "keep bottle" system, which requires members to purchase bottles of liquor from the club and to keep them at the club. Whenever the member visits, the bottles are brought out and the liquor is served. Some clubs require that bottles be consumed and new bottles purchased within a limited time. Bijo, however, either too classy or too expensive to adopt this policy, allows bottles to remain untouched for months in the service closet, where they are neatly stacked and dusted. Each bottle is marked with the customer's name, providing both a sign system of the status of the individual customer, based on the cost of his bottle (Chivas Regal, for example, is the most expensive, as everyone knows), and a substantiation—even reification—as they stand together in the service closet, of a male community established through common membership.

Service by Males

Having ordered and paid for a bottle in advance, a member will be seated and then, usually without a word being spoken, his bottle will be brought out promptly, always accompanied by glasses, ice, mineral water, and a snack for each guest. The man who has served him up to this point—a waiter or the manager—will usually prepare to pour him the first drink and then, only at this point, hesitate and ask as confirmation, "Is *mizu wari* (scotch and water, the favorite drink at Bijo) all right?" Proceeding to fill the glass, the waiter exemplifies a level of service that will continue to be prompt, efficient, and unsolicited all evening.

From this moment on, a waiter will speak only to answer questions or verify commands. He will not ask for food or drink orders but will take an order for food if summoned by a guest (or, more commonly perhaps, by a hostess in the name of the guest) and will bring out new supplies of bottled water and ice whenever he sees they are needed. His service seems to consist of foreseeing and responding to the customer's unspoken needs. Indeed, once his initial task of seeing the guest through the preliminaries is completed, his presence is practically effaced by that of the more commanding hostess. This inconspicuousness, however, has a symbolic value.

The male employees, with their silence, sobriety, and submissiveness, contrast most sharply with the *mizu shōbai* women. The waiters rank lowest of all those employed at the club; they work the longest hours, are kept the busiest, and treat customers the most politely.[1] Standing as though on guard, they smile rarely and laugh less, seldom showing any expression of emotion.

If one were to ask a customer what it is about the waiters that enhances the time he spends at the club, he would probably answer, "Nothing in particular" or simply say that the waiter expedites service. Waiters are no-

---

1. At Bijo there were always between four and five male employees: the manager, one or two waiters called "boys," a piano player referred to as *sensei*, and a cook who goes by the anglicized "cook" and remains unseen in the kitchen. In rank, the cook is perhaps higher than the waiters. The manager, also higher though possibly superseded by the rank of the piano player, is paid a salary only slightly higher than most of the veteran hostesses despite the longer hours and greater responsibility. The waiters at Bijo work from about 4 P.M. to 12:30, compared to hours of about 7 to 11 P.M. or midnight for the hostesses.

ticed, in fact, only in their failure to go unnoticed. That is, if an ashtray is not emptied, a fresh bottle of water not delivered, or the request for a song not conveyed to the piano player, then a customer's attention is distracted from whatever is happening at his table as he is forced to call on the waiter to correct the lapse. When the service provided by the waiter is at top form, however, the customer's needs are attended to almost telepathically. What the waiter is paid for, in other words, is responsiveness without presence. It is in order to be symbolically absent that he functions silently, without facial expression.[2] The customer does not want to see him, so the waiter makes himself unseen.

Drinking

The speed with which the setups for drinks are delivered is an indication of the significance given to drinking. It is expected and even required at hostess clubs. The Japanese male who does not drink here, in fact, is considered odd, unsociable, somewhat unmasculine, and almost un-Japanese. Alcohol goes hand in hand with the relaxing atmosphere of the nightlife; not only does it break down the barriers between men as quickly as possible, but it also dissolves barriers within the individual.

This function of alcohol—loosening the glue of a social order that is generally glued tight—is appreciated by far more than the businessman out to have a good time. Rules and expectations are burdensome in Japan, and women drinking alone, housewives drinking together at home, and students drinking in groups all seek a release from the various obligations of Japanese society. The behavior that accompanies the drinking—throwing up, urinating in public, dancing on train platforms, falling asleep stretched out on the seat of a train, making passes at or otherwise insulting someone normally shown respect, speaking openly about things that usually go unsaid—all such behavior is for the most part excused (yet more so for males than females).

Like insanity in the United States, drunkenness in Japan grants one an immunity from acts or behavior committed "under the influence." This was particularly true in prewar Japan, when even the charge of murder would not be leveled if the perpetrator had been drunk at the time. Today's laws are somewhat more stringent, including penalties for driving after more than one drink. Yet socially there is still a blind spot. How people behave

2. The case with the manager is a bit different, he being more visible in his role as managerial bookkeeper and stand-in host when the hostesses and Mama are busy.

when they are drunk is overlooked because, it is believed, drink changes behavior, and drunken behavior should not be judged by the usual standards.[3] The Western praise for those who "can hold their liquor well" misses the point in Japan, where many drink to achieve the freedom and the chance to act irresponsibly that come with drunkenness. The tendency is to drink hard, to get drunk, and to act drunk even when the drinking has just begun. (A parallel is the activity at American college "mixers.")

In the hostess club this logic of drink makes good sense. Tired of the rules and rituals that control their actions during the day, men use alcohol regularly, almost fiercely, after hours. With drink as an umbrella, they are protected and indulged. Thanks to the social blind spot, what they do will be excused, what they say overlooked. With a drink, they can let their feelings loose, vent a long-harbored resentment, even cut a boss to the quick; it will all be forgotten next day. But the catharsis of their remarks and behavior builds relationships that will continue in the months and years ahead.

Talking: Banter and Breast Talk

The rules, boundaries, and key components of the talk within hostess clubs are tacitly understood. The talk should be unstructured chatter about things so insignificant that they need not be recalled later. Such forgettable conversations build a commonality among men.

Conversation, I mean to suggest, is not so much a pleasure in and of itself as a means to an end. Not dissimilar in this regard to the other activities at the club, it is often undertaken with a nervous hesitation that belies the gaiety it seeks to express. Supposedly idle conversation will begin spontaneously as soon as the first drink has been poured; in fact, the members of a party will often shift in their seats while waiting for an appropriate remark from a brave volunteer. At such a time, each moment of silence seems like an eternity.

It is at this point that the hostess is assigned a table, and her arrival will

---

3. According to some studies, Japanese are genetically more sensitive to alcohol than other racial groups and react strongly to even a small amount of alcohol. Reporting on such a study, *National Geographic* has also stated that the rate of alcoholism in Japan is 4 percent of drinkers—statistically half the rate in the United States. ("Alcohol, the Legal Drug" by Boyd Gibbons [February 1992]). In my experience in Tokyo I observed that drunken behavior can occur after one sip, and have been told that alcoholics are few in Japan because everyone makes it to work the next day. If cultural constructions affect the definition of alcoholism, it is difficult to compare the rates of alcoholism between Japan and the United States.

be greeted with a sigh of relief. She will ward off a silence that could threaten the evening's objectives, launching the conversation so necessary to recreation. To smooth the conversational path between men is, in fact, a primary function of hostesses, according to most of the men I spoke with.

Although the hostess participates in the conversation, she often becomes its subject, as in the following instance. Four customers (Hamano, Agata, Mori, and Yamamoto, all from the same division in the same company) were in the club, and for about an hour I served as their sole hostess. The atmosphere was jovial and lighthearted, and the talk consisted of playful put-downs, directed primarily at Hamano, the highest-ranked among them, sexual banter about me, sometimes addressed to me, and rambling, seemingly insignificant chatter.

Hamano, speaking in English to me and his colleagues, was teased for incorporating Japanese words: "You *to* [and] me are going to Tokyo, *ne* [isn't that so]?" Because Hamano must conduct at least some of his business in English, his companions found this very amusing.

I was asked to guess the ages of the men, a common game in the hostess club, and I answered seriously forty-six, forty-five, fifty, and then jokingly thirty for Agata, who seemed the oldest, about sixty. Only one verified my estimate, while Hamano and Agata kept joking back and forth that actually their ages were reversed. Again, all laughed at this ploy.

References to sex were constant. Hamano suggested that I should try him out as a boyfriend, gesturing toward his penis and saying in English, "cock." Agata protested, arguing that Hamano would tire me out because he had "too much energy."

Yamamoto had just returned from a year in Amsterdam, and they joked about how tired he was because he hadn't seen his wife for a year and had climaxed "eight, nine times" the previous night.

Hamano said to me, "*oppai ōkii*" (your breasts are big), and then started talking to Agata about the kind of woman he liked. Agata told me that Hamano liked big-breasted women even if they were not pretty; Hamano denied this, saying that he liked pretty women even with small breasts like mine (though earlier he had said mine were big). He declared that some women have bodies of three dimensions, sketching out three increasingly large curves in the air, starting at the chest, moving to the stomach, and ending at the hips.

Agata asked me what kind of work I thought Hamano did. I replied, "*Yakuza*" (gangster). Then he pulled out a coaster and scribbled words like *oyabun* (the proper way to address a gangster boss), *chinpira* (lowest-level gangster), *himo* (pimp), *onēsan* (familiar, impolite term for addressing a woman, literally "older sister"), and *suke* (rude for girlfriend). He continued that Hamano was a *chinpira*, that I should call the Mama *onēsan* (and that it was very respectful to do so), and that Hamano was my *himo* and I his *suke*.

Agata kept telling me that I must learn a Japanese song. After he got up to sing, Mori commented on what a terrible singer he was, a routine I have often seen a man's colleagues following. Some will stick tissue paper or chopsticks in their ears, roll their eyes, or feign intolerance, but only when the singer is in fact very good.

A typical exchange in some if not all respects, the above conversation illustrates some of the directions hostess-club talk is likely to take. Introduced by the host's invitation to break rank and dispense with formal courtesies, it assumes a staccato pitch. Subjects change rapidly, nothing is discussed seriously or for too long, and there is a great deal of laughter and play. Conversation is simple and undirected, the expression of men at long last released from formality.

While the language is indeed different from that of the *tatemae* (socially expected responses) required during the day, the *honne* (true, sincere feelings) of speech expressed and so heralded during the night have their own conventions.[4] One such convention is to refer to a woman, preferably a hostess who is present, in an obviously sexual mode. Most commonly this is a remark such as "You have large breasts," "Your breasts are nonexistent" (*pechapai*—flat-chested), "Are your breasts on vacation?" "I need glasses to see your breasts," or "I think your breasts have gotten bigger." These remarks are rewarded immediately with guttural laughter. In fact, as often as I heard a comment about a breast made, it never failed to get the same reaction: surprise, glee, and release.

Though puzzling at first, considering the repetitiousness and regularity of such comments, the exaggeration of the response, I came to understand, resulted less from the content of what was said than from the fact that it was said at all. Though blatant reference to female flesh, particularly breasts, is not infrequent in Japan, it triggers in the hostess club an emotion and attitude that men are waiting to let loose. Something of the forbidden, the freedom, the frivolity that the nightlife is agreed to represent, breast talk becomes a signal that the time for play has just begun. More effective than the suggestion that propriety should be abandoned for the night—the pop-

4. I am using the words *tatemae* and *honne* as they were used by customers in conversation with me or their colleagues at Bijo. How ideological these usages are I will point out in part 3.

ular phrase "*Bureikō de ikimashōka?*" (Should we dispense with rank, regimen, courtesy?)—a statement like "Your breasts are more like kiwi fruit than melons" is the act of abandon itself. When issued by the highest-ranking member of the party and greeted with laughter, the statement signals the men's endorsement of this abandon and their acceptance of a flippancy and familiarity in their language during the evening.

Speaking of a hostess's breasts is one example of talk that falls into a wider convention of pointing to, discussing, or making fun of something—or more likely, someone—that all men present can relate to on a fairly equal basis. Such references, often sexual, frequently carry the weight of authority that men have as customers and that women must yield to in their status as hostesses. Bijo's hostesses would be laughed at and ridiculed for such perceived weaknesses as lack of beauty, old age (in their thirties), having an unpleasant singing voice, making mistakes when playing the piano (one hostess played), ineptness in servicing, being part of the nightlife with its implied dirtiness, and failing to display great interest in or knowledge of the world. Remarks of this nature were often pointed and brief—"Where did you learn to play piano—in kindergarten?" "How old are you, grandma?" and "I suppose a comic book is as much as you can read." Rarely delivering these barbs with any overt intention of being rude, the men would sit back and laugh, sure that the talk was appropriate to the place and confident that they controlled what was said and how judgment would be passed.

Talking: About the Woman and of the Man

Relying on some object, often a woman, to stimulate dialogue and rapport among men is a staple of hostess-club interactions. Taste and style, however, vary from crude, blunt utterances about the hostess to serious discussion of her. As a foreigner who was usually speaking in Japanese, I often became the butt of jokes centering on language. When this was coupled with a reference to sexuality the combination could be deadly. Not only typical but so common as to have occurred as many as three or four times every evening was the inquiry as to whether I knew certain words in Japanese. This often started when *oppai* were being evaluated and the men would say something like "*Ee, oppai toiu kotoba wa wakarimasuka?*" (Do you understand the word *oppai?*) This question was usually repeated a number of times in a tone of incredulous amusement that a foreign woman would in fact understand this term. Routinely the initial question would then be extended into a game, and I would be asked if I knew the meaning of such words as *sukebei* (lecher), *pechapai* (flat-chested), *uwaki* (affair), *omanko* (vagina), and *ososō* (explained to me as the few drops of urine which may remain on a woman after she urinates). Or, if I answered in the affirmative, I would be asked something like "*Sukebei toiuno wa tatoeba nandesuka?*" (What, for example, is *sukebei*—lecherous behavior?)

Alternatively, some men would be entertained by using vulgar Japanese in a manner they felt would elude me or by ridiculously or half-seriously trying to explain some vulgarism to me in Japanese. Others would find humor in distorting words or asking, in an excruciatingly slow cadence, "*Wa-ka-ri-ma-su-ka?*" (Do you understand?), finding humor in my presumed inability to understand. When two fairly intoxicated men were speaking to me in Japanese, one asked if I had *zubon* (pants) on. Since I was wearing a dress I found the question strange and answered no. He then gestured crudely to his own genital area and motioned as if wrapping himself in a diaper. I figured he was referring to underpants and so said yes. I was then asked if they were paper ones. This was all done in slow speech, accompanied by much laughter. Excusing myself to go to the washroom, I returned to face another question, again delivered at a very deliberate speed, "*Fuki-mashitaka?*" (meaning "to wipe," presumably in this case asking whether I had wiped myself).

More sophisticated and involved conversations are conducted as well. They can range from assessing the hostess's body almost dispassionately and with elaboration ("Your arms are very long but your torso is short. Fingers are somewhat squat but the neck is remarkably delicate") to inquiring about the woman's personal life, her daily routines, or her past. ("Do you have dreams? I wonder if they stem from your childhood. Tell me one.") As an object, the woman still feeds a talk that fills up the spaces and silences between men. By giving them something to speak to or about as a group, the hostess keeps the spotlight comfortably away from the men and on the one person at the table to whom all the men are equally superior.

A second convention found in hostess-club talk frequently involves the hostess but turns attention to the men. A man may use the hostess to show off a particular skill, demonstrate a trick, inform her of knowledge he is proud to possess, or discuss with her a hobby or recent event. Men will express themselves to the hostess or describe one another. They tell her that so-and-so is a good dancer, that his companion is a good lover, that the boss has many girlfriends, that the section chief could be a professional singer. The details come from both reality and imagination, and the stories told are both true and pretend. The effect is dual, to make each other look good and also foolish. Hence, the strategy of mutually building up and breaking down is passed back and forth; no one is permitted to become too self-confident, nor is anyone driven out of the conversation.

My fluency in English was frequently relied on to establish conversation of this second conventional type. Men would try to get a particular member of their party to speak to me in English. For one group it was the *shachō* (president) who, after much resistance, finally gave in and spoke some English words. His underlings demanded to know how he had done. I said he was great—he wasn't!—and they commented, "*Yappari*" (that figures). Everyone except the president found the exchange highly amusing; the president appeared relieved and happy he'd passed the test.

Others played this game in a much more ridiculous way. Two men, fairly drunk, kept trying to recall at least one phrase in English and finally came up with "I am a pencil." This they repeated to each other and to me, giggling each time. Many found the mere pronouncement of an English word to a native speaker of the language hilarious in and of itself. Others reacted more seriously and still others with obvious distaste. The former included those actually competent in English, who would use the opportunity to speak English either for personal satisfaction or for evidence of their accomplishment. Men who thought they should, for reasons of schooling or work, speak English or were self-conscious about not being able to do so would tell me not to sit next to them because they would not be able to converse, or would simply push me aside or explain to me, as did one man with whom I had in fact been speaking in Japanese for close to half an hour, that there was no way we could communicate because he didn't speak English.

Talking: Insult, Joke, and Pretense

Men use praise and insults to talk to hostesses about themselves. In a party of men, for example, the conversation may be something like "Hisao's good in English." "No, Nobu's the one who's better. He's a real playboy." "No, Kazuo is the one who's the playboy; Nobu's a real big shot." "No, Hitoshi's the one who's *erai* (prestigious)." Usually the building up or praise of men (to one another) is done in terms not used for evaluation during the day (that is, at home or at work). Being *josei ni moteru hito* (good with women; having a lot of women) is typical, as are comments on how good a drinker, golfer, singer, and so on, a person is. In this vein, everything said and responded to at the club is in the realm of "happy time." No one gets angry and everyone is mutually supportive.[5]

Men, nevertheless, also engage in mutual put-downs. Typically they are playful and are taken to be anything but serious. Two men were discussing their own sexual prowess or lack of it. Sato told me that Miyoshi started out by having sex seven times a night, decreasing to four times on the second date, three times on the third, once on the fourth, and after that being no good at all. He, in comparison, could do it four times a night but only once a month. Then he charged that Miyoshi, in fact, only did it once a month too, and Miyoshi replied that it was once a month to his *wife*. Sato counted up Miyoshi's girl friends: Sachiko, Reiko, Keiko, and two others. Miyoshi interjected that Sachiko was the only one, that she was his ideal woman, and that Sato could talk about her all he wanted to but he'd never met her. Keiko, he said, was another story: she's in love with Miyoshi, but Miyoshi is not in love with her. Sato said that it was just the reverse.

These men were colleagues in the same company and division and seemed to be of about equal standing. Criticism among such "friends," they told me, was simply a form of compliment. In the repartee among men many strategies are used, in addition to compliment and insult, to juggle, homogenize, and reconfirm male relations positively. One is to introduce everyone as "friends"—*tomodachi* or "homo"*dachi* as one put it (denied, laughingly, by his mates)—while refraining from articulating the true nature of the relationship. Two men in their forties told me the unlikely story that they were brothers and that the third member of their party, a man in his fifties, was their father. Subsequently the older man assumed the role of the biggest lecher (*sukebei*) among them, the common pattern between a superior and inferiors.

Men hesitate during club conversation to identify themselves in terms of business. At a club of white-collar members, one customer told me he was a bartender at the *Bōeichō* (Defense Department). When I asked another, who had told me of traveling to Brazil and about ten other countries that year, what his work was, he answered that he had been "chasing girlfriends." Two other times when I asked the question, I received no answer. Still another, in conversation alone with me, would talk generally about work—

---

5. For example, I saw one man become increasingly drunk and slovenly while other members of his group did not. He started blubbering, falling off his chair, spilling his drink, and trying repeatedly to touch the penis of the man sitting next to him. No one said anything or in any way appeared uncomfortable.

how he had worked until he came to the club that night, how work was his hobby, and so on—yet say only that his business was *sa-bisugyō* (service industry).

Pretense, preferably absurd, is a common ploy along these lines as well. Men often claim that they are *yakuza* (gangsters), for example. Joking about nationality and heritage are also prevalent. Many customers would introduce themselves or their colleagues to me as being other than Japanese. One claimed that his companion was descended from head hunters in New Guinea and another said he was descended from Scandinavians. Such absurd assertions were routinely met with a roar of laughter. When the claims were less ridiculous, however—as when one man alleged that his companion was a Korean—the laughter from the others was equally loud but the reaction from the one so depicted was a hearty and immediate "No, no, no, I'm a pure Japanese!"

In the hostess club there is little talk of the office, infrequent mention of home (specifically of wife and children), and no comment of a critical nature that is not disguised by laughter and much joking. The unspoken rule is to avoid anything that could be construed as "serious." But there are exceptions. On occasion, business may be discussed briefly. As one customer told me, for the hours spent "bullshitting," five minutes may be relegated to business. And if it's a deal that is being aimed for (in contrast to the pure entertainment of coworkers going out drinking, for example), the five minutes may make the rest of the evening worthwhile.

Another category of enjoyable interchange that is not humorous is conversation about politics, music, hobbies, and current events. In the fancier clubs on the Ginza, in fact, the hostesses are said to be well versed in such fields as politics so that they can provide customers with intellectual conversation. This was not the case with the hostesses at Bijo, although I found that customers who talked to me about Japanese-American relations, politics, and education would say that they had enjoyed the conversation.[6]

Even such "serious" conversation is, however, routinely punctuated with laughter, jokes, and asides intended, it appears, to prevent discourse from

6. Such conversations led to the appraisal I heard most often from customers: *atama ga ii* (intelligent), which seemed to add to rather than detract from my appeal as a hostess. Of course, in all that has been perceived here as "male discourse," the effects of my own position as both foreigner and observer must be considered. Both could create a distortion from that normally "spoken" at a hostess club. In regard to my foreignness, I would suggest that men behaved toward me in a manner structurally, if not stylistically, similar to that I observed operative with Japanese hostesses. Used as a vehicle to galvanize a particular kind and organization

becoming either too private (between two people, for example) or too involved. While I was discussing Japanese-American trade relations with a customer, his colleague, seated next to me, might interject a question about where my *oppai* were hiding out that night.

Singing

The somewhat illusive relationship between the serious and the light in hostess-club conversations is perhaps best exemplified by the rather recent phenomenon of singing in clubs, which represents both a break from discourse and a commonality with it. Providing, it is said, an activity by which the Japanese can enjoy themselves, it can also, I have observed, entail a considerable amount of anxiety and serious preparation.

Called generically "*karaoke*," the system is to provide accompaniment to which the customer (or the Mama, a hostess, or a piano player) will sing the words of a popular song.[7] The singing is meant to be a performance and, even in one-counter bars, will be done into a microphone. During the performance the room quiets down, and at the end of it there is applause. Lyrics are provided in books organized by *minyō*, or folk songs; *enka*, modern Japanese songs; American songs; and so on. The selection of a song is often attended to with as much care as its execution.

In Bijo the piano player starts playing at 7:30 P.M. and will occasionally sing along with his music. The Mama or a hostess may be asked to sing, and soon the customers begin to participate. A standing microphone is placed to one side of the piano, along with the accoutrements of music stand, spotlight, and a demarcated circular area to stand in. Because the tables are located a fair distance away from the microphone, this area virtually becomes a stage. The customer's singing a song, therefore, becomes an occasion, unlike the casual outbreaks of song in an American bar.

Characteristically, a customer must be urged at length by the Mama, a hostess, or his companions to sing. He will first resist, saying variously that he's *hazukashii* (shy), *umakunai* (not good), *heta* (bad), *saitei* (the pits), or

---

of speech among men, the joking about language and linguistic comprehension with me, for example, seemed simply an adjustment to my peculiar features rather than a departure from a more general approach to all women in this realm. At base, my definition still came, I believe, more from being a female than from being a foreigner and anthropologist.

7. The accompaniment is usually a cassette system in smaller bars—from which comes the word *karaoke*—and a "live" piano and player in larger clubs such as Bijo.

onchi (tone deaf). Eventually he will give in, singing at least once and perhaps a second song or, later, another song to the more or less attentive room.

One customer explained that this activity, which became popular only in the 1980s, developed when the traditional split between nighttime women of culture (*geisha*) and women of sex disappeared. Now, he said, there are very few *mizu shōbai* women trained in the arts, so the men have had to take over the singing. Another said simply that men can talk only so long. Singing gives them something else to fill their time on their night out.

Others stressed that when a member of their party sings they immediately feel closer to him. *Karaoke* allows a presentation of oneself through which certain barriers between men can be surmounted. To this end it was implied that how well one did mattered far less than simply doing it. Such sociologists as Tsurumi have argued that the worse one sings, in fact, the better.[8] To suggest a kinship of men based on inability, however, is fallacious. Though it is true that even a poor singer is applauded by a surprising number of the people in the room, and even those who are mediocre are routinely said to be good (*umai* and *jōzu*), it is also true that every man wants to be good and that the really proficient singers are recognized for being precisely that.

All men are expected to sing while out drinking with buddies at night; it is *shōganai* (inevitable). To not sing, particularly if other members of one's party have already done so, is viewed as unfriendly and distancing. To sing, therefore, becomes a sign and a promoter of camaraderie.

Singing is also a reflection of the individual. And for this reason some men practice and perfect their numbers. Many fall into what the Japanese refer to as *wan pata-n* (one pattern), performing always the same song but at least with the assurance that repetition has given them. Others will plow through the song books at length, discussing with their table what might be most appropriate to their particular voices. Singing is thus approached with a seriousness and self-consciousness not matched in conversation. And the assumption is that everyone wants to, and should, do well. A hostess who had recommended that a predominantly "one pattern" customer try a song she thought would be flattering advised him, after he sang it rather poorly, to buy a cassette of the song and practice it repeatedly for at least two weeks.

Some of the men will play up to the audience during their performances,

8. Tsurumi made the point during a lecture on Japanese social behavior given to recipients of Japan Foundation Fellowships at the Japan Foundation in 1982.

looking directly at faces or crooning to females (hostesses). Many will try to let the mood of the song (particularly the folksong) take them over, closing their eyes and coming close to tears at the inevitably sad lyrics. Nearly all who sing are attentive to the words, timing, and demeanor. Those who are not are considered sloppy and are not accorded the supportive applause at the song's end. I saw this happen only a few times, with men who were very drunk, once with a young and impatient customer, and most often with foreigners who had misinterpreted the construction and rules of the activity. As a hostess told a customer to be "serious" when he started hamming it up while singing a duet, to be untalented is excusable but to be excessively casual is inappropriate and in bad taste.

This singing, it should be noted, is not as easy as might be imagined. In addition to the appreciable anxiety of singing in front of a crowd, which includes one's coworkers, boss, and sometimes clients, is the fact that the songbooks provide only the words, not the melody. Since many of the songs are stylized, with fancy accompaniment in between, the singer, to avoid blunders, must know not only the tune but the form in which it is usually performed. For all of these reasons—the need to be fairly serious, to perform as well as possible, to be familiar with the arrangement of the selection, to just get up and do it in the first place—men are often visibly nervous as they walk up to the microphone. One man, always breaking into a sweat that he would anxiously pat at with a handkerchief, admitted that singing like this was nerveracking. The accomplishment was, however, cathartic, and the release he shared with his companions helped produce a greater relaxation for the members of his party.

3

A Type of Woman

Woman Servicing Man

Hostess clubs, with their emphasis on service by women, exist primarily to personalize the working relations of Japanese men. But why are they so successful? Men do, after all, play in environments without women and achieve a similar degree of male bonding.[1] They can play golf during the day at clubs with a measure of extravagance and attentiveness matched only by the high-class hostess clubs on the Ginza. They are picked up at their homes in hired cars, play all day at private golf courses where membership is both exclusive and exorbitantly expensive, have their own caddies and locker-room attendants, are served exquisite lunches in magnificent dining rooms, and are returned home in the hired cars that have been waiting all day.

Or Japanese men can unwind inexpensively at *yakitoriya* or *akachōchin*.[2] Here, too, in an environment markedly different from home and work, they can share food, drink, and talk. If they can afford more expensive entertainment, there are clubs that offer jazz, chanson, or stand-up comics. If not, they can still find bars with *karaoke*.

Yet the hostess club remains an ideal—not the only place to take colleagues on business but one, I was told, that is well suited, even best suited, to manly aims at night.[3] Exactly what these aims are again shifts somewhere

1. My source for this information was principally two middle-aged males in a position to both receive and initiate much business-related entertainment. One is the head of an architectural firm, the other a high-placed government official.

2. *Yakitoriya* are restaurants serving *yakitori*—skewers of meat, fish, and/or vegetables. *Akachōchin* are usually noisy and relatively cheap eating and drinking places identified by the red lanterns that are hung outside.

3. This endorsement of hostess clubs came primarily from customers at Bijo, middle-aged, white-collar executive types who frequent hostess clubs. Men who didn't have the expense accounts to warrant such forays—particularly academics, I found—would argue that the *yakitoriya* or small-bar format they used for group gatherings achieved the same prerequisites in

between work and play; and what role women play in realizing these aims shifts between the pragmatic one of work-related relaxation and the pleasurable one of masculine release.

Significantly, it is the former that women, in their positions as wives, tend to stress when explaining men's need for the nightlife. One group of women I interviewed[4] insisted that the nightlife is not about sex but about work, that men go to hostess clubs less for reasons of personal desire than because of group or business pressure, and that the hostess is pivotal in all this for the "service" she provides men with while they discuss work. Women I interviewed individually also emphasized the work component of their husbands' forays into the nightlife, emphasizing the instrumental role a hostess plays in work encounters and downplaying any attractions other than those strictly work-related.[5]

While women generally were vague about what precisely it is that a hostess provides in a hostess club—never having been in a hostess club themselves—they tend to imply that whatever a hostess does, she does because she's a woman. The implication, in short, is that the service men require is a feminine one. Women serve, and receiving this service somehow bolsters the male relationships essential to work in Japan.

The management and customers of the hostess club place the same emphasis on female service. A hostess club supplies service, and the service of a hostess club is supplied by women. It is this notion of service that persuades men to pay three, four, or five times as much for a drink in a club as the drink would cost if they bought a bottle at a store. So I was told by Bijo's assistant manager on my second day of employment, after I had failed to carry out the duties expected of a hostess, which consisted explicitly of two prescriptions—light customers' cigarettes and pour their drinks. (There were also three proscriptions—don't smoke, don't rest your

---

atmosphere as a hostess club. Other men, however—a lawyer, a cab driver, an artist—revealed that occasionally they would pay out of their own pockets to visit a hostess club with a friend, not to build business ties but simply to enjoy the presence of hostesses.

4. The group consisted of twenty alumnae of Rikkyō University in Tokyo. They ranged in age from the mid-twenties to the mid-sixties. Almost all were married and middle- to upper-class. I addressed these women in the course of conducting fieldwork during a research fellowship I received from Rikkyō.

5. For example, one woman whose banker husband was out every week night until at least midnight often sympathized with his plight, claiming (although she had never accompanied him) that the food in the restaurants he ate in at night wasn't tasty, the alcohol he drank in the clubs not enjoyable, and the women he was forced to converse with boring and unattractive.

elbows on the table, don't put your hands in your pockets in front of customers.)

While a hostess's duties are, on the face of it, minimal and no more than mechanical, they actually encode a more general posture that the hostess is expected to assume: she is to take care of and show respect for the customer. Men, in their roles as business or work partners, would cite this behavior of the hostess as highly conducive to their goal of relaxing in order to promote work relations. Not only does the hostess attend to the oral desires of the men as individuals—keeping their cigarettes lit and their drinks replenished—but she attends to the oral desires of the men as a group—keeping them involved as a unit through speech and song. It is she who will initiate conversation when no one is talking, keep it going if silence is threatening, encourage men to sing, and generally bring everyone into an exchange in which they open up and become involved. She makes sure that everyone has a good time, and she relieves everyone else, particularly the host, of that responsibility.

Besides supplying functional lubrication to a group, the hostess flatters the men in a more personal, individualized way. During my observations it often took the form of constant, exaggerated compliments: "You sing so well"; "You're very handsome"; "I bet you could make love all night long"; "You're the best joke teller I've ever met"; "What a gorgeous tie you have on!" While the Mama seemed less instrumental than the hostess in keeping interaction percolating at the table, in this personalizing, flattering role she was a real professional. Customers often identified her as the main reason they chose Bijo over other clubs, not because she spent much time at their tables (for in truth she did not) but because the level of her style and service was exceptional. Bijo's Mama was a master of attentiveness. Her appearance (wearing only exquisite kimonos and attending to every facet of her toilette with great care), her mannerisms (using feminine gestures such as covering her mouth when she talked and keeping the last finger of each hand raised), and her voice (cultivating what was called a beautiful, sexy singing voice) were all intended to impress and delight her clientele; and she flattered them further by remembering details of their personal lives, by referring admiringly to their jobs, characters, and personal attributes; and by showering them with personalized services such as seeing each one off, calling each one the next day, remembering each one's birthday.

This personal element of female service is also said to benefit business relations between men. The mechanism at work stems less from the sense of mutual camaraderie orchestrated by an outgoing hostess and more from receiving special treatment and being made to feel special oneself by a very feminine woman. One customer explained this mechanism in terms of the Mama's charms: "I flatter a client by bringing him to a club with such an elegant Mama." Others explained her appeal: "The Mama is classy herself and makes the man feel important as well."

In these more personal encounters between customer and hostess, yet a third dimension of the service expected of women in the nightlife comes into play: sexual posturing and flirting. This is what men describe as the basic, animalistic need of all men, a need that tends to be articulated in terms of what it makes of the man himself—a *sukebei*. This word, meaning "dirty old man" or "lecher," is heard repeatedly in the context of the hostess club.

Men will identify themselves as *sukebei*, refer to the others at the table as *sukebei*, question who in their party is the biggest *sukebei*, and explain their behavior out at night as that of a *sukebei*. Obviously there is a strong desire to see oneself and other men as *sukebei* in this setting. For the most part, "lecherous" behavior is limited to speech: telling jokes, commenting about women in the room, and telling stories of imaginary or exaggerated sexual escapades. Discussing his actual sex life with his wife would not be appropriate for a *sukebei*.

When the Mama or a hostess joins the table, however, the *sukebei* routines often change. The exchanging of sexual tales or barbs—"I have ten women a night, but Takai-san over here can only handle one woman and then only once a month"—may continue, but now they will most often be addressed to the woman and will frequently focus entirely on her: "I could give you good loving"; "You look like the type who enjoys good sex"; "How old were you when you lost your virginity?" "How many boyfriends do you have now and could you use one more?"

The woman becomes at one level nothing more than the medium through which men are transformed into *sukebei*. Males talk sex and the female is the sex they talk. At another level, however, men not only talk *of* women but *to* women, and out of these encounters comes a behavior I refer to as flirtation: displays of mutual interest between customer and hostess that allude to sex, romance, and sexual intimacy. The man acts as if he would like the woman for his mistress, and the woman behaves as if she would be willing to start an affair with him. There is cooing and batting of eyelashes by the hostess, provocative language, and the suggestion of a rendezvous at some future time. That rendezvous rarely occurs, however; hostess club flirtations are confined mainly to the club. Sex is built up to, but the build-up proceeds no further.

In this respect, the hostess is valued less for what she *does* for a work group and more for what she *is* to a man. And that is not just any woman, but specifically a nightlife woman—a breed apart, typified in the mass media by her willing acceptance of her own sexualization.[6] This is a woman who will have her breast size commented upon, her sex life speculated upon, and her sexual attractiveness judged and discussed in her presence. She may not engage in acts that consummate in sex, but in her midst men are reminded of sex and positioned to think of themselves as males more than as workers. As a customer confided to me, "The hostess helps us converse and relax amongst ourselves, but men also have a *sukebei* nature and women are needed to satisfy that."

Servicing the Male Group

The hostesses at Bijo were expected to arrive at work an hour before the club opened. There seemed to be two reasons for this: to have hostesses available in the event that customers arrived early and to give the impression that they were eager to serve the men. Such anticipation (of a customer's arrival, of a man's desires while at the club, of a party's need for stimulation) was encouraged by Bijo's management and welcomed by its clientele.

In preparation for the opening, the women would usually wait at the piano counter—simply wait. No specific duties were demanded of them; they spent the time polishing their nails, fussing with their hair, practicing a song, or smoking. Some women sat quietly; others conversed in groups of two or three, sometimes with members of the male staff. The conversations were more subdued but not unlike those carried on with the customers—few revelations of actual romantic, sexual, or familial relations; little serious commentary about the people they worked for, almost no criticism of the Mama, scarcely any mention of actual customers; and a preponderance of innocuous, light topics such as fashion, food, travel, and the famous

6. I use the terminology "to sexualize," as do Sigmund Freud (for example, in *Three Essays on the Theory of Sexuality,* trans. James Strachey [New York: Avon Books, 1962], 77) and Leo Bersani, following Freud (*The Freudian Body: Psychoanalysis and Art* [New York: Columbia University Press, 1986], 38, 61). In their usage, "sexualizing" means making sexual a person, a thing, or an act that was originally nonsexual. Freud uses the example of a baby sucking on its mother's breast, first for nourishment and later for sensual pleasure as well. In the latter case, the mother, her breast, and the act of nursing have all become "sexualized." It should be noted that "sexualization" does not exclude the presence of nonsexual meanings. Nursing, for example, can continue to feed a child at the same time that it gives sensual pleasure. Likewise, a hostess provides a service that cultivates business at the same time it gives men sexual pleasure. The relationship between these two "uses" of the hostess is the central subject of this book.

hot springs in Japan. Occasionally, breasts would be discussed, the women sizing up and even touching each other's breasts in a ritual reminiscent of that to be initiated and indulged in later by the customers.[7] Except for this talk of breasts, however, the hostesses strike a pose far different than that assumed in front of the customers. Now they are quiet, even sullen, with an attitude more of resignation than easy acceptance of the male behavior they'll soon encounter. Later they will play their part: one veteran told me she put up with lewd remarks and gestures only because her job required it.

When the first party walks through the door, the women all sit up straight and say "*Irasshaimase*," the perfunctory greeting spoken to all guests in Japan. At this point, most hostesses will grab a box of matches to use in lighting their customers' cigarettes. The Mama, the manager, or a waiter (upon the instruction of either the Mama or the manager) will direct the hostesses to sit with these first guests or to wait as a group for a later assignment.

On entering the club, the visitor is likely to make a quick assessment of the hostesses: how many there are, what they look like, how well they are dressed, whether any are spectacular. On the basis of this assessment, the hostesses at Bijo were judged, by the many customers I explicitly questioned, to be mediocre. Their number was small, only four to nine women for a clientele that peaked at thirty-five to forty-five customers after 9 P.M. Their looks were considered commonplace, with no one hostess standing out. Beauty in the *mizu shōbai* sense commonly is assessed by three criteria: (1) age—the younger, the more beautiful; (2) dress—the more expensive and refined the clothing, the classier and more attractive the woman; and (3) so-called natural beauty—pretty face, lovely hair, petite or busty figure. Customers quickly perceived that the average age of the Bijo hostess was about twenty-five; her usual dress, either street clothes or muumuu, Chinese dress with a slit up the side, or a variety of sexy attire, such as clingy top and long cotton skirt; and her looks average or at least not remarkable. These women could in no way compare to the younger, prettier, and more elegantly attired hostesses of top-rated clubs in the Ginza or Akasaka, and yet it was precisely for this lack of distinction that the Bijo hostesses were valued by customers.

---

7. These breast rituals mimicked but did not parody those engaged in by men. In other words, when women did to themselves what, in the context of club routine, was done *to* them (by men), they were not making fun of the process but rather appropriating it as if it were their own.

As Yamada, a fiftyish frequent customer, articulated it, Bijo's women were *futsū*—common, normal, usual. They were not unapproachable; in Yamada's meaning of the word they were not so gorgeous as to be a fantasy of ultimate desire, but not so fantastic either as to remind men of their own limitations and insecurities.[8] These women made a guest like Yamada, who was well established but not wealthy or prominent enough to gain entrance to the Ginza and Akasaka hostess clubs, feel comfortable, partly because of what the women were—average rather than those categorized as professional or veteran *mizu shōbai* women—and partly because of how they behaved—taking care of and showing respect for the customer.[9] Appearance may be what is first noticed about a hostess, but behavior and service are often most appreciated.

Which hostess the customer is assigned and the number of hostesses granted depends on several factors: how busy the club is, how large and important the party, whether a customer has indicated a preference, and, if so, whether the management can or wishes to satisfy it. Only infrequently do customers at Bijo request a hostess; it is a common practice, however, in other hostess clubs. The customer pays a large fee for choosing his hostess and retaining her for the evening. At Bijo, by contrast, all the hostesses were ultimately at the Mama's disposal and adhered only to her commands and to her policy of rotating the hostesses often.

Directed to a table by the manager or "boy" or sometimes at the command of the Mama, a hostess will approach the table with an *"Irasshaimase"* and ask, perhaps humbly, if she may sit down. Although when and how much she participates in (or precipitates) conversation will vary, she will always pour drinks and light cigarettes, actions that symbolize as well as constitute most concretely the *sa-bisu* (service) expected of her. These "es-

---

8. This notion of idealizing perfect beauty but preferring to deal with a secondary class was expressed by many of the men I talked to. The rationale was that men would be stymied and immobilized by a woman who was too beautiful, made aware, as it were, of their own physical imperfections. By contrast, a woman who was less than perfect but still attractive could be approached and enjoyed.

9. The numbers would vacillate—three (Eri, Machiko, Keiko) had many years experience in the nightlife and were considered veterans, all having been with Mama since the start of Bijo, and Eri having worked in her previous club. The others came and went, some staying one night, others a week, still others for months. Some had had previous *mizu shōbai* experience, others not. The latter included Mayumi, a college student (*joshidaisei*) who worked at the club to make money to buy a car, a would-be musician who could not yet live off her musical skills, and two or three women known as O.L.s (office ladies), who worked in offices during the day.

sentials" of service may at times, although infrequently, be the hostess's only involvement with customers.

Positioning the ice bucket, bottles of mineral water, and bottle of liquor directly in front of her, the hostess will act as the constant intermediary between the men at her table and their alcohol. Anticipating what she assumes is their desire, she continually replenishes and re-ices all the drinks. A man articulates only his wish for her to *stop* pouring, in fact, and even then will probably be cajoled and encouraged by the hostess to drink more.

The lighting of cigarettes is even more automatic. Picking up a box of matches (imprinted with the club's name, address, and phone number) even before the first guest arrives, she will hold on to it for the entire evening, learning to jump instinctively at the mere motion of a customer's hand toward his cigarettes. This is by no means a casual act of politeness. It is a ritual a hostess must become most conscientious about observing and was the only task I was ever reminded to perform.

The men tend to be oblivious to these services unless the hostess fails to perform them. I saw one customer sit with an unlit cigarette dangling from his mouth waiting for a hostess positioned five seats away to strike a match for him. Another chided a hostess for allowing his glass to remain unfilled. Unnoticed or not commented on was the far greater eventuality of a cigarette being promptly lit and a glass being punctually filled. Some men would mutter their thanks (*ah dōmo*), and, very rarely, a man who had spent time in the West might prefer to light his own cigarette.

It takes no great skill to light a cigarette; men in Japan and elsewhere do it all the time. But the lighting of the cigarette takes on a symbolic importance in the hostess club. It imbues the man with the heightened status of the customer and strengthens the male experience. Even the lowest-ranked member of a party, who lights the cigarettes and pours the drinks when a woman is not present, is hereby freed by the one person outside the group—the female hostess.[10] She is not allowed to smoke and can drink only in moderation or at the urging of a customer to keep him company.[11] Because of these differences from the men, she fosters their similarity to and with each other.

10. In Japan, the custom is to serve one another, taking turns filling and refilling each other's *sake* cups. Though the custom is intended and perceived to be reciprocal, lower-ranked members of a group tend to be more aware of it.

11. I once transgressed this understanding. Around 11 P.M., when no guests were in the club, I asked the manager if I could help myself to a beer. Everyone found this highly amusing, and thereafter I was called a *nonbe*—a lush—as if a hostess who drinks when she doesn't have to or is not doing so to serve the customer is consuming alcohol for the wrong reason.

The hostess's role is to help create a *group* out of a table of individuals. To restate, the role most basic to her is to change and vitalize the relations among men by her act of serving. Asked at times to sit in silence, usually because the men are discussing something of a business or serious nature, the hostess is nonetheless kept at a table for a period I've observed to last as long as an hour and a half. Thus it is not for her voice, which she is denied on such occasions, but simply for her presence that she is most valued. She is there, even when she doesn't speak, to remind the men that their reason for being at the club is not only to be together but to have a good time. And to have a good time requires making it plain that they are having a good time together.

This agenda of mutual self-enjoyment in a group is not so easy a task for men as it may appear. One customer described its complexity in this way: "We must come in and show the client a good time. But after a hard day I'm tired, too, and unless I know him well, I don't know what to say or what we could talk about that he would enjoy." Like others, this customer believes that the party hosting an outing is ultimately responsible for the enjoyment of all those he hosts. Also like others, he is grateful to have the hostess assume this responsibility: "If a hostess can liven up a table and get everyone to relax, it makes my job that much easier."

Two hostesses at Bijo, Eri and Machiko, were highly praised by the customers for their ability to orchestrate lively interactions at the tables they served. Eri, in her late thirties, had worked for years in the *mizu shōbai* but also had a day job, typing assignments on commission out of her home. Judged to be average in looks (the two most common remarks about her appearance were that she was very old to be in this business and had a pudgy stomach), Eri tended to wear clothes that were somewhat cheap— Indian-print skirts with clingy tops, outdated suits, cocktail dresses that were sometimes floor length. Machiko, about twenty-five, and also a veteran of the *mizu shōbai*, was attractive but never used makeup and usually wore a simple shirtwaist dress. Because her gay lover owned a bar where Machiko worked nights after leaving Bijo, she had no time to do laundry, and she often wore the same shirtwaist dress for days in a row.

Men to whom these women were assigned were usually treated to some remark by the hostess as soon as she joined the table. From Eri, it could be a reference to her breasts or her tan; she might look down as she pulled out her shirt, for example, and say, "My tan really extends all the way to my nipples." Machiko could be more blatant still—asking who would like to touch her breasts, then taking a customer's hand and guiding it to her breast.

Machiko was the more audacious of the two. Far more inclined to be physically demonstrative, she would lean over the laps of the customers, caressing a hand or holding a knee. Throwing out barbs to the men at her table—"I bet your penis was the size it is now when you were ten"; "Do you fart more in the morning when you wake up or at night when you're sound asleep?"; "I read an article about someone who could climax as he urinated"—her tendency was to shock and insult, all in a teasing manner that was taken to be amusing and that would provoke men into similar exchanges among themselves. Though she was known as a live wire, Machiko could accommodate herself to a guest who preferred calm and could converse quietly and tastefully. She had a beautiful voice but would only sing at the demand of a customer and then usually insist that he join her in a duet.

Eri was less lively and innovative. Treating all the customers the same, she could be overly assertive, bulldozing her way into conversations and then controlling their direction. From my Western perspective, this seemed less than desirable on occasion, particularly when the men were conversing well enough on their own about something that they appeared interested in pursuing and that Eri was likely to know nothing about. Even then, however, the men would sometimes comment on how skilled a hostess this veteran was and would describe her as the type of woman who knew exactly how to take care of men.

Once this praise of Eri was made after she had been sitting, along with another hostess and me, with two men. When we were assigned to the table, the men were already immersed in a private conversation, talking about golf in the serious fashion that Japanese often adopt for this sport. Thinking that speech on our part would be intrusive, I remained silent. Eri and Haruka, by contrast, spoke up at once and carried on a dialogue, mainly about the men: "Don't you think he looks strong?"; "Did you notice his tie, it looks European"; "His shoes are very sleek, don't you think?"; "I can tell they play golf because they both have such tans." Now and then they would try to break into the men's conversation by asking them questions: "Do you play golf every week?"; "Are you very good?"; "Is golf a difficult game to learn?"; "Do you think even a dummy like me could learn how to play?" At first the customers would answer questions politely but perfunctorily and then resume what was still basically their own private conversation. In about fifteen minutes, however, the women's involvement had increased and the men's attempt to converse seriously about golf was abandoned altogether.

Although two customers did complain to me of what they called Eri's boring and invasive style, far more admired her ability to produce and sustain a conversation at the table. Without fail, Eri was a woman who could and would talk, and without exception, Eri was a hostess who could and would make those at her table talk as well. From the minimal pouring of drinks and lighting of cigarettes to encouraging the men to sing, asking if they wanted food, and wondering whether they weren't too hot or too cold, her technique came close to one of "taking over." From merely anticipating the man's needs, she at times came to define them; and from servicing male desires, it seemed that it was her desires that occasionally demanded the service. This is to say that while the first aspect of a hostess's service—ensuring that all men in a party limber up and engage in a group dynamic—is valued, it can expand into a form of coercion that is felt by some to be oppressive.

Flattering and Personalizing the Male

In all the strategies listed so far that the hostess uses in servicing the man, the pleasure gained is often that which can be shared by a group. In her hands and using her as diversion, men can relax with one another as friends and relate to one another without the divisions or tensions that operate practically everywhere else. But a man also takes pleasure in being singled out, in being recognized apart from his group and having his individual qualities addressed. In brief, a man enjoys not only assimilation with other men who, in terms of male desires, appear much the same, but the differentiation of himself from everyone else.

At Bijo, the Mama was an expert in dispensing this particular service. Her main objective, it seemed, was to structure relationships that appeared—and more important, felt—specifically personal. That is, she treated each customer as if he alone were special and as if he alone had caught the Mama's fancy.

Bijo's Mama would give her personal service in a number of ways—by greeting the guest by name and by recalling details of a previous visit, reminding him of whatever he had chosen to speak of, from headaches to a fondness for Italian food. Nothing is too trivial, so long as the man himself has offered it as personally significant or at least worthy of mention.

The Mama's memory for such details was seemingly inexhaustible. Recalling even the names of friends brought to the club months before, she would begin almost every conversation with a tidbit gleaned from a previous encounter at Bijo. Each customer, no matter how infrequent his visits to the club, was thus awarded a continuous relationship with the Mama; her terrific memory would also result in scoldings for those customers who stayed away from the club too long.

In her attempt to obligate a customer through personalizing a relationship based on money, the Mama used her memory of visits to comment on his presence as well as his absence. The guest who was made to feel temporarily guilty for not having visited Bijo sooner was also reminded that his presence has been notably missed. The Mama thus reflects back to the man an image that he has created, by repeating to him only the discursive fragments of conversation by which he has already indicated that he prefers to be known. If the Mama has pursued and acquired information about him elsewhere, she does not mention it.

Directing her attention solely to one or, at most, two or three guests at a sitting, Mama speaks in a quiet, almost conspiratorial voice. To keep her few moments with a customer private, she would often shoo away any hostesses already at the table. Not particularly astute politically or intellectually, as some women in the *mizu shōbai* reputedly are, the Mama discusses appealing topics that a man is not likely to pursue with other men and especially not with his wife.

The Mama is a good listener but in no way a passive conversationalist. She would sustain dialogues with concern, flattery, and flirtation. Speaking at times in a whisper, she would pick up on, reflect, and then enhance whatever the man felt most at ease with about himself. She would ask him for advice on matters she knew he could handle and compliment him on qualities he was straining to achieve. Though she would hold a hand or touch a shoulder, she mainly caressed his ego. To be told that he is handsome, charming, a splendid singer, makes a man feel good even when objectively it isn't true.

On the one hand, Mama attends to the man as subject, perceiving his needs and intuiting his desires. She asks the hostess he has admired to sit with him, keeps encouraging him to sing when she knows that is his inclination, seats him away from the air conditioner when she remembers that cold air bothers him, and makes other arrangements for his comfort and pleasure. Responsive to the wishes he expresses or implies, Mama also strives to become included in this list of his wants.

The Mama's attentiveness, however personal it seems, is routinely granted to every guest. Attempting to spend at least a few moments with each customer, she also personally sees each customer off when he leaves, calls each new guest the day after his first visit, sends all of her customers cards on their birthdays and New Year's, and mails them chocolates on Valentine's Day. Though every customer systematically received the same treatment, this fact did not diminish its appeal.

As a customer becomes a regular, Mama uses gifts and phone calls to secure and extend the relationship and thereby increase obligations on her customers. Often they would come to Bijo, for example, on a particular evening only because Mama had called them that day, requesting that they visit. When she gave her big *buyō*, traditional Japanese dance recital, all of the customers were implored for months to attend and presumably to contribute to the expense, which was charged entirely to the participants, and while complaining out of earshot, many did.

Seeking to dispel anonymity, distance, and unconnectedness for her customers in the nightlife, Mama acts to personalize the relationships she has with them in various ways. Another of her strategies is to objectify and personify herself, in effect providing a mirror in which a man can flirt with his own reflection. Self-designed as a beautiful, refined, desirable woman, she achieves a subtle perfection in appearance and flirts with a coyness that is lent dignity by the gestures of a traditional lady.

Having built up the image that the customer wishes to project, the Mama does not wait for reciprocal treatment but will direct attention to herself, if need be, on her own. Sure of being complimented, she may ask a customer what he thinks of her new kimono or hair style. On receiving such orchestrated praise, she responds without the so-called typical modesty of Japanese femininity, voicing instead a simple "*hontō?*" (really?), thereby signaling that the compliment is something she's well aware of.

Mama's voice is celebrated for its beauty. Staging its exhibition, she will single out one guest to be her partner in a duet, encourage him if he resists, and then select a song from a separate list that, I noticed, comprises her repertoire. She will then overshadow her partner in performance, singing with a volume and a seriousness that reveal her perception of herself as a professional. To memorialize the event, Mama has a waiter photograph her and her partner. The waiter will then ceremoniously hand the photo, autographed and dated by the Mama, to the customer. As both image of her and evidence of a relationship (if only through song), this picture will be shown off and examined all evening; a flashlight is made available specifically for this purpose.

Bijo's customers not only treat these performances seriously but also visibly delight in them. They exclaim and fawn over the Mama, taking real pride in her stardom and accepting the illusion, created by her, that at some level she belongs to her customers.

The ideal the Mama can personify for her audience is that of a metaphoric, stand-in, pretend, temporary, or potential mistress. Flirting with one man as if she means it, she allows the customers he brings in to think that just maybe she really is his. Her art could be said to be that of giving away nothing yet pretending to be accessible (and getting away with the pretense). I remember one customer, Hanno-san, who, after spending an hour with the Mama at dinner and ten minutes with her at his table, asked her what she had done with the five man (50,000 yen, about $250) he had given her as a birthday present. She nonchalantly replied that she had added five man of her own and purchased a beautiful kimono. When baited for the additional money, Hanno-san handed over five more bills, which the Mama immediately counted, joking that one was missing. Slipping the money quickly into her kimono, she smiled coquettishly but did not voice a single word of thanks. When he asked for a single kiss, he was presented only with the Mama's cheek. The Mama then smiled slyly and rushed off to another table. Gazing after her in feigned or real amazement, this sixtyish man muttered that at least he could have expected a kiss. The hostess sitting with him, however, quite seriously attempted to convince him that he had, in fact, been lucky. He had, after all, shared dinner with the Mama; with a woman so much in demand, this in itself was a great honor.

Still young and attractive enough to be desirable and concealing the fact that she already has a patron, Mama cultivates the illusion that she is still available. What flatters the customer is the possibility that her flirtatious signals can be taken seriously. But playing this game can become boring, as Hanno-san admitted to me. Realizing that a woman of the Mama's age and means must have a patron, he had found the attractions of the game wearing thin. Nonetheless, even though the Mama's flirtatious performance had become wearisome, Hanno-san felt that the impression she made on customers he brought to Bijo was motivation enough to keep coming.

Sexualizing Male Play

Eri joins a table and is told her breasts look particularly flat. Akiko sits down, and the men wonder aloud if her breasts have grown at all since she turned twelve. When I am talking with a guest about England, he asks suddenly what my bust size is and how it compares with that of other foreigners. The men always laugh at these comments—not a snicker but a hearty guffaw, a laugh that seems to achieve a release—getting it all out, unwinding from the day, cleansing them of tensions and resentments before heading home. It is this laughter and release that men will say is one of their prime objectives in going out drinking at night.

Alluding to women's breasts, the men speak at such times *of* females but mainly *to* other males. And what they speak of is themselves, not of being Yamaguchi from X section at Y company but of being "the biggest *sukebei*

I've ever seen," "a *sukebei* who has ten women a night and wants more," "a *sukebei* who took me out last night and introduced me to a whore," "a *sukebei* who can't get it up but dreams of it all the time," "a man who couldn't find a wife because all the women knew he was a *sukebei*." The tone is jocular, the gesture friendly; pointing out a woman's breasts—a body part most indicative of the female's otherness—brings out the "other" in the man himself, the dimensions of his personality that men say must be repressed not only at work but at home as well.[12] Shifting from a remark about the female to one about the male—"Your breasts are small. What a *sukebei* I am"; "What melons she has. *Sukebei* is his middle name"—men frequently proceed to a discussion in which, by self-proclamation, they open up and reveal themselves in ways they do only rarely anywhere else—for example, telling a boss off, letting a coworker know that he had done something offensive, disclosing private dreams of the future, or telling others about a hobby one has or an invention one has made.

There is also a tendency not only to segue from breast talk into talk about one's self but to deal with woman as object from the subject position of the sexualized man. This can take several forms, exercising different dimensions of the *sukebei*/male/customer position men acquire in the context of the hostess club. One is that of going beyond language and touching the woman, usually on one or both breasts. Such touching, at Bijo at least, could be characterized by what I call "the pat," a ritualized bop to the breast that ends almost as soon as it begins. Less a caress directed to and intended for the woman, it seems a gesture engaged in more for the benefit of the other men. That is, just as a man will call a woman's breasts flat and look to the other men, who all laugh, a man will place his hand on the breast of a hostess and look not at her but at the rest of the males.

An instance of this behavior occurred one evening when, seeing off guests downstairs, I noticed another hostess returning to her club after making similar farewells. Three men who had been drinking at that club approached her. They did not seem to know the hostess, but as they passed, one reached out and patted her breast, without a murmur or even a glance. The men kept moving, but they laughed together loudly. The woman had no visible reaction: no words, no facial response, no protest. The encounter had lasted only a few seconds.

While touching can include other body parts and involve a more pro-

---

12. Men would say that even at home they are aware of their social responsibilities, and women would tell stories of hearing that their husbands were the "life of the party" when out at night, while they remained uptight, taciturn, and serious at home.

longed feeling or pawing, these short, ritualized pats to the breasts were by far the most pervasive form of male touching at Bijo, directed almost never to the Mama or to novice hostesses but regularly to the veterans, who would often initiate or manipulate the movements. Thus the pat to the breast (much like the remark about the breast) signifies a second aspect of the *sukebei* role: possession. The female body becomes, in a sense, possessed, and the male (as *sukebei*) is the proud possessor.

Sexuality, in this context and this construction, has inequity built into it. In the relationship between customer and servicer, males become the party not only of sexual desire but of sexual rights, and females become not only sexually desired but sexually owned. As Bijo's manager told the hostesses in one of two staff meetings he held during the four months I worked at the club, one reason hostesses are employed is that men have a *sukebei* nature. When they make lecherous gestures, either verbal or physical, a hostess must be willing to put up with them. Most important, she must never show anger. There to serve the man his cigarettes and drinks, she is also there to serve, within limits, his sexual needs.

Reaching out to the woman's body as assuredly as he would to his glass of liquor or plate of bean pods, the man is in the position not only to desire but to have. That the man as customer is allowed to touch the hostesses confirms both a change in his "world"—from the duties and control outside the hostess club to the pleasures and release in it—and a change in his position. Instead of bending to the system, the man finds that the system accommodates him. The woman need not be cajoled, enticed, or consulted; she may simply be "taken." The man thus becomes the "taker," a position that begets power, masculinity, and pleasure.[13]

It is from this position that customers react to the bodies of the hostesses in two other ways. The first is a more extended commentary on the women's physical appearance. Unlike the brevity of so-called breast talk—the one-liners about a hostess's breasts that end in guffaws—this body talk often involves many parts of the woman's body and can be conducted in a serious or at least semiserious tone of voice:

Guest 1: Akiko has very pretty legs. She's only nineteen, you know.
Guest 2: Yeah, she's a *joshidaisei* (university student).

13. Sexual behavior grounded in a gendered relationship of unequal power is also the structure of rape, sexual abuse, sexual harassment, and, according to some feminists, all sexually-based heterosexual relations in Western culture (see, for example, Dworkin 1981). Here, the sexual privilege accorded to male customers in hostess clubs institutionalizes the

Guest 1: She really looks slender, but she has no breasts whatsoever.

Guest 2: Maybe as she gets older, they'll grow.

Guest 1: Amazing, no breasts whatsoever to speak of. I mean, nothing at all.

Guest 2: Yeah, not even the hint of a breast.

Guest 1: (as Akiko walked back to the table from singing) You know, her ass is surprisingly large.

Guest 2: Yeah, she's very big there. Yet she looks so slender and has no breasts at all.

"Having" the woman, in this manifestation, entails less the mere physical presence and more the aesthetics of a display, there to be looked at like the furnishings and the Mama's dress. The hostess is expected to please, of course, in the service she renders, in the appearance she provides, and in the lecherousness she allows. And while the appearance of the hostesses is the area most criticized by customers about Bijo—one man saying that the Mama, the decor, and the general service were all superb enough to make Bijo "first class," but the hostesses' dress and beauty brought it down to a "second class" club—still the men assess how the women look, as if there were a standard of appearance and as if they were its author, or at least its judge.

The direction of "the look," of course, goes predominantly one way. Women *do* discuss how men look, but the discussion is complimentary and is usually centered on clothing and accessories as evidence of social standing: "nice Italian shoes; they must be expensive"; "a Pierre Cardin tie—classy"; "a Gucci watch; you must be important." In contrast to the woman's attempt to glamorize or inflate a man's looks, the man's impulse is generally to strip the woman down. She becomes nothing more than her sexualized body parts and is stripped to what she "naturally," "actually" is: a woman with little breasts and a large butt, a woman with coarse hair and pudgy, though cute arms, a woman with fat legs but large breasts—in general, a female who is to be seen and judged by the harsh but authoritative eyes of the male. Significantly, men neither relish nor accept comparable treatment. Twice, after conversations when all the hostesses' breasts had been evaluated and discussed at length, I tried to ask the men about the size of their

sexualization of male privilege. Significantly and consistently, a new fad in hostess clubs in the early 1990s has been "sexual harassment" (*seku hara*) clubs, where hostesses dress the part of O.L.s. This comes in the wake of Japan's first sexual harassment case, won by the plaintiff to the puzzlement and amusement of Japan's male population (*New York Times*, 17 April 1992).

penises. The reaction was immediate. They blanched, coughed nervously, and immediately changed the topic. The hostesses, however, laughed gleefully and patted me on the back.

Although some of the things customers say about the hostess's body can be overtly crude as well as rude—"Your vagina looks wide"; "Do you wear underpants? Are they made of paper?" or "Maybe you're not even a woman—your breasts are so small"—such remarks are made in a tone that doesn't appear intended to insult and doesn't appear to be taken as insulting by the hostess. Many comments on appearance, in fact, are directed openly to the woman, whose tendency is to accept and agree with them wholeheartedly:

> Guest 1: You're certainly pudgy, aren't you?
> Hostess 1: You're right about that. I'm a real chubette; chubby arms, chubby legs, chubby tummy.
> Guest 2: How flat-chested you are!
> Hostess 1: Yep, I am. I have nothing down there, nothing at all.
> Guest 2 (speaking to me): I can't stand your hair. It flops all over your forehead. You should brush it away. (He leans toward me to brush my hair off my forehead.)
> Hostess 2 (speaking to me): *Otōsan* (referring to the guest who had addressed me) likes women with their hair up and off their faces. That's the reason he likes me, you know.[14]

This move, to address the woman's body not only in her "absence"—referring to or touching it as a means of establishing a particular rapport among men—but in her presence, signals the second form of male objectification or sexualization of the female within the club. Besides moving from talking *about* her to talking *to* her, men may proceed even further and say they desire her. Of course, even an initial breast remark ("What knockers you have") can be accompanied by a statement of desire ("and I'd love to touch them in bed with you one night"), but what I'm describing here are more intimate encounters, usually between one male and one female, that can include long, private conversations; whisperings back and forth; caresses of the hand, shoulder, and hair; and confessions, often mutually expressed, of sexual or romantic interest.

One rather strained engagement I witnessed took place when a man

14. *Otōsan*, literally "father," is used in the club for customers who come often or are important. Keiko told me that she used this term with customers she'd like to make her patrons.

brought his wife and son to Bijo to celebrate the son's new job. Another hostess, Sachiko, and I were seated with the party, and while I tried to speak with the wife, who was visibly uncomfortable, the son vacillated between our conversation and that between Sachiko and his father, which had warmed up immediately. All but ignoring his son, the father devoted his attention to Sachiko, cuddling up to her, caressing her hair, asking her to sing, kissing her fingers, patting her breasts, and, with repeated insistence and specificity, trying to set up a date with her at a love hotel on Saturday night.

Whether this particular date transpired or not I have no idea, but the official club line was that liaisons between customers and hostesses were neither encouraged nor allowed. In fact, I sensed that on occasion they did occur, but if they became obvious or extended the hostess involved would be fired or asked to resign. Soon after this encounter, in fact, Sachiko was no longer working at Bijo—why, I didn't find out. Far more common were flirtations between customers and hostesses—some brief, some longer, some highly stylized, some more personal, some physical, and some with no touching at all—that would end when either the hostess was moved to another table or the customer walked out the door. Like a snapshot of two lovers, the scene is one of attachment, but the picture is framed by the club. Hence, while men and women may profess to love one another here, the understanding is that this is a form of play, one that will not usually lead to a relationship, sexual or romantic, outside the club.

The manner in which this play usually proceeds is that a customer will flirt with one hostess and then with a second, who has taken her place; or he will continue his romancing with a different hostess at each of three, four, or even five clubs he may visit in a particular night; or he will persist with his advances toward one hostess even though she has for months refused to date him outside the club. In my own experience, I had men say they adored me, desired me, thought I was beautiful, wanted me for their mistress, and then either turn to another hostess and reiterate the same sentiments or leave the club and stay away for months, forgetting my name before their return. Other customers, more ardent in their pursuits, would continue asking me out without any encouragement from me.

What the man seemed to gain in these encounters was a kind of romantic exercise rather than an emotional or sexual experience. Assured that most hostesses would at least play along, the man would act as if the woman was his heartthrob, and she would respond in kind. The lack of sincerity appears quite irrelevant to the Japanese. In fact, I was told that only Westerners mistake a gesture of sexual interest displayed in the hostess club for a willingness to bed down elsewhere. A Japanese told me of an American who had propositioned a flirtatious hostess and had been shocked when she took offense, considering him rude and even perverse. She, after all, had only been playing the hostess game. While Japanese customers proposition hostesses, they can be joked with and put off.

Exaggerated claims of love and adoration and hyperbolic compliments are not meant to be believed so much as enjoyed. Play calls for a suspension of belief; and in the hostess club playing is an experience a man can count on. He need not worry whether he'll really be liked, whether a woman will really find him attractive, or whether a female will be willing to flirt; he knows what he can expect, and the expectation is reassuring.

As a customer explained to me, when I asked if the canned performances of the hostesses were demeaning to a man, "Men are *sukebeis*, but they only have limited time and money to act out being dirty old men. The men who come to a hostess club like this are at least middle-aged; they don't have the energy to chase women all night. When they buy a woman a drink here, they know she'll pay them attention. A man feels good when a hostess tells him he's hot stuff. And if he still wants sex, there are places to go for that, too."

Part Two

Mapping
the Nightlife
within Cultural
Categories

Introduction

In *Nihonjin no Ishiki Kōzō* (*The Structure of Japanese Consciousness*), Aida Yuji, who represents a school of Japanese scholarship generically referred to as the *nihonjinron* or debate about Japaneseness, addresses the question of what constitutes Japanese behavior.[1] Concerned, as are other *nihonjinron* scholars, with the issues of where Japanese culture comes from and what it consists of today, Aida embarks on his investigation with an assumption about Japaneseness already in place—that the culture of Japan is unique and that its cultural uniqueness explains divergent behaviors, from the tea ceremony and flower arranging to the ethics of hard work and company loyalty.

In this context, Aida addresses the practice of Japanese male workers congregating at bars and clubs after work.[2] First, he describes a foreigner's reaction to this behavior, which to the foreigner appears very strange:

> One night a fellow worker who is also a good friend and I took a *gaijin* (foreigner) who was in Japan observing our company to a bar. It was around 11 P.M. and seated next to us was a group of workers from an electron microscope company heatedly discussing some issue. The foreigner was surprised at this and asked what possibly

1. The *Nihonjinron* refers to a discourse that is engaged in at many levels—popular, scholarly, political—and hence encompasses academic treatises and research projects devoted to the subject (archaeologically, linguistically, historically, sociologically) as well as to the type of conversations and discussions TV hosts, newspaper reporters, and housewives will have about it. For a general description and critique in English, see Mouer and Sugmimoto (1986).

2. Female office workers—significantly gender-labeled O.L.s (office ladies)—will also drink together (and with male coworkers) after work and attend such company-sponsored events as *enkai* (office gatherings). Yet the practice of going out with employees or clients almost nightly to expensive clubs, and using company money for these sessions is most heavily engaged in by *sarariiman* in or headed for management positions. Although women now constitute 40 percent of the labor force in Japan, only 1 percent of them hold managerial positions (*Wall Street Journal*, "Reluctant Feminists: Women's Movement in Corporate Japan Isn't Moving Very Fast," 6 June 1991).

could workers from the same company be doing together at an hour
like this. I surmised that they were probably reflecting on upcoming
marketing strategies for their microscopes and was probably not far
off. The foreigner, however, found this to be strange and remarked
that Japanese companies are different [from American companies]—
working their employees until even midnight without giving them
overtime pay. He added that that's why Japanese companies give him
a strange sensation of being fearful (*kowai*). (1972:66–67)

Contrasted to the foreigner's perspective, in Aida's account, is that of a
Japanese, who finds workers' drinking sessions familiar and acceptable.
Due to a cultural principle the author refers to as *kōshi kongō* (literally "the
merging of private and public"), Japanese workers are said to see nothing
strange in the convergence of the public realm of work and the private realm
of nighttime socializing. In fact, there *is* no clear-cut private-public distinction, for work doesn't definitively end at five o'clock, and the worker has no
personal identity that doesn't somehow incorporate his work. As Aida puts
it, "For the whole 24 hours (a day), a worker can't forget that he's a
worker" (1972:67).

In this passage Aida employs two techniques common in *nihonjinron* discourse. One is to position a Japanese behavior by stressing its differences
from behaviors found in other cultures. The second is to explain Japanese
culture in the same terms that are used to describe it—as ways of behaving
that are characteristically Japanese. By these techniques Aida makes the
drinking sessions of workers seem both distinctly Japanese and the outcrop
of cultural ideas that all Japanese innately and uniformly share. Consequently the practice of worker outings is seen as an icon and paradigm of
Japanese culture, and Japanese culture is seen as explaining and legitimizing
an industrial practice—that is, Japanese workers go out drinking together
after work because they are Japanese, and because they are Japanese, workers go out drinking together after work.

Such a treatment of culture is *essentialist* in the language of anthropologists. This means that behavior shaped by a number of factors, including
politics, economics, history, and class, is explained primarily or only in
terms of culture. Aida fails to point out that workers are encouraged by their
companies to drink with one another after hours and that their refusal to do
so could affect their careers. His description of the phenomenon is therefore
selective and his explanation of it apolitical, suggesting that culture rather
than the conscious policy of corporations is responsible for the behavior.

Like Aida, I found that most Japanese regard the custom of company-supported outings as familiar, acceptable, and natural. If inclined to explain it at all, most choose to do so by rooting it in more generally established or codified cultural behavior. Few speak of what actually goes on among men out drinking at night "for work," and fewer still consider the implications these sessions have for other realms of social life such as leisure time, family, gender, and class.[3] Rather, the tendency is to essentialize this practice by discussing and accepting it as culturally Japanese.

My goal in part 2 is to examine the cultural terms Japanese use in discussing nighttime drinking at company expense. As I will argue in part 3, these terms convert a practice institutionalized by corporations into an ideology that shapes the behavior of workers, a gendered division of labor, and a commodified sexuality that channels masculine energy into work. Following Roland Barthes, I use the concept of naturalization—that behavior structured by historical, social, political, and/or economic institutions is made to seem "natural" by conceptualizing it as cultural (1972). If drinking with coworkers is a fact of culture rather than industrial policy, in other words, its institutionalization and the effects of this institutionalization are both harder to recognize and harder to resist.

In this part of the book I am interested only in laying out the cultural categories through which nighttime drinking at corporate expense enters the worldview of Japanese. The ideological maneuvers that make use of these categories (and use them as an "alibi" in Barthes's terminology [1972:123]) are discussed in part 3. Let me be quite clear: I am discussing a hegemonic or popularly accepted view. Not all Japanese subscribe to the corporateness of nighttime drinking so willingly or naively. Some see this behavior as an example of the corruptness of Japanese corporations. Some also view the constant merging of leisure and business as a mechanism that benefits business and the leisure industry but works against the well-being of individual workers and their families (see, for example, Nada 1992). Those within the middle or upper echelons of corporate society, however, are those most likely to participate in business-paid entertainment and most likely to view it as culturally valid. It is this perspective that I am interested in here, and I will examine it in terms of the cultural behaviors, theories, and customs used to explain the "Japaneseness" of corporate entertainment.

3. None of the accounts I have read that refer to business-supported male entertaining in the *mizu shōbai* give a detailed account of what actually goes on. The most descriptive is Yoda (1981), which is not specifically concerned with nighttime entertaining at company expense.

My data in part 2 come from three sources: interviews with Japanese, comments made in the context of conversations engaged in or overheard at the hostess club, and published material—essays, books, articles, and *zadankai* (roundtable discussions)—that focuses or touches on the subject at hand. The speakers and writers represent a variety of positions and perspectives: wives who accept such behavior from their husbands; men who are expected to adopt such behavior as company workers; sociologists and counselors who consider the behavior in terms of family dynamics; reporters and commentators who put the practice in the context of Japanese patterns of sexuality, parenting, and social relationships; and scholars who discuss the behavior when writing about the ways in which Japanese play, work, establish subjectivity, and deal socially with others.

Explanations of why Japanese men engage in corporate-sponsored drinking sessions vary. They can be grouped in five categories, at least one of which is mentioned by each speaker or writer:

The hostess bar is . . .

1) a factor of Japanese notions of *place* and identity;
2) an outcrop and feature of Japanese *work* patterns;
3) a structure of the Japanese *family* and the *gendered division of labor* rooted within the family;
4) a realm of and for *play*, which has a separate status in Japanese culture; and
5) a domain of *sexual license* whereby Japanese men can express, and have traditionally expressed, a sexuality away from family, home, and wife.

Each of these rationales is taken up in a later chapter, but in practice they often merge or overlap. The tendency is for a discussion coded in one way to switch codes along the way. A man begins by talking about work and establishing good trust relations among men who work together, for example, and winds up telling me of his need to release frustrations related to job and home with a woman whom he need never see again. This seguing is an indication of the complex cultural meanings and ideological potential that the hostess-club corporate ritual holds in Japanese society.

I would like to add a word about my own position on many of the ideas, opinions, and theories presented in part 2. Generally these views privilege a culturalist explanation. They justify corporate drinking by its Japaneseness, giving it an identity that is linked to other behaviors in the culture. Factors of history, economic interest, political motivation, and practical consequences are often overlooked, reducing the complexities of an institutional phenomenon to the essence of a culture. Of these tendencies I am critical, but I will not always offer the reader my specific criticisms of each position presented. My goal here is to lay out the cultural ideas that support corporate entertainment by framing and legitimizing it as cultural custom. All the perspectives represented in part 2 serve this function, and for this ideological role the texts and perspectives in this section were selected. I point out the ideology of the cultural assumptions in part 3. In part 2, so far as possible, I let the voices of Japanese speak for themselves.

4

Social Place and Identity

Hierarchy and Difference

Two concepts that continually surface in discourses about the Japanese are that they are very "group-oriented" and that their construction of self reflects and embeds this group orientation. Some, myself included, attempt to root such cultural behaviors within specific historical and social relations: relations, for example, of gender, class, and work through which "group orientation" is differentially produced and realized. Yet in the popular and regularly quoted texts on Japanese character and society—Nakane Chie's *Tate Shakai* (*Japanese Society*), Minami Hiroshi's *Nihonjin no Shinri* (*The Psychology of the Japanese*), and Doi Takeo's *Amae no Kōzō* (*The Anatomy of Dependence*), for example—there is a shared and uncritical conception that what characterizes and distinguishes Japanese society, universally, homogeneously, and trans-historically, is the embeddedness of its people in organizations that construct their behavior, identity, and relations with others.

Nihonjinron scholars have frequently rooted Japan's "groupishness"[1] in the cultural responses Japan has made historically to a series of geographical, ecological, and racial conditions. Living on an isolated island endowed with few natural resources, with a terrain so mountainous that only about 19 percent of the land is arable, and with a number of potentially cataclysmic environmental features (earthquakes, volcanoes, typhoons, tidal waves), the Japanese have survived and flourished, it is often argued, only through

---

1. Two terms for "groupishness" are *shūdanseikatsu,* which literally means "group life" and is used by teachers and parents to describe the life children enter when starting school (see Rohlen 1989 and Peak 1989), and *kyōdō seikatsutai,* "one big happy family" or "one collectivity," which was the term used by a Japanese *sarariiman* to describe how "Japanese style management" was characterized for him at a seminar. As we will see, he criticized this concept (Tsuda 1987:118).

hard work and social cooperation. According to many, racial homogeneity has also been an important factor in this successful development.[2]

For centuries the Japanese have cultivated rice, a subsistence crop that demands backbreaking labor and periodic and absolute cooperation among neighbors.[3] Such practical incentives to a communitarian ethos have been supplemented and codified over time by a number of religious, political, and legal institutions. During the Tokugawa period (1603–1868), for example, the newly centralized government of the Shogunate instituted the policy of the *goningumi*, dividing villages into five-family units, with each unit accepting responsibility for any wrongdoing by an individual or family. Cultivating the group as the unit of both loyalty and penalty, the community developed the practice of *murahachibu*—punishment by ostracism from the village or the group. *Murahachibu* is a word still used today to indicate ideological ostracism of a person who does not conform to the ways or mores of a perceived group. And group loyalty and responsibility are still cultivated in various school and work practices,[4] and stressed within the languages of religion, family, and the state.[5]

2. Racial homogeneity is a key element in the *nihonjinron*, and its premise underlies much that Japanese say about who and what they are. While prime minister, Nakasone alluded to this racial oneness of the Japanese, as contrasted with the ethnic multiplicities of America, which, he said, make America a much more difficult country to control and manage. This position has been widely criticized by non-Japanese and by various Japanese as well (see, for example, Mouer and Sugimoto 1986).

3. For a fairly standard version of the *nihonjinron* that traces major Japanese social traits to its history of rice cultivation and particular ecological, geographical, and historical conditions, see Ishida 1974. A customer at Bijo who tried to explain male outings to me used rice cultivation as a parallel to corporate endeavor. "Japanese men work hard *and* together, just as Japanese rice farmers have done traditionally, and hence must also relax together" was the gist of his explanation.

4. In preschool (*yōchien*), children are grouped in four-person or two-person groups called *han* to pursue various activities (Tobin 1989; Lewis 1989:149–50; Allison 1991). Performance is often judged by the *han* rather than by individual participation, and this tendency to conduct activities, judge performance, and form identity according to group membership is pursued at many different levels. Work practices such as lifetime employment, QC circles, seniority wage structures, all-enterprise unions, and job rotation stress the tie a worker has with the company. For descriptions of some of these practices, see Rohlen 1974; Dore 1973. For a critique of how ideologized and overstated they can be, see Sugimoto, Shimada, and Levine 1982.

5. To oversimplify, the languages of religion, family, and state include the *ie* system, a system treating the family socially and legally, under the Meiji Family Code of 1898, as a corporate unit, and the Imperial System, which, until the end of World War II, was a state religion centered on the emperor. Under both the *ie* and imperial systems, the individual was identified (and still is, culturally, and socially, to some extent) according to his or her place within these wider units. For a readable account of these social institutions, see Hendry 1987.

Scholars such as the highly noted and frequently cited Nakane Chie, an anthropologist and the first female professor at Tokyo University, link Japan's groupishness less to the structure of family and more to a social principle of "verticality." Labeling Japan a *tate shakai*—vertical society—Nakane writes that it is a society where the group or groups one is currently a member of outshadow membership in the groups one may have been born into, such as the family. What these groups will be for the adult depends heavily on gender. For a female the group is the family she marries into; for a male it is first the school or university he graduates from and next, and most important, the company he works for (Nakane 1970).

Ba (frame) is the concept Nakane uses to explain the attachment the Japanese have to any group they belong to. A particular frame (a club, school, company) is shared by a number of people and signifies a shared attachment, a shared commitment, and a shared identity. The individual becomes "framed" by this association and assumes the social identity, status, and behavior of the group. Japanese behavior is therefore bound by and to particular frames rather than guided by universal laws or values that would transcend the specific context of the individual's own frame. This means that when decontextualized from their own group, the Japanese tend to behave without order or rules. That tendency may explain why, when riding the public trains, visiting tourist spots, and/or traveling abroad, Japanese have been accused of "lawless" behavior. It also means that changing groups is extremely difficult and that the behavior and identity of a person who makes such a change may shift dramatically overnight.

Although members of particular groups share a communal link, Nakane is very careful to point out that such communality is neither equivalent to nor conducive to a structure of similarity of and between the members. Rather, she notes, it is the framework of the group itself that encourages and demands the production of difference. In Nakane's words, "Without either 'frame' or 'vertical links,' it seems to be almost impossible for the Japanese to form a functional group" (1970:59). By this she means that there is a social imperative to rank people hierarchically in Japan and that it is within and by the mechanism of groups that Japanese are ranked. She explains:

> The vertical relation . . . becomes the actuating principle in creating cohesion among group members. Because of the overwhelming ascendancy of this vertical orientation, even a set of individuals sharing identical qualifications tend to create a *difference* among themselves. (1970:25)

As Nakane elaborates with various examples, difference is the premise of almost every social relationship in Japan. Until this difference is established, two people will not know how to behave toward one another. The custom of exchanging *meishi* (name cards) upon first introduction satisfies the need to produce difference: one's affiliations (company, division, rank) are inscribed on the cards, allowing recipients to assess differences in status. For those affiliated with the same group, differences in status can be determined by age, gender, seniority, progress, and promotion within the group. But no matter how it is effected, ranked difference is the principle, Nakane argues, by which Japanese are structured to interact and position themselves socially.

This linkage between a deep commitment and attachment to one's group and the position and behavior of the rank one assumes within that group is made repeatedly by Japanese and often in a language that implies how inaccessible such a concept is to the thinking of a Westerner. The suggestion is that Westerners possess a different notion of self, a self as somehow extractable from the group. The individual Westerner may also be committed to groups, but her commitment is different.

"Front Culture" and "Back Culture"

The Japanese use the term *honbun* to express the socially contextualized concept of self. Minami Hiroshi defined *honbun* as "the position everyone is put in that is appropriate to their activities in a system of justice" (1978:206). Translated loosely as "position" or "place" (or "duty" or "part"), *honbun* doubly encodes place: a person's identification by his or her *location* in groups and the *location* of those groups within the wider society. Determined by where one is "at" in society (school and work are Minami's example), it nonetheless transcends the dimensions of mere time or material space. A worker's *honbun* (*shain no honbun*), for example, means he remains a worker past the hours of "work" and outside the physical boundaries of the workplace.[6] In this respect, *honbun* differs from the concept of duty (*kinmu*) and marks the person in a continuous "24-hour-a-day" fashion (Minami 1978).

While various Japanese have refuted this concept or at least denied internalizing or acting upon it in their own lives (see the various testimonies of

---

6. By this process a woman's identity and ranking become that of her husband, unless she is unmarried or in a professional or managerial position herself.

sarariiman and their wives in Tsuda 1987, for example), many see the principle of *honbun* and the social interrelatedness (*ningenkankei*, literally "human relations") it fosters as the feudalistic "foundation" of Japan's modern capitalist economy. Minami calls it the fusing of public with private: "For most Japanese their public time or work eats into their private time and lives. The public life of company workers wrests almost all of the personal time from the moment of leaving work until midnight parties (*enkai*) (1978:207)."

Aida uses a similar example—workers from the same company drinking together at night rather than returning to their separate homes—to make the same point: "We mix personal and public in Japan and it increases our work output. It suits Japanese to think of themselves as workers 24 hours a day" (1972:67). In Aida's discussion, however, the emphasis is not so much on the relation between the person and the group as on the nature of the interpersonal relations within the group. Aida refers to these relationships as having two tiers: a front (*omote*) and a back (*ura*), or a hierarchical structure (*tate shakai*) and a human and humane backing (*ningenkankei*) to that structure. The structural component is the affiliations—the hierarchical imperative to structure all social relations according to a principle of ranked difference. This aspect he presents as essential but cold, one that is incomplete without the personal relationships (*kojin teki kankei*) which infuse the structural ties of hierarchy with humanity and warmth. Aida considers the duality of this package the uniqueness of Japan, stating that in America there exists only a "front" structure without the "back" support of human relationships so treasured and essential in Japan (1972).

To illustrate the "humanity" of "back" relationships, Aida describes a questionnaire (frequently cited in discussions about Japanese work attitudes; see Tsuda 1987, for example) that asked Japanese to select which of two types they would prefer for a boss. Type A is considerate, fair, even-tempered, and no taskmaster. He leaves work on schedule and neither makes demands on his workers nor indulges them in ways not strictly work-related. Type B occasionally becomes angry and unreasonable; he's basically fair in evaluating the work of his employees yet is sometimes swayed by his own feelings; and he looks after his workers in ways that are not separate from strictly work-related matters. According to Aida's data, 80 percent of those polled in Japan selected the Type B boss (1972:64).

Aida has argued that this humanity or humaneness (*ningenmi*) is the most important quality of a Japanese leader or boss. A good boss will cushion his employees by accepting responsibility for their acts and by comforting them when they fail or make mistakes. Aida uses the example of an employee sent out to land a contract; the Japanese boss must be concerned not merely about the success or failure of the negotiations (as, Aida claims, would be the situation in America) but also about the psychological state of the employee if he fails. But though the boss will "humanly" understand his workers, the humanity he expresses will not negate the hierarchy separating employer and employee in the work relationship. Instead, the hierarchy is humanized; and *because* it is humanized, the maintenance of hierarchy is assured and sustained (1972:63, 65, 68).

In Aida's words, a boss must be "humanly above" his underlings; this is the most important qualification for his position (1972:63). What precisely this means, however, even Aida admits is slippery. What it is *not* is simply the "front" relationship (*omote kankei*) of hierarchy; nor is it merely official or rational concerns that a boss in America or Europe might feel contained by. It comes closest to being a buddy substitute, an *oyaji* (chap, fellow, old man, one of the guys) (67), one who can personalize a work relationship of work so that neither the relationship nor the person is strictly limited to the arena of "work." And with this, Aida returns to the point he and Minami agree on: Japanese merge the private and the public in a manner neither familiar nor comprehensible to Westerners.

Aida adds a final concept—that of "self-denial" (*jiko hitei*), which he argues is the "original premise for us as Japanese" (1972:161). If a person is too self-assertive, the dynamics of Japanese social relations cannot be established. Hence, self-restraint must be learned, and the inclination to *awase*—to make a fit with others whose needs and desires one must always consider—placed first. This is the basis of "human reciprocity" (*ningen sōgo*), of sympathy displayed for one another despite the dimension of hierarchy, and the ability, as Aida puts it, to see the child in the other. "I am a child; the other too is a child" (1972:164).

For those highest in the chain of structural hierarchy, this social expectation to "think of others" and "deny the self" intensifies rather than lessens. According to Aida,

> For a normal worker (*hirashain*) it is okay to just think of oneself. But once a person rises even a little and has, for example, three people working under him, he must think of the company plus those three workers. Once this becomes 30 people, 100 people, and more and more, he must lose sight of himself and think instead of these many others. Rather than thinking of oneself (*jiko*), a boss must be other-

oriented. And for a company boss (*shachō*) this is particularly true. Under the Meiji Constitution the pinnacle of all this was the Emperor who had no realm of privacy whatsoever. (1972:64)

Logically and culturally similar is the concept of *amae,* or dependence, which Doi Takeo (1971) has argued is, in its intensity and pervasiveness, unique to Japan. Besides the dependence a mother encourages in her child, *amae* also signifies the psychology of any hierarchical relationship in which the person in the inferior position is psychologically and socially dependent on the superior. The one hierarchically on top bears the heaviest obligation, and the structure of hierarchy is, once again, underwritten by a language and system of human relatedness uncritically considered to be uniquely Japanese.

5

The Meaning and Place of Work

The *Sarariiman*

Gendered Division of Labor

Work in Japan is considered a male realm. That is, although a larger proportion of women than ever before are now working in salaried jobs outside the home, work is still considered, ideologically and culturally, an activity that is more important for men and that identifies the male more than it does the female. A woman may work, but her social status and place in society is not defined primarily as worker. When a man works, by contrast, it is to his work that he commits most of his energy, time, and loyalties, and it is as worker that his place in society is assigned.

Various practices and institutions encourage this masculinizing of work in contemporary Japan, and most borrow from divisions present in the family. As noted by sociologist Yuzawa Yasuhiko (1982) in a study that is admirable for its consideration of complex factors, Japan's gender roles have been formed and differentiated clearly within the family. According to a multitude of surveys, questionnaires, and interviews that Yuzawa conducted, the overwhelming responsibility placed on women by their children and husbands is management of all matters of home, family, and domestic maintenance. By contrast, the single constant expectation of a father/husband is to be the financial supporter of the house. Yuzawa concluded that a husband who doesn't work has "no meaning" in Japan (1982:64). Restated, the "meaning" a Japanese male has, even for his family, is situated in a realm separated from the home: his work.

Though conceptualized often in such homely phrases as "the husband manages outside matters; the wife manages inside matters" ("*ottō wa soto-mawari tsuma wa uchimawari*," quoted in Yuzawa 1982:74), the relation between female and male labor within the family hasn't been and isn't always one of bifurcation. When husband and wife manage a small business or independent shop, and when they are farmers or blue-collar workers, their labor is often cooperative or more equally defined (Bernstein 1983; Kondo 1990;

Yuzawa 1982). Yet such postwar developments as rapid industrialization, which requires more white-collar labor; increased urbanization and price inflation of urban land space, which distances the residences of urbanites from their workplaces; and smaller families and family units, which focus the woman's role on mothering fewer children, have spread a "new middle class" (Vogel 1963) with families sharply divided along gender and labor lines.

This new class is the class of the *sarariiman*: the white-collar worker whose position in a large company is the standard goal of youths whose parents are, or wish their next generation to become, comfortably middle-class. The security and status offered by big companies—for example, lifetime employment and a wage structure based on seniority (*nenkō joretsu*)—are greatly desired, but contrary to the Western assumption, such rewards are by no means standard in the Japanese workplace. Lifetime employment, for example, is common only for the highest in the hierarchy of workers and only in the largest of companies.

For such beneficiaries of the corporate system, loyalty to a company is a matter not merely of traditional ideology but of good common sense as well.[1] The longer a person works for a company, the more he gets paid and the more he loses by switching to a different job. Considering the longevity of this connection, a worker's relations with his coworkers, his bosses, and his company become a dominant, almost permanent part of his life.

Competition to achieve a *sarariiman* position in a prestigious company has become increasingly intense in Japan, and success depends almost solely on one's academic record. Some jobs, in the largest and most reputable companies or in the highest-ranked branches of the government, are annually reserved for graduates from designated universities. And many other jobs with high status, good pay, and security are filled by graduates gleaned from the highest-ranked universities. The hierarchy of Japan's universities is widely established and accepted; admission is highly competitive and is based solely on entrance examinations.[2]

Preparation for these examinations is called "examination hell" (*shiken*

---

1. Rodney Clark has written that the practice of lifetime employment, along with concomitant notions of the company as family and employee loyalty to company, were popularized in the first two decades of this century. While these concepts were expressed in traditional-sounding language, the ideology was really modern (1988:105).

2. See Horio 1988; Rohlen 1983.

jigoku). It is a period of intense study and supplemental instruction (through *juku*—cram school, *yobikō*—preparation school, or *katei kyōshi*—private tutors) that can last as long as several years.[3] The phrase "pass with four, fail with five," which means that you pass the exams if you are willing to sleep only four hours a night and fail if you indulge in five, refers not only to the effort expected of Japanese youth but to the ideological coding of the entire process. Because entrance exams test memorization of set "facts," so-called innate intelligence is not examined, nor is intelligence alone sufficient for success. Rather, it is mainly effort—the ability and willingness to work hard and bend to the expectations of the system—that determines who will be admitted to the university and who will be headed toward the most successful positions in society.

While females compete as well, the pragmatic and social meaning of their efforts is often tallied differently. In 1983, 32 percent of Japan's women continued their education after high school, constituting 90 percent of the student population in junior colleges but only 22 percent in four-year universities (Fujimura-Fanselow 1985:474).[4] A very small percentage of students at Japan's top-ranked Tokyo University are women. This reflects the social fact, as a female student at the university told me, that graduation from a prestigious four-year university can actually inhibit rather than advance a woman's employment prospects. Though the Equal Employment Opportunity Act of 1985 (which makes no provision for legal enforcement) forbids sexual discrimination in the workplace, jobs and career expectations are still gender coded. Office work that includes preparing and serving tea to male workers is mostly reserved for O.L.s.

Executives I interviewed lamented this discrimination but claimed that

---

3. Public education ends at the ninth grade, so that all children must take entrance examinations in order to enter high school. At that level, however, other factors are taken into consideration during the selection process, among them the student's academic record and the teacher's evaluation report, *naishinshō*. There is also the so-called escalator system of academic progress by way of lower schools attached to universities. A student who enters such a school will proceed to the higher levels without having to face further testing. Entrance examinations and possibly interviews, however, determine entrance at whatever level the student seeks admission. My sources quoted two years as the standard preparation time for examinations at both high-school and university level. The prospective university student who is not accepted by the school of his choice may become a *rōnin*, a masterless samurai, studying full time at his parents' expense to retake the examinations, which are offered only once a year. An artist friend of mine was a *rōnin* for three years before being accepted into the highest-ranked art school in the country.

4. What is also interesting is that the relative percentage of women entering university as opposed to junior college is less today than it was in the 1950s and 1960s (Fujimura-Fanselow 1985:474).

it didn't pay to move women into managerial slots (that would reward four-year university graduation, for example) because they "always get married and leave." Female company employees used to be forced to retire when they married, and such "retirement," women told me, is still customary or is ideologically encouraged by male management today.[5] When a woman is expected to work only until she marries (30 percent of women marry between the ages of 20 and 24, 78 percent are married by age 29, and 90 percent are married by age 34 [Kodansha Encyclopedia 1983]), attending a four-year university can become a liability rather than an asset. Still, the coupling of work and education that operates for males is not necessarily inoperative in the case of females. Rather, as both male and female interviewees asserted, the notion of work is merely different; university education is considered good preparation for women in their roles as mothers (who, as kyōiku mama or "education mothers," manage the test-taking process and preparation for their children) and for the supplemental work they can fit in prior to, during, and after motherhood.[6]

Sarariiman and the Structure of Work

Men who successfully pass into the ranks of sarariiman at big companies (bulk of the clientele at Bijo) regularly use three phrases in their discussions about work: "ranked hierarchy," "hard work," and "attachment to the company." In The Lives and Opinions of Modern Generation Sarariiman (Shinsedai Sarariiman no Seikatsu to Iken), Tsuda Masumi (1987) offers testimony and group discussion by sarariiman and their wives. The men agree that if a man wishes to rise and be successful in a company, he must face tough competition, he must work hard, and his attachment to the company must be based on a willingness to abide by and conform to the way things are done there.

5. The proportion of women in the labor force is high (40 percent), but includes part-time workers, whose proportion in the female labor pool has also increased in recent years. Thus, while more women are working, more women are doing so on a part-time basis, which can be up to 37 hours of work per week and which offers no benefits, little security, and low wages (Juristo 1985).

6. One woman with a law degree and three children told me that education was less essential for her daughter because she had another way to make a living: by marrying. Her sons, by contrast, had to earn subsistence by themselves. This woman added, however, that she would push her daughter to become trained in some skill just in case her daughter either never married or became divorced. Interestingly enough, she herself had been forced—by her parents, not her husband—to give up her own occupation (as lawyer) when she married.

Where the men differ, however, is in how they experience and interpret these obligations.

The men Tsuda spoke with always described their work as hard but conceptualized and discussed it in varying ways. One worker calls it a feature of "Japanese-style management" (*nihon teki keiei*):

> When I started working I realized, and was surprised at, how hard they work the people. My overtime is, on the average, 150 hours per month. In busy months it reaches 200 hours. According to the regulations of the union it is not permissible to work more than 50 hours per month overtime for three consecutive months, so I can only record the appropriate amount and I work the rest of the hours for no pay. . . . I had learned before working about "Japanese-style management," so I thought "So this is what they mean." (Tsuda 1987:120)

Another worker describes the excessive and strenuous work schedule that was demanded at his company the first year. He articulates the demand not in terms of company expectations or policy but as an attitude toward work that he, as a worker, should have been able to display but failed to deliver: "I intended to be very *mōretsu* [diligent, eager, enthusiastic] in my work, but my evaluation gave me only average ratings. I wonder if being late [a single time that he has previously described] was the reason?" (Tsuda 1987:121). A third worker equates the amount of work expected of him with pay levels and ultimately with the success and status a worker can achieve: "[At my company] there isn't much overtime, the boss too takes it easy, there are many days off. . . . On the other side, however, the pay is low" (121).

While stressing different points, these workers adhere to a commonly held work ideology: hard work = Japanese work style = success. Roughly similar was the way in which many of these men and many successful businessmen calculated the rigors of the entrance exams they had all survived. "It is horrendous and personally painful," one man told me, "but Japan needs some mechanism for selection, and anyone who works hard enough is rewarded."[7] From such a point of view, dimensions of the system that an outsider might consider arbitrary, excessive, or unfair—150 hours of over-

---

7. Quoted from an interview I conducted with a middle-aged male executive in a large company whose own son was then enmeshed in *juken benkyō* (exam preparation). He added that diligence rather than innate intelligence was being tested and that this was good because diligence is the quality big businesses in Japan need in their employees. When asked about the agony and stress it can produce, he answered that he and all his friends went through it and that the process would make his son tough as well.

time without pay, for example, or exams that test only memorized bites of "knowledge"—tend to be conceptualized by those within the system as matters less of structure than of personnel. That is, responsibility is shifted from the institution to its workers: work hard, compete with others, criticize higher-ups—but only privately. Coupled with this is an attitude of resignation; though the worker may be displeased with some aspect of the system, he will be more inclined to put up with it than to try to change it or leave the job.

Goya, a *sarariiman* in his late thirties, expresses deep frustration with corporate practices:

> When I first entered the company, everything was great. Every night all of us would go out drinking and walking. Then there was the oil shock. . . . Even though I've done everything right—I was raised in a *sarariiman* family; I studied and graduated from university; I applied myself, worked hard (*ganbaru*) in the company—but I feel frustrated (*zaisetsu o kanjiru*) as if my way of working has little "ripening" (*minori*). (Tsuda 1987:28)

Goya traces his problems to what Minami and Aida refer to as the "human" backing or "back culture" of Japanese institutions.

> There are three things required in order to be successful with management:
> 1) Make sure the boss (*shachō*—head of the company) knows you.
> 2) Make sure you are highly evaluated by your immediate superior. In my case the *buchō* (division head) thinks I'm well suited to my work. (Actually, I hate my work, but . . .).
> 3) The evaluation of one's work.
> I am now a "transparent person" (*tōmei ningen*). I don't push my own ideas. Rather, I go along quietly, calmly, with the ideas put forth by my superiors. Whatever the *buchō* (section head) and *kachō* (department head) say, I put my head down and don't counter it. For me this is terrible (*iya*), but I become a "transparent person" in order to be successful.
> From the beginning to the end, there *is* no other path. (Tsuda 1987:30–31)

Articulating the commonly voiced sentiment that in order to survive and be successful there is no path (*shikata ga nai*) other than entering a company and staying with it, Goya experiences company life as personally oppressive and stressful, a fact he blames almost entirely on the much-touted "human relationships" (*ningen kankei*) of Japanese corporations. In the testimonies of other *sarariiman,* complaints about superiors or the "human involvement" of work outweigh those mentioned about any other aspect of the company environment, including hard work. Younger workers complain relatively more about the workload.

One man tells of a boss (*jōshi*) who criticized employees even for their way of walking and talking and was never satisfied (Tsuda 1987:69). Another cites a boss who would shift criticism he received from higher-ups onto those beneath him (73). A third speaks of the "dirtiness" (*dorodoro*) of becoming a *kachō* (division head)—how so many are promoted because of connections they have with the head of the company and wind up doing little work (119). Still another laughs at the concept of *kyōdō seikatsutai,* the "one big happy family" mentality of Japanese-style management he learned about before commencing work. He points out that not all workers are subsumed under family: O.L.s, for example, are called the "flower of a company" but in fact prepare tea; his boss did not invite one worker to a dinner at his home and ordered the others to keep the dinner a secret (118–19).

Another man (Ishihara) uses the phrase "a world of drama" to describe the posturing that those ranked higher in a company's hierarchy can subject their inferiors to. He describes two bosses, one of whom would humiliate him in the presence of his customers:

> During business hours there are customers all around. But even in front of them he would yell at me: "*Omae* [rude address for "you"]— get the abacus and bring it to my desk!" The customers look at me and my pride completely dissipates. Every day this continues. (Tsuda 1987:126)

The other boss, ranked two steps higher than Ishihara, did not graduate from a university. For a time, Ishihara and this boss have to work together until two or three o'clock each morning. The boss berates him constantly: "Even though you graduated from a number one university, I bet you can't do this, right? Even though it's something that even a woman could do" (128). One night, after ordering Ishihara to clean up his desk for him, the boss invites Ishihara out for a drink and, while drinking, quizzes him, "Hmmm, something's bothering you, right?" (128).

While complaining isn't rare, very few of the *sarariiman* whose comments are gathered in Tsuda's book are critical about work. In fact, those who are most positive speak of their satisfaction with relationships at work.

These are workers who speak of good bosses: superiors who look after their subordinates by shouldering responsibility for them, cushioning them against blame for mistakes, recognizing their good work and pointing it out to superiors, taking them out drinking on a regular basis, having such personal characteristics as modesty, sympathy, "cleanness" (that is, not being susceptible to bribery), and interacting "humanly" with them by noticing a new haircut or asking about their children (Tsuda 1987:71–72). With a boss who is working by one's side, as it were—making the same demands on himself as he does on his subordinates—the attitude seems to be that one is neither inclined nor entitled to complain about the workload the company assigns.

The "Company Person"

Even such workers speak freely of the rigors of the *sarariiman's* work life, however. None describes his workload as relatively easy and light unless he also admits that at his company the pay is low or that opportunities for advancement are limited. The standard description is of an arduous schedule and a demand for intense commitment. Significantly, the language used to convey this intensity at and for work is most often formulated in terms of attitudes or types of workers: the *kaisha no ningen* (company person) is a worker so devoted to the company that he rarely goes home; such adjectives as *mōretsu*—intense, keen, furious, strong—and *bari bari*—intensely devoted to working hard—encode the same all-encompassing commitment to work. The assumption held by almost all *sarariiman* is that unless such an attitude is adopted, promotion through the ranks will be stymied. Or, viewed slightly differently, the more successful a *sarariiman* is, the more he is expected to give to his job. As one worker put it, section heads and department chiefs never go home.

Some of the men spoke of those who have failed the system or been failed by it—the *madogiwazoku* (literally "the group who sit by the windows"). Due to the principle of lifetime employment, men who have not lived up to the norm of the Japanese worker cannot be fired. Instead, they are given meaningless work to do in peripheral jobs. Their fate is to be pitied, but here their stories are used to illustrate not victimization of workers so much as corporate severity. Few men aspire to become part of the *madogiwazoku,* so they codify the "company person" ethic as being not necessarily desirable but inevitable. Beyond their power to change or resist it, company life is what they must accept if they want to make good.

Still, the suturing of self to work and the merging of personal and public life, accepted and ideologized by both Minami and Aida as being structures of "the Japanese self," are sometimes questioned. One man, a department chief, admits that he is not a "company person"; he spends Saturdays and Sundays at home with his family, pursues his own hobbies, and conceives of his "life" (*seikatsu*) as resting outside the company (Tsuda 1987:37–38). Others are "playing the game" only reluctantly: "What we long for is: to leave work on schedule, to be able to play with our kids on Saturdays and Sundays, and to read books" (66). Or they question the wisdom or necessity of coupling their self-interest with the interest of their company:

Even if I put out an [original] idea, there's no one here who will accept it. This is a discouraging feeling. Should I be working for the company or should I be working for myself? Lately this question has got me very perplexed. (130–31)

A few men even question what is usually considered a positive and healthy practice of corporate behavior: drinking at company expense when the office has been particularly productive.

Whenever we exceeded our fixed profit ceiling, the branch manager would say, "Let's go drink." And everyone would go drinking. I don't hate drinking, but going out means that my return home is even later. (Tsuda 1987:127)

Another worker relates the following incident:

Once I returned from a business trip at nine at night and went straight to the dorm. The next day I was scolded by my boss—"Why didn't you return to the company last night? That you didn't show up at the *enkai* [company drinking party] and join us with some alcohol was very indiscreet [*fukinshin*]." So I apologized, but the atmosphere at my company—even on holidays—is work, work, work. (124)

All of these speakers can obviously distinguish between work and personal life; drinking with coworkers, even if it's enjoyable, is considered to be work. That company drinking is a unifying ("human") process for all is also challenged. One man remembers being positioned between his *kachō* and *buchō* one night at a club and having to endure listening to the complaints each whispered in his ear about the other all evening long (Tsuda 1987:71). Another recalls a former boss of "the old school" who ordered him to attend all *enkai* (company drinking parties) to pour the drinks for everyone else, but not to consume any alcohol himself (127).

Significantly, the references made to company-sponsored drinking are more specific when they are negative. It is as if a negative criticism requires justification, while acceptance can be very general:

> Saying all this I still have to say that I think of my company as superb (*subarashii*). Why? Because it's a surprisingly "clean" company. The boss and his workers go out drinking at company expense, and businessmen don't use company money for personal reasons. (Tsuda 1987:68)

The function and pleasure of work-related drinking sessions is thus assumed rather than analyzed. Drinking becomes a sort of language; long established, shared, and consensually understood, it is referred to as a general, generic experience, not distinguished nor recalled by details of specific nights. Treated in this fashion, company drinking is meant to stand for what is good about a working environment. The practice of drinking at company expense with one's boss is the mark of both a good workplace and a good superior.

Implied in this evaluation, however, is a definition of work that includes some of the human connectedness that scholars like Aida, Minami, Nakane, and Doi characterize as being particularly or uniquely Japanese. Among *sarariiman* for whom this definition constitutes a "common sense" view, the complaint that drinking with coworkers or bosses at night takes them away from family or home is rarely, if ever, voiced.[8] For such workers, extending the workplace into this realm of "not-precisely-work" does not impinge on a time or space reserved for family or home. Because it is not exactly a "personal" zone defined in the usual family and domestic terms, it isn't viewed as a sacrifice of nonwork time.

The *sarariiman's* frequent visits to Bijo and other *mizu shōbai* establishments seem to add something to work without subtracting something from family or home, yet they take place in a social and physical location somewhere between these two domains. Men go from work to bars and clubs,

---

8. I am using "common sense" here as Roland Barthes does (1972): ideas about the world that are so taken for granted that we don't articulate them through a conscious language. According to Barthes, these are the structures that "naturalize" specific relations of power in our societies and determine the place any of us will assume within them. John and Jean Comaroff (1990) call this level "hegemony" and oppose it to "ideology" at the other end of a fluid continuum which is more conscious and formulated more clearly in language.

and they leave these bars and clubs to continue on home.[9] "Humanization" of work is possible during these outings at least partly because men find the transitional location appealing. They are engaging in a work-related activity that isn't work and is separate from the office; and though headed toward home, they aren't home quite yet.

Much of the discussion, however vague, about corporate drinking refers to how it augments and humanizes work relations. But those nightly visits to the hostess clubs also have an impact on the family. While going from work to bars may add something to a man's job, it certainly keeps a man away from the home. Yet Japan's divorce rate is low by Western standards. Further, as I was repeatedly told during my discussions with Japanese men, it is the man's duty to his family that motivates him to stay with a company for life, work hard, and do nothing to jeopardize his career (such as coming home early to play with the kids).

What is sometimes called the traditional American conception of opposition between work and home and Americans' alignment of "self" and the "personal" with home life (see Schneider 1968) seemingly does not apply in Japan. To understand the meaning and practice of corporate drinking sessions, one must first consider the cultural patterns of family and home.

9. I don't mean to include all Japanese here. Obviously there are various experiences, constructions, and patterns of Japanese home life—couples who practice sexual fidelity and men who spend, or want to spend, considerable time at home are not nonexistent, as I'll point out. I argue, however, that when a practice such as company-paid drinking becomes socially and corporately institutionalized, it has a systematizing effect on behavior, including (in this case) that of home, family, and gender.

6

Family and Home

A Male Perspective on Marriage and Home

Probably the first question a Westerner will ask me when I describe the nightlife drinking of Japanese men is, "Why do Japanese wives put up with it?" That a Japanese man would drink with other men, away from wife, children, and home, is more comprehensible to Westerners than the female response to this behavior. Usually Westerners also wonder how a wife could endure her husband's absence from home. Such questions reveal our own assumptions about marriage and family—that a husband should not spend his evenings flirting with strange women, that a father should be a presence in the home, and that a wife has a right to demand that these rules of marital behavior are observed. The corporate practice of nighttime drinking, on the other hand, reveals and constructs a different set of assumptions.

In my interviews as well as in Tsuda's, wives were generally more articulate and forthcoming than were husbands in discussing a man's work schedule from the perspective of family and home. Men were more likely to speak of their absence from home in terms of their presence somewhere else. One customer at Bijo, for example, mentioned that he joins his family for dinner perhaps once every six months. He then spoke not of what he was missing at home or how much he missed it but of the need for a hardworking and successful executive like him to spend his time after office hours in the nightlife. Bantering with a colleague, this customer turned his absence from home into evidence of industriousness and made it the subject of good-natured competition:

> "Let's see, when *was* the last time? I thought it was once a month, but . . ."
> "That often? You're slipping these days. I only make it home once every six months."

Of course, these remarks were made in a hostess club, an atmosphere that encourages joking and exaggeration and inhibits serious discussion about home. But even outside the club, men were either reluctant to speak at length about home and family or spoke only in terms of mother and children, placing themselves on the periphery of the family circle or even outside it.

One of the few exceptions was Takada, a man in his late forties who was owner and boss of his own architectural business. He talked at length about his family and the respective roles he and his wife play:

> I work hard and long hours. Work is very stressful, so when I return home I don't want to hear about any problems my wife had in her day—quarrels with the neighbors, a bad test score by my son, a faucet broken in the kitchen sink. A good wife will manage everything at home and neither ask her husband for assistance nor relate to him all the various things and events that have filled up her day when he returns from his job.

Takada emphasized the importance of a wife's not only handling all domestic matters but also maintaining relative silence about them. I asked him about this point. Was it just that he didn't want to know about the problems, or that he would feel pressured to solve them, in addition to all the problems he had already dealt with during the day? Takada was definite—he really didn't want to hear much about family or home when he returned late at night, tired from work and drinking. He wouldn't elaborate on why he so coveted silence from his wife, but he did admit that he preferred to keep silent about the life he led away from home. Takada's lack of interest in his wife's life apart from him was complemented by his unwillingness to share with her his life of working and drinking.

Living in a world entirely apart from the home, Takada spoke of this separation not with sadness or a sense of loss but with irritation that he was required to be home at all. Being with his family appeared to evoke no feelings of comfort or pleasure; Takada described family-shared Sundays and vacations as time that he endured rather than enjoyed. He spoke of his son mainly in terms of the boy's hobbies, study, and school, matters that he knew little about and left almost entirely in his wife's hands. Though obviously interested in his child, he seemed to feel no need for involvement with him.

For Takada, the huge number of hours his job demands, both day and night, does not impinge upon time he should or would like to spend at home. Thus, Takada's duties to work and home present no contradiction for him. When asked what he would change about his life if change were possible, he says he wishes for more personal time away from work *and* home.

In other words, while work is clearly marked as a source of anxiety and pressure for Takada, home is *not* its antithesis.[1]

As the testimony of Takada and other female and male informants shows, the *sarariiman*'s absence from home stems as much from constructions of home as constructions of work; work is where he must be, and home is where he'd prefer not to be. Not surprisingly then, Takada spoke of his drinking with clients and employees in terms of both work and home: the release alcohol brought from the tensions of work was facilitated by drinking in a space other than home.

Female Perspectives on Marriage, Home, and Male Work

Wives' accounts and interpretations of male absence vary according to whether or not the wife takes her husband's perspective. When speaking for their husbands, wives carefully word their responses in terms of demanding work and long hours—even if these include hours of drinking: "He has to work hard"; "It's inevitable and can't be helped (*shikata ga nai*)"; "Japanese men are diligent and hard-working"; "That's the way it is for *sarariiman* in Japan." But even when their attitude is sympathetic, their descriptions of precisely what their husbands do until midnight or their explanations of why such late nights are necessary to their husbands' careers are usually vague.

Some wives picture their husbands' work environment as bleak and harrowing and imagine that this bleakness extends into their evenings. Ikura pitied her husband for having to spend evenings at bars, drinking and talking with strange women. She treated these evening sessions as added burdens for her husband, tasks that were as onerous as his workdays. Other wives I spoke with avoided speculating about how pleasurable or unpleasurable these evenings actually were and instead categorized them simply as a part of a man's work.

A group of female alumnae of a Tokyo university whom I interviewed asserted that the nightlife Japanese men enjoy at company expense is about work, not sex. When I asked them to elaborate, none revealed any knowledge; and they preferred to remain uninformed about the details of their husbands' nocturnal jaunts. Nakamura, however, had heard descriptions of her husband's drinking behavior. He told stories, joked with the men, flirted

---

1. This conception of home—a sphere defined in part by its contrast to work—is important in American culture. See Schneider 1968.

with the women, and drank heavily. He would never behave this way at home, she told me, nor would she want him to. Explaining that this is "male behavior" in which women rarely indulge, she accepted these nighttime engagements as being a condition both of her husband's work and of his masculinity.

When wives address from their own perspective the deprivations their husbands' jobs impose on home and family, some admit to a sense of loss. Nakamura was one of the few who confessed to once believing in an ideal marriage, a romantic partnership in which husband and wife both worked and maintained the home. Born near the end of World War II, she had attended law school in the 1960s and took a part-time job at the time of her marriage. Her husband, newly employed as a *sarariiman* in NHK, the national television network, was equally committed to assuming parallel roles inside and outside the home and spending much time together as a couple. Both perceived this image of marriage as deviating from the Japanese norm.

At first the plan was successful. They worked during the day and reserved evenings for time together. Soon, however, their plan was disrupted by what Nakamura called outside forces—work (for her husband) and motherhood (for herself). Her husband was pressured to work longer hours and extend these into evenings of work-related drinking; and partly because of his increased absence, the responsibilities of parenting fell almost totally on her. After four or five years, Nakamura said, their "ideal" marriage had congealed into a traditional, gender-specific one. Their worlds had become separate, their relationship sustained by the roles they managed separately and largely in each other's absence.

Nakamura's story emphasized the weight and inevitability of social forces. Though she and her husband had desired something different, the family structure they wound up with was created less by their own desires than by the operations of the "outside." According to Nakamura, the demands on her husband as an upwardly mobile white-collar worker had the greatest impact on their behavior and thus their marriage. Nakamura did not blame her husband for spending time away from home, nor did she express bitterness, nostalgia, or a longing for a different type of domestic existence. As she put it, they once had hoped to be mates and lovers, but now they'd become more like brother and sister. This lack of companionship in their marriage did not threaten it, she explained. Rather, their marital pattern now conformed to the norm: husband and wife leading separate lives and achieving social camaraderie with others—golfing buddies and drinking companions for her husband, and female friends with whom Na-kamura could enjoy dinner and the theater.

Not all Japanese women find such a divided marital style acceptable. Some decide to pursue full-time careers outside the home. By all accounts, however, it is a rare husband who, even with a wife working full-time, will assume more of the traditionally female chores of child rearing and domestic management (Yuzawa 1982). The expectations and pressures of the husband's job are not reduced simply because his wife chooses to work; increased absence of mother from the home doesn't usually result in the increased presence of father.

Some women find the demands imposed on family and home life by a husband's job unacceptable. One woman in her late twenties said that she encouraged her husband, a *sarariiman* in a large corporation, to resign his position and find one that would allow more time for the family. After a few years of work he complied, becoming manager of a convenience store with shorter hours but less pay.

Two other women in their late twenties told me how they wished their husbands would be better companions for them and better fathers for their children. Their husbands were *sarariiman* who spent most evenings and often at least one weekend day at work or work-related activities (golfing, seminars, drinking). One of the women wondered if her husband had affairs and if some of his late-night engagements were more personal than business. Though the thought was painful, she'd never asked her husband, assuming that any affair would eventually end. Because a marriage is based not on a man's sexual fidelity but on his ties of duty and responsibility, she explained, philandering on his part would neither threaten the marriage nor result in separation or divorce.

The other woman told a slightly different and, in a sense, more distressing story. After a day of devoted mothering she'd fall asleep at nine o'clock with the kids. Then, at whatever hour her husband returned home, usually well after midnight, she would get up and prepare his meal. She didn't mind doing this, she said, but she was upset by her husband's lack of communication—no remarks about his day, no questions about hers. After he ate, he would read a book for as much as two or three hours, never turning to her for companionship.

This woman was by many measures conventional, yet she questioned what is—in broad outline at least—the structure of conventional marriage and family in middle-class Japan. Her husband fulfilled his role as good provider, and she was a good housewife and mother, but she wanted something more—a husband with whom she could build and share a relationship and a father with whom the children could play and interact. Her husband's absences and lack of involvement left her lonely and disappointed with their marriage.

Although the absent husband/father was mentioned in most of the women's accounts of *sarariiman* family life, few women expressed such an intense longing for their husbands. Many are resigned, like Nakamura, to the family's truncations, attributing their inevitability to Japanese corporate practices. Others speak of their mother-focused families without any mention of loss, impoverishment, or regret. For these women, the removed husband/father is a fact of life; for some, it's even preferred.

Mother and the Home

Yuzawa (1982) has pointed out that financial support is often the sole contribution a man makes to his family. Apart from this financial component, he argued, most households in Japan are run by females. If a husband/father should die suddenly in an accident, there would be an initial psychological shock, a continuing financial loss, and a social stigma attached to the child.[2] In every other sense and particularly at an everyday level, however, there would be no change, no hardship, and no problem whatsoever (1982:70).

In Yuzawa's terminology, Japan is currently in an "age where no father is needed" (*otto fuyō jidai*). The family structure that now exists is relatively new. Traditionally, the role of the father was much more central in Japan, as it continues to be in farming families where husbands and wives work cooperatively. Now, however, most Japanese men are viewed first of all as financial providers. The husband's role is often referred to as "Sunday carpenter and repairman-husband." Observing that for a fee even those services could be carried out by a non-family member, Yuzawa concluded that "in this age where physical labor and power are not needed as they were in earlier ages, the usefulness of men as husbands has really decreased" (1982:72).

In light of such family conditions, Yuzawa became curious as to why Japanese women would want to marry in the first place. He canvassed fe-

---

2. Yuzawa explains that once a child reported on a school questionnaire that her/his father had died, this would be considered a handicap (1982:70). I have also heard that job applicants and suitors whose fathers or mothers have died are considered "risky" by potential employees and fiancés or fiancées.

male students at his university and learned that 98 percent positively desired to get married even though "they knew a husband isn't necessary" (1982:73). Yuzawa proposed three reasons for this desire: (1) in the eyes of society, having a husband makes a woman more acceptable and, in this sense, makes her life easier; (2) most women state that they want children, and motherhood outside of marriage is socially proscribed; and (3) women not only want but need a husband's income even if they themselves work, because gendered pay differentials are great and become increasingly greater as Japanese women get older.[3]

Considering how difficult it is for Japanese women to support themselves—particularly when they leave the job market to bear and raise children and then attempt to reenter it later—Yuzawa emphasizes *necessity* over mere desire as the motivation of Japanese women to marry (1982:73). I also heard financial dependence given as one of the main reasons some women have stayed with their husbands. And despite the common Western stereotype of the complacent Japanese housewife, at least a third of the women I interviewed spoke of divorce, of dissatisfaction with their marriage, of irritation with their husbands, of dreams of different lives, and of fantasies about other men. Yet not a single one of these women was actually contemplating divorce, and the reason given was never romantic or moral but always financial: they couldn't cope without their husbands' income.

Japanese women stressed their keen desire for and attachment to children as the more compelling reason for wanting to marry and stay married. As I was told by many of the women I interviewed, the role they assume upon marriage is more that of mother than of wife. While the position of wife carries status from the husband, the position of mother provides an emotional and social relationship over which the woman herself has primary control. Motherhood becomes her place and her realm of expertise, one in which her competence is much greater than her husband's. He can bring home a bigger paycheck, but she can manage family and home so well that his contribution in this realm is judged to be meager, even unnecessary.

This aspect of Japanese marriage tends to be overlooked by Westerners, who visualize the unfortunate, subservient woman left at home while her husband carouses late at night. There *are* Japanese women who would like

3. According to Yuzawa's figures, if a male makes 100 (dollars, yen, etc.), a female makes 90 when she's in her teens, 70 when she's in her twenties, 55 when she's in her thirties, and only 50 when she's in her forties and older (1982:73).

their husbands to be home more often, but a male's absence from home is rarely viewed as the removal of a vital family part. Life operates fully and smoothly without the man around, so long as he provides the necessary financial support. Asked to identify a dream or fantasy about changing their lives, most women would agree with Kazuko, who wishes merely that her domestic life could be a little less busy: "If asked what I would like at this stage of my life more than anything, I would answer—to just take it easy and do nothing for a while, take a trip or go shopping at a relaxed pace" (Tsuda 1987:50).

Significantly, Kazuko does not wish for a husband to spend more time at home. She does, however, include two additional wishes that involve her family. The first is a wish she has for her husband: "More than anything I'd like my husband to be very successful at work, considering that he works so hard" (Tsuda 1987:50). The second, a wish she makes for herself and the children, relates to the first: "There are also many things that I'd like. A car, a piano for my daughter, a trip abroad" (50). And it is in this connection that Kazuko mentions her husband's nights out:

> He has entered the "kachō competition" (kachō sensō). Now, in the real meaning of the word—company life (kaisha no jinsei)—he's at the starting line. . . . To this aim, since meeting and interacting (tsukiai) with his superiors and coworkers is so important, I never complain about his coming home late at night. (49–50)

In a children's book entitled Tokei ("clock" or "time"), how well integrated the families of mother and children can be and how this integration diminishes the importance of the father are encoded symbolically. Intended to teach children the mechanics of telling time, the book takes a family through its morning routines in fifteen-minute intervals. At the top of each page are the figures of mother and children eating together, brushing teeth, going to the bathroom, telling each other good-bye. Alone at the bottom of each page is the father, going through his home-based activities all by himself: drinking coffee, eating breakfast, reading the newspaper, departing for work. Equally symbolic is the custom of setting a place at the dinner table for the absent father. According to one of my interviewees, the mother points to the plate and reminds her children that it is because their father is working so hard for them at a job that he can't join them for dinner at home. The message conveyed is that the man's role, even within the family, takes place (and takes him) outside the home. The point also made is that the meals and lives of the children and wife go on just fine in the man's absence.

The mother's role in grounding and maintaining such familial integrity when the father is largely absent can hardly be exaggerated. Her presence, in almost every sense of the word, is constant and crucial. Even when the mother works outside the home, her role as mother is not reduced or replaced by that of the father. It is she who manages everything from broken bicycles and skinned knees to housecleaning, the household budget, the children's schooling, and the egos and psyches of all the family members. As Yuzawa's research has pointed out, whereas wives and children are quick to identify the sole duty of a husband and father as financial supporter, husbands and children include an entire range of expectations when speaking of a wife and mother (Yuzawa 1982:65).

Mother-Child Bonding

Volumes have been written about the Japanese mother's relationship with her children.[4] To be brief: The mother's role within the family structure has long been a predominant motif in Japanese folklore, religion, and literature (Buruma 1984; Kawai 1988). Since the end of World War II, with the nuclearization of the Japanese family and the rapid reduction of family size to a mean of 1.53 children (1991 figures [Asahi Journal 1992]), women have come to center their mothering on fewer offspring, in some ways tightening the bond between child and mother. Other factors have contributed to this heightened relationship: industrial changes that have taken more men away from home; increased urbanization that, coupled with an obscene escalation of urban land prices, has forced many Japanese to travel for hours to reach their places of work; and an intensification of the educational process, which has molded mothers into educational supporters, thereby increasing their children's reliance on them.

These forces have taken men farther away from home and pushed women farther inside. The word for housewife, oku (literally "inside"), reflects the woman's location inside the home once she marries. Of course, there is much she is expected to do there: manage the house, raise the children, take care of the husband. But even when these jobs can be handled with a margin

4. See Doi 1973; Yamamura 1971; Juristo 1985; Fujita 1989; Kyutoku 1981; Imamura 1987.

of time to spare, leaving the house can be interpreted as selfish or inappropriate. A housewife in her late thirties, quoted in Tsuda, is apologetic:

> I play tennis once a week; go to tennis school; and am a helper at my childrens' schools. I feel that I really fill up my time by myself (*jibun de*), but I also think that I've begun to neglect the care I should be giving to my husband (*shujin no sewa ga tenuki ni natteru koto wa*). (Tsuda 1987:50)

And with reason, as indicated in the story of a husband, told by one of Yuzawa's interviewees:

> At the time he was in his 30's, working . . . at a big company. . . . One day he happened to look out the window of his office and saw his wife playing tennis. They'd been married for eight years and had no children and she had asked him if he'd mind her playing tennis once in a while. He'd said no, go ahead. Yet when he saw her playing tennis that one day, sweat started pouring out of him and he had a reaction of disheartenment. (Yuzawa 1982:69)

If the Japanese term for housewife suggests the homebound role of women, the Japanese views of motherhood *demand* it: A woman's place, as mother, is by the side of her child, particularly when s/he is preparing for the entrance examinations, first for high school and then for university.

The stories of *kyōiku mama* (education mother) are legendary. Even when children are very young, a dominant social pattern (from which, of course, there are mothers who deviate) is for mothers to give them endless support, doing everything from preparing midnight snacks and tea to sharpening pencils, attending their own cram school, and checking homework to assist, inspire, and monitor children during their ordeals of exam preparation. This mothering intensifies for at least a year immediately preceding exams. I have known women who for that time period (*juken benkyō*) temporarily "check out," forgoing their usual extradomestic activities (hobbies, clubs, getting together with friends, helping out at their children's schools, and so on). They position themselves ever more firmly within the home and ever closer to their child; the intensity of this attachment affects not only the mother but child and father as well.

Particularly when interlaced with this educational imperative, the mother-child relationship is overdetermined, bringing mother and child together in a bonding that further encourages the exclusion of the father. One man, describing the *juken benkyō* (exam preparation) process his son and wife were then undergoing, spoke of his wife's behavior with derision. She was forcing the boy into constant study, and the boy, though obedient, was resentful. The man's reaction was to stay away from home even more, say nothing about the matter to either, and let them work it out on their own. Significantly, he could barely speak about either wife or son without mentioning the other, so close was their togetherness.

Some scholars have noted that tendencies always implicit in the mother-child bond have become more pronounced in contemporary Japan. One result of the educational pressures is the infantalization of the child. Excused from household chores in order to study, children are raised to expect and allow themselves to be taken care of. And when the grown-up child is a male, the pattern of gender interaction has been fixed: the behavior expected of one's wife mirrors that of one's mother.

A second, related trend is an eroticizing of the mother-child bond. Sensationalized by the press with stories of mother-son incest (*boshi sōkan*), the sexual closeness, if not actual incest, between Japanese mothers and their sons has been described by serious scholars (*Gendai no Me* 1980; Sano 1991; Mizuno 1982, Ishikawa 1982). Their explanations trace not only the priority given to the parental over the marital relationship in a Japanese family but also the increased absence of the husband and the intensifying (due to the educational system) of the mother-child connection. With no man around, a mother and son who are in each other's company for most of each and every day may cross the invisible line from interdependence and affection into a realm of sensuality or sexuality. Some Japanese scholars view such relationships as an extension into sexuality of the most intimate relationship in Japanese society. They further argue that mother-son is the only gauge for female-male relations in Japan and that even lovers and spouses will assume these mother-son roles.

Sano Yoko, a woman writer, explores this issue in an article dealing with the question of why Japanese men cheat (*uwaki*) on their wives. One man claimed that it wasn't cheating since he thought of his wife as mother, which meant that sex with her would be incest. Another man, calling his wife "natural" (*tennen no tsuma*), recalled that after his first infidelity he had run home to tell his wife, expecting her to be "naturally" indulgent. Sano considers this relationship between husband and wife to be juvenile and emotionally stunted, more like the relationship between a three-year-old and his mother (1991:94–95). Pointing out how such childishness is not only tolerated but also cultivated by women as mothers, she complains that "Japanese women are flirting with their own sons" (95).

Sano concludes with a discussion of female sexuality (which she sarcastically labels "wantonness"—*inran*), lamenting the tendency of Japanese women to direct this to their sons instead of a more appropriate person—a husband or another man. Urging women to give up this overindulgence of and involvement with their sons, she tells mothers to cut the boys loose and make them grow up. Sano ends, however, on a discouraging note. Repeating the words uttered by a mother about her son, "He's just so cute, I can't help but love him," she notes that the son referred to is a twenty-year-old man (Sano 1991:95).

7

Structure of Japanese Play

In his book *The Structure of Japanese Consciousness* (*Nihonjin no Ishiki Kōzō*), Aida Yuji (1972) considers the custom of Japanese workers going out as a group to drink together at night. He discusses two significant aspects of this behavior: the dynamics among the men, and the social space within which this male dynamic takes place. As a cultural essentialist, Aida tends to perceive much of what the Japanese do as unique, explaining both *what* goes on and *where* it goes on in terms of Japanese cultural categories.

Aida's term for the location or social sphere for such drinking is "the world of the outlaw" (*gedō no sekai*), a sphere in the "back culture" (*ura bunka*), which Aida differentiates from the "front culture" (*omote bunka*) of public structures such as work, family, school. According to him, Japanese regard front culture as an edifice that is socially necessary but humanly false. In the realm of back culture, they can behave toward one another on the basis of who they really are and how they really feel rather than according to a behavioral pattern that is mediated and determined by social place (Aida 1972:57).

Aida says that Japanese not only recognize the difference between these two sides of their culture but also appreciate the place and role of each and believe that both are necessary to Japan's social sustenance. By contrast, he writes, Americans and Europeans prioritize the front culture of social propriety, and this causes all behavior falling outside these strictures to be automatically labeled as deviant. No matter how much the outlaw in Western popular culture is romanticized, s/he is literally positioned outside the law. In Japanese culture, the outlaw can operate in a manner at odds with social correctness, or front culture, yet still have a place within an order that is culturally sanctioned as back culture (Aida 1972:58).

The Western view of outlaws, as presented by Aida, constitutes a category of persons: outlaws are outlaws for life, presumably. In Japan, outlaw refers more to a subset of behavior and to the social space within which that behavior takes place. Japanese can enter easily into the world of the outlaw, and they can leave it just as easily. The example Aida gives is of a man becoming frustrated both at home and work and seeking a way to resolve this frustration by having contact with the opposite sex (1972:58). In the United States, were such a man to seek relief from daily frustrations with a woman he picked up in a bar (part of the outlaw world), the dalliance could prove dangerous. He doesn't know who the woman is, whom she is involved with, what she may come to expect, nor how she'll behave after this one night. A Japanese man can play safely with a woman at a bar or club precisely because these establishments, and the women in them, *are* part of a structured outlaw world.

As Aida elaborates, the realm of the *gedō* (outlaw world) has its own order, its own morality, and its own way of doing things. In Gion (the Kyoto *geisha* district), for example, several basic rules have traditionally been in effect: (1) even if the wife of a patron dies, the mistress has no right to become his wife; (2) if a *geisha* bears a child, the child remains illegitimate and is not socially recognized by his father; (3) a man cannot just casually abandon his mistress, and if he does, the community of Gion will no longer allow him to enter it; and (4) activity and affairs in Gion can in no way upset the peace and harmony of the man's family (Aida 1972:59–60). These rules prescribe behavior not only in the *gedō* but also between the outlaw world and the outside world. One can play freely here but only by remembering the rules of play—and the rule that play remains inside Gion's borders.

It is toward such an ideological space that Japanese men head when going out in company groups to drink at night. Male behavior, once there, is both informed by and guided by this placement. Yet the particular dynamics of coworkers who socialize in groups outside of work are, according to Aida, driven and explained by other cultural traditions as well. One of these is the custom of dissolving resentments about a superior by expressing and sharing them collectively, a practice Aida traces to the *idobata*—gossiping by the side of the well—which dates back three thousand years in Japanese history. In this modern version are two key elements: a content of bad-mouthing a boss (*uwayaku no waruguchi*) and a form of human interaction that operates on the tacit understanding that no one in the group will reveal what has been said to anyone outside the group (1972:56, 62).

Such a practice would be impossible in Western societies, Aida writes, because Westerners wouldn't keep the shared criticisms secret. They lack a conception of the kind of group he calls a *pon yū* (buddy), which operates on the principle of a "consciousness of companions" (*nakama ishiki*), safe-guarding the privacy of the group and its members. Aida regards this as a special feature of human relationships in Japan and finds it a liberating and useful device of the individual. A Japanese can "open up" (*uchitokeru*) to friends while drinking and not have to worry that what he reveals will go beyond those in the group (Aida 1972:56,7).

But there is another aspect of this behavior that Aida doesn't critically assess except to say that it is stress-relieving: the content of the opening up and the manner in which it is linked to (and perhaps demanded by) particular human relationships. Aida cites a study showing that when workers from the same company go to a bar to drink, there is one constant element in their talk—complaints about the boss. The complaining follows a set pattern. At first, concrete grievances are aired, but as everyone gets drunk, the complaints become generic—a complainer may say, "He doesn't understand a person like me at all" (1972:66). Although the speaker resembles a spoiled child, according to Aida, his coworkers nevertheless indulge him in this expression of frustration.

Aida fails to explain why a drinking place elicits the same type of expression from all the participants nor why this frustration isn't or can't be expressed anywhere else. He does blindly assert that for Americans and Europeans there is no such "place" for directly relieving the frustrations that arise from the human relationships at work (Aida 1972:57). Further, particularly in American culture, there is the assumption that a man can relax at home with his wife and kids. This assumption in turn rests on a premise, not shared by Aida, that home doesn't create its own set of frustrations. Yet he does not address the question of why family and home can *not* relieve work-related tensions for a Japanese man and why bad-mouthing a boss is so systematically and persistently the format for opening up among coworkers. The fact that work groups not only indulge in but in fact depend on specific forms of collective engagement such as joint complaining about a boss is nowhere established or problematized in Aida's book.

The Pleasures of Nightlife Play

Yoda Akira (1981), in a book entitled *Otoko ni Totte Onna towa Nanika?* (*What Are Women to Men?*), also examines the behavior of Japanese men in the bars and clubs they frequent in the company of fellow workers. Unlike Aida, Yoda tends to explain the nighttime conduct of Japanese men in terms of universal (as opposed to culturally specific) male psychology. Yet what Yoda addresses and describes are the behavioral patterns specific to Japanese men; and the position from which he speaks is that of a man who has experienced and enjoyed Japanese nightlife firsthand.

In response to the question why men don't drink at home, where the price is much less, he explains that the psychology of drinking would be much different at home. Men can't "relax" there (*kutsurogu*, the same word Aida uses in this context, which also means to feel comfortable, familiar, "at home," as we use that phrase in English). At home a man is still a husband and father; he can't converse with family members the way he talks with a bar hostess, and so he can't reveal himself and be "frank." And for all these reasons he can never "remove the spirit of tiredness," even if his body becomes refreshed (Yoda 1981:25).

Saying that what men want after work more than anything is to become "not husbands, not fathers, but plain old men" (1981:24), Yoda identifies four conditions of nightlife that make this feeling possible. The first is being in the company of friends: "That's because even if we have already been drinking [at another bar with, for example, a boss], we're still uptight as long as there is a work connection. Only when we can drink without this tie of work can we finally relax" (24). Though Yoda makes a distinction here between close friends and work-related friends, the difference seems one more of degree than of kind. That is, "good friends" are not a separate set of relations; they are more likely to be a subset of all the relations one has that are work-connected—those for whom friendship and work have merged. That such a merging is not true of the relationships one forms with all fellow workers, even those one drinks with at night, is significant if not surprising.

The second feature is the content of the conversation, which consists mainly of insignificant chatter between hostesses and customers or complaints about superiors: "The conversation with hostesses and friends at this 'one more place' is, generally speaking, totally nonsensical and trivial (*tawai nai mono*). We grumble about our superiors and do a lot of bad-mouthing about our colleagues" (Yoda 1981:24).

Other scholars have referred to this structure of *asobi*, or male play—drinking while conversing about things that don't (in any other context) matter. A group of academics convened to explore the meaning of play in (post)modern Japan describe this particular pleasure in much the same words as does Yoda:

—When I am asked, "How do you play?" I can't say that, in the end, I just drink.
—You're right. . . . But you know there's really only drinking; drink-

ing and bullshitting about nothing in particular (*kudaranai*). This is a big part of play.

So much so that one could say that only this is play. (*Heibonsha Karucha—Today* 1980:92–93)

The third condition of a successful night out with the men is that the individual becomes "spiritually" refurbished and cleansed of the tensions that build up at work during the day. Yoda adopts a functionalist view here, stating that nighttime drinking in bars is, for this reason, not only beneficial to men but necessary: "To a man, it is unwinding the tension built up from a day at work. And if this tension isn't unwound yet builds up day after day, it will break the man's spirit. . . . So for us, who are men, we must go to these places . . . in order to protect our spiritual health" (Yoda 1972:25–26).[1]

The fourth condition is what Yoda calls "the desire for self-confirmation" (*jikokenjiyoku*) that is encouraged and satisfied by the hostesses at a club (1972:27). As Yoda explains it, all men wish to be "noticed, respected, and confirmed by others," but such recognition is as difficult to achieve at work as it is at home, though for different reasons. At work one's position is as coworker (*dōryō*), and to be too self-assertive is considered a "minus" factor that will inhibit one's chances for success (28).

At home, too, no one is impressed by a man acting full of himself and overly confident. Here the reason isn't that such a stance is inappropriate but that it simply doesn't work: wife and children know the man on an everyday basis and have known him for years. They will not give him the approval (*mitomeru*) without which he begins to feel foolish in life. A hostess, however, will. Satisfying a man's desire for recognition is, in fact, one of her principal jobs. Whatever the man reveals of himself is accepted and magnified by the hostess.

One should note in this connection that in Yoda's usage the term *self-revelation* doesn't necessarily mean a revealing of the self that is completely

---

1. Yoda doesn't explain the mechanism by which certain nightlife male behaviors trigger the release they supposedly do. Merely connecting them in description, he gives no reasons why the behaviors work: "You can say whatever you want to, sing even badly at *karaoke*. . . . For a man, this is how he unwinds from the tension built up at a day at work. If his wife could see him like this, however, she would find his behavior simply stupid. . . . But for a man, it is reassuring to see other men's faces as they sing to a piano or *karaoke* in a bar. The faces seem innocent and carefree. . . . If the rhythm is off or the notes are not quite right, nobody cares. As long as the man is enjoying himself and immersed in this form of self-expression, that is all that matters" (Yoda 1981:25–26).

accurate. In fact, it is the opportunity to project an imagined and desired construction of the self, one whose acceptance and approval by the hostess is guaranteed, that constitutes the pleasures of self-revelation as Yoda describes it. The "back culture" thus doesn't lend itself so much to truth and reality as Aida would have us believe.

Leisure and Recreation as Release from Work

The drinking a man does with colleagues in a hostess club or bar is fun, relaxation, release, unwinding—concepts that are in turn defined by what they oppose: tension, stress, duty, hard work.

For a symposium organized to discuss leisure and recreation in Japan, one scholar analyzes the relationship between work and play:

> With work there is a world in which rules have become exact. These are rules which maintain our cooperative life and we have responsibility to support that. Yet it becomes dreary [insan] and eventually we all reach the point of hurling at one another like atomic bombs. Play is placing oneself physically in a place distinct from that. Or, in other words, from within that play, one can look out over the world of work and from that perspective, the whole structure of work, including its defects, can be seen. (*Heibonsha Karucha—Today* 1980:128)

Play is thus viewed as an activity that not only removes a person from work but also provides a removed perspective through which work can be assessed or reassessed. This is a version of Yoda's safety-valve theory of the nightlife: it offers a necessary though only temporary escape.

Another scholar makes a similar point when discussing his fondness for the Japanese game of mah-jongg. The money he wins at mah-jongg has a sweetness that his paycheck from work could never match. Even so, he limits the amount of money he will withdraw from the bank for his bets and limits the time he spends playing the game. Without such boundaries, "playing" would become something else, and the person playing would become what is disparagingly called an *asobinin* (literally, "person who plays") (*Heibonsha Karucha—Today* 1980:43–44).

Amanuma Kaoru (1987) has written on the Japanese concept of *ganbaru*, translated as tenacity, persistence, doggedness, and hard work, which in its imperative form, *ganbatte* ("hang in there"; "don't give up"), is what Amanuma calls *the* cultural key word of Japanese. He proposes that the notion of leisure or relaxation carries a negative connotation in Japan. A number of native words can be used as equivalents to *ganbaru*, but there are few words for its opposite, relaxation. Such Japanese words as *hima* (free time) or *yoka* (time to spare) don't carry a positive value, and the concept of vacation or relaxation is usually expressed by a foreign word, thereby exoticizing and distancing its usage.[2] Concluding that Japan has a cultural apparatus that encourages hard work and repels relaxation, Amanuma links the modern constructions of relaxation (*rirakkusu*) and leisure (*reja-*) to work in two ways. First, these concepts are largely defined in relationship to work—as a means to relieve stress and tension built up primarily from work or as the actual intervals of time when one is not at work.[3] Second, the model of work has invaded the manner in which Japanese relax.

> Japanese are a people who also *ganbaru* [work hard] at their leisure. This unconscious sentiment of working hard even at leisure is perhaps something that penetrates through all Japanese people. And it differs from people of other cultures. While Europeans and Americans, for example, can enjoy leisure for weeks, even months at a time . . . about the tops for a Japanese is five days. Doing nothing makes Japanese somehow uneasy (*fuan*). (Amanuma 1987: 132–34)

As Amanuma describes it, there seems to be a contradiction in this work-leisure relationship. While such leisure activities as vacations are constructed so as to radically oppose and provide an escape from work, attitudes about work still guide attitudes toward vacation and determine their length. Amanuma cites the case of a female office worker who went to an island for a two-night, three-day trip. Determined to come back with a good suntan, she worked so hard (*ganbaru*) at it that she died of overexposure (1987: 134).

The length of vacations as well are often circumscribed by considerations of work. Although men I spoke with said their companies allotted them three to four weeks of vacation annually, all said they'd take less time off for fear they'd be regarded as too "selfish" and not sufficiently devoted to their

---

2. The words that are borrowed come from the French word *vacance* and the English words *vacation, leisure, relax,* and *recreation,* which have been Japanized but are retained in the syllabary (*katakana*) as Japanized foreign words (Amanuma 1987:131).

3. Amanuma's argument is linguistically based at this point. When *reja-* (Japanization of "leisure") is translated into native words it becomes *yoka* ("time to spare," "off hours") or *hima* ("time," "spare time," "time off"), and when *rirakkusu* (Japanization of "relax") is translated into native words it becomes *kinchō o toku* ("relieving tension") or *kutsurogu koto* ("be relaxed," "lounge around," "be comfortable," "be relieved").

jobs. The result is intense, frenetic, short vacations, often to faraway, expensive spots. One family I knew went to Hawaii and back in less than a week.

For some of these reasons, Tada Michitaro admits that Japanese are perceived to be "poor" (*heta*) at play, a perception he explores in his book *Play and the Japanese* (*Asobi to Nihonjin*) (1974:42). The assessment is based on foreign judgments that Japanese are very "serious" at play and that many forms of Japanese play (for example, *pachinko*, mah-jongg, and drinking in bars) are unhealthy in that they are insufficiently differentiated from everyday life. Both judgments are based on the typical Western definition of leisure and relaxation as separate from work, which, as has been shown, does not apply in Japan. Tada disputes them on the grounds not of the observation but of the interpretation. That Japanese *may* have a tendency to play not far from where they work and even, at times, with attitudes like those of the workplace does not mean that they reject play but that play in Japan is culturally different from play in the West.

Whereas Asanuma looks at such leisure activities as vacations (which, though short and compulsive, are clearly demarcated from everyday life), Tada examines what Japanese do more routinely in order to relax and have fun. At the time of his research, the four most popular leisure activities in Japan were golf, bowling, *pachinko*, and mah-jongg (1974:33). One of Tada's most interesting discussions focuses on *pachinko*, a game in which a player sits in front of a slot machine—in a *pachinko* parlor with hundreds of machines—attempting to guide small steel balls into holes. Skill is awarded with meager prizes of cigarettes, crackers, and soap.[4] Tada, himself a player in his youth, considers *pachinko* a postwar phenomenon. Though its appearance actually predated World War II, its popularity has greatly accelerated recently. Between 1965 and 1972, for example, the amount spent annually on *pachinko* went from 3 trillion yen to 8 trillion (Tada 1974:43, 45).

The structure of this play, as Tada describes it, is significant. *Pachinko* players play alone and usually when fatigued or bored. The game serves to refresh them.

> It is a play that completely relaxes both body and mind. One doesn't look from side to side at all. Even if the man sitting to one's side completely collapsed, a *pachinko* player wouldn't notice. I think the sense of solitariness and fatigue runs very deep. (Tada 1974:45)

---

4. Many scholars and visitors to Japan have written about the fascination accorded *pachinko* in postmodern Japan. See, for example, Barthes's analysis in *Empire of Signs* (1982).

A French observer of *pachinko*, Roger Caillois, has written that the effect it has on players is hypnotic, paralyzing, and addictive and that it is a "pitiable" form of play (quoted in Tada 46). Tada discounts this assessment, however, as ethnocentric. He argues that if the game is viewed from the perspective of the social realities and cultural categories of the Japanese who are playing, the most avid *pachinko* players are those who work in factories during the day. For them, the structure of play—placing balls in holes in a machine— resembles the structure of their work. Japanese move easily from work into play, and *pachinko* can be played immediately (requiring neither partners, like mah-jongg, or a long commute, like golf) and quickly. Tada writes that the close connection between work and play is pervasive in Japan, and discounts any intrinsically negative effects of Japanese play.

This conceptualization of play as distinct from yet aligned to work also applies to hostess bars and corporate drinking. Tada does not explicitly address this subject, but he does mention two other Japanese behaviors that are pertinent. One is what he calls, borrowing a term coined by Miura Shumon, the "television mold" of Japanese leisure (*terebikata reja-*). Referring to a study, he notes that most Japanese men on their days off listen to the radio, watch television, read the newspaper, nap, and generally take it easy (Tada 1974:34).[5] Despite their claim that they prefer such separate and special recreative activities as golf and mah-jongg, their leisure is, then, even less separated than those games are from everyday life and work and even more easily assimilated to them. Again, Tada's view on this matter is not that Japanese are working too hard and relaxing too little but that the styles with which they pursue both work and relaxation are best understood as being culturally Japanese.

A second behavior of the Japanese at play that is as mundane as watching television or napping and is valued for its very mundaneness is drinking. Drunkenness, Tada notes, is recognized by many Japanese to be a form of play much like any other. The joy of "forgetting decorum" (*fureigi*) and car-

---

5. Nada Inada, a writer and psychiatrist, notes in 1992 how napping has become forbidden to the wearied *sarariiman* on his days off, although they listed it in 1991, in response to a questionnaire, as their preferred activity on weekends. "Leisure" has taken on new meaning as a result of a heightened mass media campaign. "'Leisure' now implies going out and doing something"—spending much time and much money taking one's family to an amusement park, for example. Nada laments this development, concluding that while Japanese have started "playing" a lot in the past twenty years, it is a form of play that is constructed in "the interstices of work" (1992:24). Nada's critique here contrasts significantly with Tada's perception and acceptance of such patterns as "Japanese."

rying on has been a traditional pleasure in the culture, rooted perhaps in the *omikoshi* rituals, where neighbors join together to carry the *omikoshi* shrine on their backs, weaving collectively in and out of the neighborhood as they become collectively drunk.[6] Tada calls these rituals a joining of the sacred and the profane; the pleasure of collective drinking, he says, comes from a similar joining of opposing states—work and play (208–11). Interestingly, he does not discuss any benefits of solitary drinking.

Tada writes that drinking frees the man from everyday constraints and that being with others creates a sense of unrestrained freedom. Noting that the concepts of free (*jiyū*) and unconscious (*muishiki*) are considered contradictory or incompatible in Europe, he asserts that this is not the case in Japan. Rather, to be conscious of things is a restraint that can be broken when drinking with companions: "The individual feels free in this collective setting, or, put the other way around, it's only within this collective setting that the individual feels free" (Tada 1974:211). Tada adds that not only is the individual brought outside of the self, as it were, but that within this state of collectivity the ties (*tsunagari*) between individuals are strengthened and the similarity and compatibility of all persons is recognized. Should the state wish to imprint such a message, political and even military force would be needed. But when such social imprinting is done without force, and through the mechanisms of custom and cultural traditions, Tada ponders what is being expressed.

Tada is what can be described as a cultural essentialist. His explanation of the connection between forms of play and structures of work is that, rooted in the culture, it is a relationship that was established long ago in the past and continues to have contemporary effects. For most of the scholars quoted in this chapter, the view taken of play-work connectedness is similar: based in the culture, it is what is natural for a Japanese. The naturalness of, for example, working late at night by playing at a club, is the worldview I will challenge in part 3.

6. At base this is a religious ceremony, the *omikoshi* being a shinto shrine and the *omikoshi* ritual being a leaving from and a returning to the shinto temple. For an English description, see Bestor 1989; also see Hendry 1987 for a succinct account of how this ritual fits into larger meanings and rituals of religion in Japan.

8

Male Play with Money, Women, and Sex

Most of the Japanese discussions and discourses conducted about play or "back culture" or "world of the outlaw" concern men only. Because men are the subject of most of the research, male forms of play are highlighted. Women are not totally ignored; Tada (1974), for example, uses terms for play and childhood games that are gender neutral or shared. But the tendency is to define and conceptualize play in relationship to work, and work, as an occupation and not just a job, is treated as primarily male specific.

Females and Play

Japanese women both work and play, of course, but how they work and how they play are not nearly so institutionalized or usually so public as these behaviors are on the part of men.

Women I knew who were mothers or housewives and did not have full-time jobs outside the house often pursued activities that a Westerner might consider recreation: going out to lunch, playing tennis, studying English, joining other mothers and their children for picnics, frequenting the public baths. Often these occasions were described as enjoyable, but enjoyment was rarely the primary motivation. Typically there was another rationale— for example, self-improvement (studying English) or social interaction for the kids (group picnic). Lacking a "good excuse," the women often expressed feelings of embarrassment for their imagined self-indulgence.[1] Play seems easiest to manage and conceptualize for women when it can be fitted into the social roles of mother and housewife they're expected to assume.

1. Tomioka discusses this inclination to find an excuse for leisure activity or recreation as being characteristically Japanese (1980:93).

This is true of men too, of course, who justify their play in the nightlife by connecting it to work.

Yet housewives are limited not only in their available modes of recreation, which are few, but also in their ability to "indulge" in play.[2] Domestic labor is not considered to require or deserve the same type of "break" that male labor outside the home merits. Mothers and housewives don't speak of escape, nor do they speak of what they do as work. Hence play for women has a different meaning and a construction that is subsumed within, rather than distinguished from, the activities they engage in domestically. Interestingly enough, when I asked women if they "played" with their husbands, most laughed. Some used the word to refer to early months in their relationships with their husbands, when they'd spent leisure time in each other's company—playing golf together, going out for a drink, visiting jazz clubs, eating out. What brought these times to a halt were not only increased workloads for the husbands, but also childbirth. Play then became a word women associated with children more than with husband and one they connected to their role as mother more than as wife. Simultaneously, male play became something their husbands were pursuing without them, in connection with work, and outside the house.

How and why domestic labor is undervalued in relation to outside employment is a complicated issue and one I don't intend to address at length here. What is of immediate relevance, however, is how work is linked to play and how gender is factored into that relationship. The key component appears to be money. Though the contribution women make to family and home is calculated and valued in various cultural and social terms, money is not one of them. Money is, by contrast, the medium that both measures male labor and that male labor represents. It is also the medium that in capitalist economies acquires goods, determines the standard of living, and, in the case of Japanese capitalism, purchases and mediates most forms of male play.

2. The custom of hiring a baby-sitter to watch one's children is not popular in Japan, and men who might be willing to watch the children are often home only on Sundays, if they are *sarariiman*. This leaves women largely alone with their children. One woman I knew had never been away from her four-year-old since the child's birth. The woman had no relatives living close by, no friends who offered to take her child, a husband who was rarely at home and, when home, wanted to sleep. Some of the mothers I knew took turns looking after each other's children if they had doctor appointments and so on. Some also had mothers close by who provided child care—more, in fact, than mothers-in-law, even if the latter were living in the same domicile. Altogether, though, women with small children who are not using day-care facilities seldom get away on their own.

Money and *Kōsaihi*

Money and women are connected in the nightlife, and both stand for and structure the recreation men pursue while out together at night. Yoda (1981) speaks of the connection between money and women in two ways: Money purchases women, with the type of woman purchased reflecting how much money is spent; and the type of woman obtained through money determines the likelihood of sex. Yoda refers to a woman as a symbol, apart from what she actually does. The geometry is that the prettier and classier the woman, the better she reflects a man's status—and this coding works for the entire package of nightlife: how many places one goes to, how each place is rated, the quality of the furnishings, and so on.

As Yoda describes it, the packaging of women as a currency to flatter and build the male image is used most heavily by *sarariiman* in top industries. Entertaining clients, in the practice of *settai* at company expense, is conducted in high-class clubs with high-class hostesses to "heighten the image of one's business" in businesses where "image making is necessary" (Yoda 1981:30). First-class and second- or third-class drinking places are not significantly different in "substance." What does differ are the furnishings, the service, the women, and the price, all essential to creating the right image.

In a book devoted entirely to the Japanese corporate practice of using *kōsaihi* (company expenditures for recreation) and its relationship to tax law, Tabe Shiro (1986) emphasizes the aspect of image making and its connection to money, if not always to women. Recreation expenses in Japan, he writes, "are an indispensable expense of industrial operation" (Tabe 1986:1). While, on the one hand, it seems a useless expense, in periods of low economic growth and high competition, expenditures for *kōsaihi* actually increase (2).

In 1982 a new tax law severely curbed the deductible portion of a corporation's *kōsaihi*.[3] Nonetheless, *kōsaihi* expenditures have increased annually, reaching about $35 billion spent nationwide in 1991 (Sakaiya 1991).

As Tabe has pointed out, the amount of *kōsaihi* is differentiated by industry. The biggest spenders are trading companies, securities companies, and construction businesses (Tabe 1986:197). According to a ranking of the 200 top-spending companies of *kōsaihi* that has been issued by the magazine

---

3. The Reform Bill states that for companies with capital exceeding 50,000,000 yen ($25,000), *kōsaihi* isn't recognized as a pecuniary loss. In the case of large companies this means that 100 percent of their *kōsaihi* is now taxable (Tabe 1986:203).

Shūkan Daiyamondo annually since 1979,[4] the ten biggest spenders are trading companies—the first being Mitsuibussan and the second, Mitsubishi-shōji (figures date to the publication of Tabe's book, 1986). If *kōsaihi* were calculated based on the amount spent per company employee, the biggest spender would be not Mitsuibussan but Hattori Seiko, which spent an average 1,200,000 yen ($6,000) per employee annually. The second-ranked company was Takajima, a trading company, which spent more than 1,000,000 yen per male worker per year.

Tabe pays more attention to how much is spent on *kōsaihi* and by which companies than on the structure of *kōsaihi*. There are pages of figures, but accounts of how the money is used, with what agenda, and to what effect are scarce. Instead, Tabe mentions the need for trading companies to "actively promote their industrial image," and he quotes an executive at a securities company:

> *Kōsaihi* is an expense expended towards amicable relations between customers (*ningenkankei*). In transactions on the money market the feeling of mutual trust is indispensable. This is particularly true in the case of securities companies because transactions involving large sums of money are made without exchanging contracts. (Tabe 1986:204)

As this man explains, *kōsaihi* for golf and drinking is used to encourage the signing of contracts but also to reward the customer once the signing is completed. A branch manager of a bank makes the same point—he receives a set amount of money from the head office each month for the express purpose of enticing customers and thanking them for their business. Another branch manager, this time of a securities company, says that *kōsaihi* is also used as incentive and reward for one's own workers: "When business is good, *kōsaihi* goes up, and when business slips so does *kōsaihi*. The idea is that in order to fully justify using *kōsaihi* (for ourselves) we really have to work hard (*ganbaru*)" (Tabe 1986:214). (The speaker is referring to entertainment at the intracompany rather than intercompany level. In times of lower profits a company will cut back *kōsaihi* spent on entertaining its own

---

4. At the time of the KDD incident in 1979, when it was discovered that huge amounts of *kōsaihi* had been used by the company to pay off politicians, public interest became focused on *kōsaihi*. Tabe quotes the editor of *Shūkan Daiyamondo* as suggesting that the ranking they do is somewhat skewed by the fact that financial reports are not made available for all companies. Securities and trade companies may be outspent on *kōsaihi* by insurance companies and pharmaceutical companies, as the manager of Bijo also suggested to me (Tabe 1986:201, 207).

employees but at the same time continue or even increase the amount spent on clients or potential clients.)

Of course, what *kōsaihi* is used for differs from one company to another, and different uses impact on the meaning and structure of the *kōsaihi* operation. Yet in Tabe's description it is the symbolism of *kōsaihi* that is important, not what *kōsaihi* is actually used to buy. In this equation, the more spent, the more valuable the symbol. A branch head reports that if he holds a drinking party at a fancy restaurant and then proceeds to a high-class club for a "second party," the tab could run to as much as 100,000 yen ($500) per person for the one night. If he takes six people, the 600,000 yen ($3,000) spent may use his entire *kōsaihi* allowance for the month.

If the Japanese tax office is to be believed, companies have been in an "economizing" mood since the imposition of the new tax law, and spending in the nightlife—the preferred but most expensive form of *kōsaihi* recreation—is gradually being replaced by less expensive recreational activities like golf (Tabe 1986:208).

One executive notes that even at 60,000 to 70,000 yen per person ($300–400), golf is much cheaper than "one drink at a *ryōtei* [high-class Japanese restaurant]" (Tabe 1986:208). A Mama of a Ginza club also observes a shift: *Sarariiman* from trading companies who used to be her biggest customers are less common in her club than the heads of small- and medium-size companies and those with undefined sources of money. The manager of another first-class club says:

> In our club too 60% of the customers were formerly manufacturing (*bussan*) people. But now, they'll say, "I can't spend more than 10,000 yen ($50) on that client." That means everyone has become clever and seems to use cheap places like *karaoke* bars or bars in hotels. (Tabe 1986:206)

Even in these times of financial cutbacks, however, Abe, the manager of Bijo, told me in 1988 that the fanciest clubs on the Ginza—the type that cost $400 or $500 per hour for one customer to drink, talk with hostesses, and soak up the atmosphere—would never cease to exist. The appeal of these places is too great, even though the higher class the club, the easier it is to go bankrupt. The use of such clubs for company outings on *kōsaihi* may diminish, but if a Japanese man has money, Abe declared, he longs for nothing less than a top-class club.

Why this desire exists among Japanese males, Abe couldn't say, but he contextualized their nightlife (*mizu shōbai*) behavior this way: *Sarariiman* start going out to bars and clubs on *kōsaihi* in their twenties and thirties, usually taken there by their bosses; in their forties and fifties they go on *settai*, treating or being treated by clients; and in their sixties or older they've become wealthy and *erai* (eminent) and just drop in after work, even paying the bill out of their own pocket. Over time, drinking in the nightlife becomes habitual, and even without the business incentive or the company funds to go there, men go anyway, paying for it on their own—what Abe refers to as the *sarariiman's* "bad habit" (*warui kuse*).[5]

Why Japanese men don't go home to drink is due in part to this patterning of their work/play lives away from home. It is also due to the attitude of their wives, who not only believe that a man's drinking is for his work but also correlate his absence from home with success at his job. Since coming home late from work becomes a sign of a man's success, women try not to imagine what else might be keeping their husbands away. In Abe's assessment, many Japanese men *are* having extramarital sex (*uwaki*). Their partners tend to be either young women in the company or hostesses, neither of whom would be likely to pull a man away from his wife and family. If wives sense this, they keep quiet, Abe says, partly because they calculate that to endure for the present may mean a payoff for them in the long run: If their husbands become successful, they could even become *buchō fujin* (wives of department heads). In addition, Japanese women don't usually have incomes of their own and couldn't divorce anyway; and so they keep things peaceful and hope that everything will be all right.[6]

Abe thought the *mizu shōbai* was already changing in 1981. By 1986–87, when I returned to Tokyo and interviewed him again, corporations were entertaining more often in cheaper places, at golf, or by staying at one hostess club rather than moving from club to club as was the practice ten or twenty years ago. He predicted that it would change further if men in fami-

---

5. *Sarariiman* abuse the *kōsaihi* system as well, by fabricating a business deal in order to go drinking, either on their own or with friends. Bijo's manager claimed that *sarariiman* in their thirties and forties are notorious for doing so. He also spoke of a second abuse of the system— a client calling up someone in the company he is doing business with to "suggest" that he be taken out that night. Abe said, in this context, that there are two types of *settai*. While business negotiations are progressing, *settai* is legitimate, but when clients ask to be taken out at company expense after the deal is completed, it is not. A friend of mine confirmed that this abuse occurs, based on her father's experiences.

6. According to Abe, women, like men, have affairs (*uwaki*), though this part of Japanese life isn't publicized. Women's partners tend to be men they're acquainted with, though a journalist, Chiba Atsuko, told me she thought their partners were more often people they *didn't* know beforehand, such as door-to-door salesmen and foreign students living in Japan.

lies with two incomes and no children began to involve themselves more with their wives and home; if a new generation of *sarariiman* started to say no to a superior's invitation to go out and drink; and if men generally developed a new attitude toward their wives. In Abe's words, "If Japanese men would develop the habit of treating their wives well, the *mizu shōbai* would not be so popular."

Male Desires in the *Mizu Shōbai*

Yoda has described the pleasure of going to a top-class club and merely sitting next to a beautiful woman—what he calls "showing one's face" (*kao ga kiku*):

> One aspect of this nighttime carousing is . . . reconfirming one's social status and being able to display it to another person. . . . A first-class club connotes a first-class clientele. To show one's face in such a place allows a person to display his social standing to his friends and others. (Yoda 1981:29)

But most Japanese men are less interested in the prestige of being seen with a hostess than in the pleasure of having her as a potential sexual partner. Interviewees of mine have concurred: being doted on by a beautiful hostess "looks good" in the eyes of their friends, but they would prefer the doting to be more than symbolic.

A woman obtained with money rather than through marriage or romance is generically referred to as a *mizu shōbai* woman, and her appeal is widely acknowledged, even by Japanese wives. One woman in her forties, whose husband frequented the nightlife routinely on business, described her image of the *mizu shōbai* woman: she has a loose and carefree manner; her style, in both clothing and speech, is provocative; she is ideally young and pretty; and she will say things and do things that no self-respecting wife would. This woman could understand why her husband would find such a woman desirable, but she would not admit to feeling threatened by the other woman's desirability. Her attitude was that such a woman had a place where her husband might visit but where he would never stay.

This woman's vision resonates with Aida's depiction of "back culture," where "outlaw" behavior is allowed and expected. It also conforms to Liza Dalby's assessment of why Japanese wives accept a husband's relationship with *geisha*, the traditional woman of the night who is skilled in various arts such as dancing or playing the samisen. They are two distinct relationships with two distinct kinds of women (Dalby 1985:169).[7] The relationship is acceptable because it is separate. The arrangement, one should note, is gender specific. Most husbands said they would sue for divorce if they learned their wives had been unfaithful.[8] Their reasons varied; the primary one was that such behavior in Japan is not customary. Play in an institutionalized "back culture" is permitted for husbands but not for wives.

The *mizu shōbai* woman evokes male sexuality, yet not all women in the *mizu shōbai* will contract for sex. In fact, the relationship between sex and money in this world is one of inversion: the more expensive and classy the club, the less the possibility of sex with one of the women; and, conversely, the sleazier and cheaper the club, the greater the chance. This principle of the more money, the less sex is not absolute, by any means, for establishments in the *mizu shōbai* are categorized not only by price but by service as well. These can include services that are not sex-related—chanson (French singing) clubs, comedy clubs, *karaoke* bars—as well as sex-specific ones. In the latter group, places are differentiated precisely on the basis of a particular sexual service offered: *no-pan kissa*—"coffeeshops" (*kissaten*, from which *kissa* is derived) where the waitresses are without underpants (*pan*), whom the customers can watch but talk to only to give orders; *shi-suru pabu* (see-through pubs), where naked women swim in a tank of water but have no contact with customers; *nozoki pabu* (Peeping Tom pubs), clubs where women are positioned to be "peeped on" in some fashion (for example, by customers looking up through a glass floor simulating the floor of a subway car; the women are lacking underpants); *osawari kyabare-* (touching cabarets) where there are different prices and "sets" for the touches women will give and receive (fellatio or "help in ejaculation" [*hassha no tedasuke*], where the woman "caresses" the man's penis until he ejaculates); *karaoke no-pan kissa*—*karaoke* bars where the hostesses wear no underpants and offer to sing with customers; *pinku saron*—darkened clubs where men are serviced in their booths with, depending on price, masturbation or

---

7. Dalby accepts the wives' attitude toward *geisha* at face value—as being a traditional practice in Japanese culture which, for that reason, is acceptable to all parties. I will suggest later that there are other ways to assess this behavior—that is, that "traditional" ideas are sustained when they also fit into and support current economic, family, and educational relations.

8. One man explained to me that wives were like "possessions" and that only husbands are entitled to them. Another man, a manager of a *pinku saron*, said it wouldn't matter as long as he never found out. The idea, in principle, of his wife being as unfaithful as he was, didn't upset him. Yet were he to discover an infidelity, divorce would become a matter of honor, something he'd be almost forced to do considering how marriage is viewed in Japan.

fellatio; and soaplands, high-priced brothels offering various forms of intercourse.

This list is hardly complete, for differences are invented in the nightlife as ways to package and sell sex. Fads come and go quickly, *no-pan kissa* disappearing one day only to reappear the next as *karaoke no-pan kissa* or *video no-pan*. Even so, the list is representative of the Japanese sex industry (*sekkusu sangyō*), which sells women sexually even when it is not selling intercourse. Percolating throughout the country, it operates in rural communities, small towns, and urban centers (*Gendai no Me* 1980). Yet for all the constants of its business (men are the customers, women are the prime attraction, money is exchanged), there are differences. Most obvious of these are the sexual services and the prices.

One feature of the Japanese sex industry found most incomprehensible to foreign visitors is the degree to which sex in some establishments is flirted with but eventually deflected. The deflection is often built into the packaging of the sexual enticement; women are kept distant through no-talking rules, glass floors, see-through tanks, cubicles, stages, and so on. Often the degree to which the women will be available to the men but also restrained—look but don't touch—is clearly specified at the entrance to the establishment and by the format, as, for example, at the *no-pan kissa*. Men enter knowing what they will and will not get.

There are also places where sexuality is suggested, but to achieve what is suggested is not guaranteed. This is increasingly the case as clubs become classier and more expensive. Yoda calls this the business of offering the "dream of sex":

> "If things go well" is the expectation. However, in most cases, this expectation is no more than a hopeless dream. . . . This is a business trick of hostesses. They must give the impression that someday they *will* go with the man and without that impression, men won't keep coming back. (1981:31–32)

Men fall for this trick for two reasons, according to Yoda. The first is a certain vulnerability men experience in the nightlife, which Yoda exemplifies by referring to the sweet but programmed words of the "pullers-in" (*kyakubiki*) who stand outside certain bars hawking the wares of the women inside:

> If one summarizes their insistent words, it would go something like this—"These beautiful young women are waiting for attractive men

like yourselves. You are very masculine so you could get these women immediately to fall for you. Furthermore, the price of this club is especially low." . . .

Half of the men who are so pulled in to the club become drunk immediately. Their judgmental powers are weakened, but their sexual impulse, by contrast, is heightened. After having given the club such an exorbitant amount of money, the man feels "I've been very shallow. I will never go there again." However, after several months, he may in fact go to the same club again. It's because men are weak to the words of the puller-in. (Yoda 1981:31)

Yoda implies that no sexual consummation has occurred and that most men are unhappy about this. They keep going back because they hope to have sex with the *mizu shōbai* woman.

Men have this expectation that someday, maybe, they will get the hostess. So hostesses are not what can be called amateurs (*shirōto*) . . . and if sex *does* occur between a hostess and a customer, it's different than if it occurred with a real amateur. There are no traces afterwards and there's no worry of this being brought into the family. In the case of having a relationship with a hostess, it's safe. (Yoda 1981:32)

The particular pleasure of the *mizu shōbai* woman, as presented by Yoda, is that one can have a purely physical relationship with her. What the man wants depends not on the woman's personality but on her agreement to relate through body alone. To quote Yoda, "One is looking for a sexual relationship without spirit (*seishin no nai*)" (32).

Paid-for Sex(uality)

In the book *Hikisakareta Sei* (*Sex Which Has Been Torn to Pieces*), edited and published by the magazine *Gendai no Me*, the same point is made: Men don't mind paying for sexual relationships.

When one pays cash, there is something guilt ridden about it. At the same time, it's easy to negotiate and the sex act can proceed without complication. Also, even at the first encounter with a woman, a man is assured of intimacy and is assured that the woman will put her whole heart into it. Also he knows no scandal will result. (*Gendai no Me* 1980:166)

The editors note that money is a constant in nonmarital sex; what differs is how the money is paid and how much. Men of power have mistresses, paying them in jewelry, clothes, cars, and apartments. Men without power pay cash direct, going to soaplands, for example, to purchase sex on a time-by-time basis. The difference is financial only, for male desire crosscuts class and occupation. Take the following example of a union organizer:

> As a socialist I would like to deny the sexual behavior that money mediates. But, in fact, in my circle of friends, everyone, as soon as they have money, runs off to a *toruko* [soapland] or cheap cabaret. That's because they see the big dignitaries on the nights of important union meetings indulging in "sex carnivals" [*sei no ka-nibaru*]. Such a form of sex play is absolutely the same that the big shots in companies are indulging. The only difference is that for the union members, the gap between *tatemae* (social propriety) and *honne* (real, sincere feelings) is bigger. (*Gendai no Me* 1980:162)

While sex through money represents (male) power, sex from money also represents (female) eroticism—yet the meanings of *erotic* and *female* here are quite specific. As the editors of *Gendai no Me* present it, the appeal of a paid-for woman is her willingness to do what the male customer wants while telling nothing about herself. Women working in the *mizu shōbai* tend to keep their private lives secret from customers: "After all, the guy in the darkened booth getting a blow job isn't interested in whether this woman has a child or a family" (1980:175). They keep their private lives secret from their fellow workers, too. And they keep to themselves desires they may have in common with "conventional" women, such as getting married and having children. While working, they suppress their own personalities, which may be strikingly different outside the club (175).[9] In place of their

9. The editors of the book comment on how interesting it is that so many *torukojo* (prostitutes) are "optimistic and defiant." Though they are in a position where they have "no path of retreat" (*tairo no nai*), many still hope, largely in vain, for marriages (*Gendai no Me* 1980:175). For hostesses in the sleazier *pinku sarons*, it is said that sex is merely something they do in the shop, while planning or fantasizing about fairly conventional lives later: "They put their bodies in the center of this alienated (*sogai sareta*) sex, yet the concept of 'a woman's happiness' follows them: for young hostesses, the hope is for marriage; for middle-aged hostesses, it is for the growth of their children" (176). The editors also cite many cases of women whose hopes for marriage and family are crushed when the men in their lives discover what kind of work they are doing or have done. One woman notes the double standard of men who leave their wives for working in the places they themselves frequent (174–75).

true selves, they assume the post of the *mizu shōbai* woman and play it as well as they can.

> In order to do business a woman must use her *buki* ["weapon"] to the maximum. . . . This *buki*, these women know very well, is different from what constitutes the conventional woman's femininity and superiority. . . . It is the female weapon of not denying or refusing to be touched, of exposing her bare skin rawly. These women are selling a piece of their flesh . . . and what they're giving and satisfying in the men is a sense of immediacy. (176)

The point is reiterated here that while women who wear clothes that reveal their own bodies and who touch men sexually to titillate theirs could be judged as "sex starved," the motivation for their behavior is much more financial than sexual. As one writer puts it, "Creating an imaginary world is connected to selling it for money" (Mizuno 1982:94). According to the authors of *Hikisakareta Sei*, many motivations propel women into the *mizu shōbai*: young women want the money to buy clothes, wives in their thirties with families need to supplement their husbands' incomes, college students need cash for an overseas trip, O.L.s aim to open their own businesses with their nightlife earnings (*Gendai no Me* 1980:172, 174). Unlike the women who worked in the *mizu shobai* to help their impoverished families or because they were sold into prostitution by their parents, women today enter the business willingly to make money; and money—as much as 1,000,000 yen per month ($5,000) as a *torukojo* (prostitute working in a soapland), three or four times what they could make as an O.L.—is what they make (167, 175).

If what my sources told me is true, the quality that most accurately defines a *mizu shōbai* woman is that everything she does is motivated by money. She may have many good qualities, but sincerity isn't one of them. This is also, of course, her appeal. Because her behavior is money-based, the man need not be at all concerned about her approval. In fact, she always approves—because this is what she's paid to do.

Men's Need and Desire to Be Taken Care Of

Why are Japanese men willing to pay so much for services with no more than overtones or promises of sex? A number of scholars writing about sexuality in Japan, particularly male sexuality, indirectly address this question. Narabayashi Yoshi, a sex and marriage counselor, has observed from his clients that the rate of primary impotence is on the rise in Japan. In contrast to secondary impotence, which occurs years after a man has been functioning sexually—often in middle age—primary impotence develops at the time when sexual activity should just be beginning. More and more Japanese men are suffering from this obstruction, and most, according to Narabayashi, are on what he refers to as the "elite course": those who are preparing for or have passed entrance exams into Japan's top-rated universities, which pave the way to prestigious white-collar careers (Narabayashi 1982:21–22).

As measured by the standards of academic and occupational achievement, these males are successful—in fact, among the most successful in Japan. Yet in order to secure this success, they sacrifice their sexuality, particularly in the years during *juken benkyō* (preparation for entrance exams). For such adolescent males particularly, Narabayashi notes, erotic fantasies are characteristically incomplete (1982:23). For example, one man, in the course of his treatment for impotence, began ejaculating in his sleep to fantasies of women who were always faceless. There is a haunting similarity between these faceless women and the women of the *mizu shōbai*. It is not surprising then to learn from Narabayashi that even his clients suffering from impotence with their wives could usually perform sexually with a prostitute.

One man explains the difference this way:

> It's because I receive it being done to/for me [*atarimaedayo yatte ita-daku kuseni*] which isn't strange at all. When I say "You do it so I can receive it," of course I can perform. But a man can't do that in marriage, right? When married, one has to do it rather than having it done to [*yaranakereba naranai*]. And because of that, I become no good. (Narabayashi 1982:21–22)

Other scholars similarly note a decreased sexuality in young, upwardly mobile Japanese males and a tendency to seek sexual satisfaction in a public domain with a prostitute rather than in a private one, as with a wife or girlfriend. (See, for example, Mizuno 1982, Oshima 1970, Fukuda 1982, Wagatsuma 1982). The social reasons given are generally two: the tightness of the mother-son bond and the pressures of work. Fukuda mentions the latter in responding to a comment Narabayashi has made about there being some sense of "violence" (*hageshisa*) in Japanese males: "We were speaking of 'violence' (*hageshisa*). For example, entrance exams are incredibly brutal and brutally competitive. So is industrial life. After being absorbed in that,

maybe men emerge who are meek in all other facets of their lives"
(1982:25).

Oshima Nagisa puts it somewhat differently. Work doesn't weaken men
sexually so much as it deprives them of the time and energy to actually have
sex: "If one is made to work 12 hours in a day, there's almost no possibility
for people to have sex. So sex becomes a problem related to labor"
(1970:26).[10] Some of the men I spoke with said that work kept them so
busy they could only manage the simplest sexual arrangements: talking
with hostesses or having sex with prostitutes. Why these men would mention only women whose services require payment and not their girlfriends
or wives seems odd. Narabayashi's explanation points to the role of the Japanese mother and the fierce bonding she makes with her son during his entire life but particularly during the period of exam preparation.

> Wagatsuma [speaking about a conference at which brothels were
> discussed]: It was said that *toruko* [soaplands; brothels] aren't about
> sex. Sexual satisfaction is a secondary, even tertiary concern. It's more
> about men being taken care of from A to Z like a baby. In the *toruko*
> they're washed, caressed, completely taken care of. This is the
> pleasure.
>
> Narabayashi: And for most of them [males], this is how they were
> raised as well—having everything done for them. Particularly at exam
> preparation time, who was taking care of their handkerchiefs and
> almost everything else? So they grow up to be men who can do it at a
> *toruko*, but can't with a partner in marriage. (Wagatsuma 1982:22)

The implication here is that males become so attached to their mothers in
their pre-adult years that they either can't duplicate this closeness with a
wife or sexualize the structure of the mother-son attachment, enacting the
relationship with a paid-for woman more easily than with a spouse. The
emphasis is on how men need to be taken care of, treated indulgently, and
flattered.

Stories are told of boys who report dreaming about sex with their mothers or actually having it (Ishikawa 1982; *Gendai no Me* 1980). Cases are also
cited, however, of males who display an inhibited sex drive: boys who write
to advice columns, for example, wondering whether their inexperience with

---

10. The reference is to women and to the female labor of childbirth as well: "Giving labor
and bearing children: these too are forms of labor. And once children are born, a woman too
has little time and little energy for sex" (Oshima 1970:26).

masturbation is abnormal (Narabayashi 1982). Some scholars, including Fukuda (1982), Wagatsuma (1982), and Narabayashi (1982), interpret such dulling of sexual interest—boys who don't masturbate and whose erotic fantasies are characteristically unimaginative or meager—as the result of repressing desire for the mother. The drive is there, but because the object of one's lust is socially unacceptable, it is blocked out.

There are also suggestions that Japanese males are becoming somehow feminized or weakened in the absence of strong masculine models. Not only are boys spending extended periods of time within the home and close to their mothers, particularly during preparation for examinations, but they are doing so in a setting where the father is seldom to be seen. There is neither a gender balance in parental influence at home nor a cultural mechanism to disrupt this imbalance. Wagatsuma refers to initiation rites in certain so-called primitive societies that dislodge the intensity of a mother's relationship with her adolescent son. Symbolically expunging all traces of femininity from the initiates, the ritual surrounds the boys with males and "maleness." Structurally similar, according to Wagatsuma, were Japanese practices that stopped after World War II: taking a new army recruit to a prostitute, for example, so he could "become a man." The disappearance of such rituals has led to the Japanese male becoming extremely *otonashii*, a word that is translated as "gentle," "mild," or "meek" and is used to describe a valued trait in females. As illustration, Wagatsuma cites a new social fact: whereas crimes committed by females have increased in recent years, those committed by males are on the wane (1982:25).

Ishikawa notes the passing of such male rituals as masturbation contests in university dorms, whose demise he also traces to the end of the war. Now he describes a situation where males are far more reserved and inhibited in the company of other males, going so far as to hide their penises from one another when bathing together during a school trip (1982:25).[11] Significantly absent from these discussions and discourses about males is mention of the ritualizing they do with other males in the nightlife.

Sex Tours

Though in scholarly writing there is marked inattention to the sexual relations in Japanese male group behavior, the reporter Sano Shinichi has investigated a sexual practice that Japanese men indulge in routinely as a group.

---

11. Group bathing is a common practice on any group outing.

This is participation in "sex tours" (*baishun tsua-*, literally "prostitution tours"). Providing a carefully studied ethnography (*Sei no Ōkoku—Empire of Sex*, 1981) of how groups of Japanese men fly overseas and descend collectively on the brothels of a foreign Asian land (mainly Thailand and the Philippines), Sano treats the group more as a context in which sex is pursued than as a structure that contributes to the organization and meaning of the events. In other words, Sano doesn't regard the collectiveness of sex tours as particularly significant, nor does he view sex tours as the type of male ritual both Wagatsuma and Fukuda say is now absent in Japan.

What Sano observes, however, correlates with observations made elsewhere about Japanese attitudes toward play, money, and sex. One such attitude is the single-minded compulsiveness with which Japanese sex tourists court their objective, staying only a few days and for one purpose. Organized much like the "sets" at various sex establishments in Japan, payment and sexual service are transacted as a package and the man simply decides which package he wants, not how to construct or negotiate a transaction himself. A hotel manager in Pataya Beach, Thailand, called this arrangement "fishing," which he contrasted with the "hunting" style of Germans. Implied is that Japanese like to know precisely what they're getting ahead of time and to proceed, with businesslike efficiency, to the scheduled sexual program. A survey conducted by the *Kokusai Kankō Shinkōkai* on the Japanese sex tours in Southeast Asia depicted typical sex tourists from Japan:

> They are very hasty and have no interest in the beautiful nature or cultural heritage of the area. Many of them come from the lower or middle class with a level of education that is not very high. Their manners in public are not commendable—for example, they'll open the zipper of their pants in order to retrieve money out of their underwear. They are very aggressive about sex and are looking constantly for girls. They say it is because they work so hard in Japan and that they never have time for sex there. (Quoted in Sano 1981:37)

Japanese sex tourists display another common trait—maintaining a distance from their sex partners. Aside from the language barriers and the nature of the transaction, itself distancing, Filipino and Thai prostitutes say that their Japanese customers are particularly aloof. Their insistence on engaging the woman at no other level than the physical one of sexual acts has led to nicknames for these Japanese tourists: "duck" in Thailand and "monkey" in the Philippines, references to their being crude and "oversexed" (Sano 1981:33–37, 60–63). Further, Sano has observed, there is a racial and nationalistic arrogance, a tendency to sexualize a hierarchical relationship that these Japanese assume exists between their country and other Asian nations (63). Why Filipino and Thai women are found to be attractive rests partly in their difference from Japanese women—"Thai women are subservient. They don't whine like Japanese women today" (40)—and partly in the price, far less than women can be bought for in Japan today.

The behavior of Japanese sex tourists has been criticized both in the countries being visited and by women's groups and female politicians in Japan, among them Doi Takako, the former head of the Socialist Party, who visited the Philippines expressly to investigate these sex tours. The criticism involves the purpose of the tourism (sex) and the behavior of the tourists, who are generally uncouth and unrestrained. Sano, however, makes a distinction between the outward display of crudely direct and arrogant sexual manners, the inward psychology of these Japanese men, and the manipulation by which they are managed and used by the sex tour operators. He writes that many of these men are likely to be miserable, pathetic, middle-aged men who are somewhat paranoid about sex rather than sex animals. They are probably good husbands and fathers who work hard for the family, and would not even be able to speak to women themselves (Sano 1981:39).

The sexual chauvinism for which these Japanese men are so commonly criticized is conditioned, according to Sano, by two factors. The first is being with others: a man who is shy and reserved acts haughtily in a group. The disinclination of solitary Japanese to talk much is one of the features Filipino prostitutes most often find distasteful about their Japanese customers. The second factor is the structural meaning of travel in Japanese culture: to travel is to be socially removed and absolved of all behavior that would be socially unacceptable at home. Sano cites, in this connection, the adage "shameless behavior during a trip is to be scraped off one's mind" (*tabi no haji wa kakisute*). He also draws a connection to the Tokugawa (1603–1868) governmental policy that maintained strict regulations against travel. To be so rigidly confined to one's physical place produced among the common people an incredible thirst to travel; and travel became associated with other forbidden or asocial desires, including those for sex and alcohol (1981:79–88). Even today, Sano claims, liberation is associated with physical dislocation from the places where one lives and works, and travel is viewed as a means of sexual pleasure.

While Sano's book does not touch on the behavior of those men who enter the nightlife in Japan and associate with women while in a group of males, it describes a phenomenon with structural parallels. Men go in groups to engage in an activity that involves women, has overtones (or more than that) of sex, and is often paid for by some association. One "sex tour" to Thailand was the prize of a *fukubiki* (a kind of lottery) from Yokohama East Side Merchants Association (Sano 1981:37–39).

The practice of sex tours has been described and contextualized within economic, social, and cultural relations. It has not been analyzed, however, in terms of the dynamics of what concretely takes place between men and women in such settings. Such is my objective as I turn back to Bijo in part 3.

Part Three

Male

Rituals

and

Masculinity

Introduction

One night I was hostessing at Bijo. The men were regular customers who wanted to know what this foreign hostess was doing in Japan. I told them that I was an anthropology student, linked to a university in Tokyo, and that I was doing research on modern Japanese behavior. They were intrigued and thought this admirable, but what precisely was I studying? I answered that I was investigating what men such as themselves were doing in a place such as Bijo routinely at night. They asked me to explain further. I said that I was researching the *mizu shōbai*, specifically the practice by corporations of sending their workers and clients into bars and clubs to drink at night at company expense. At this they laughed heartily. One of them gave me a hard pat on the back. "Well," he said, "you've finally managed to come up with a Japanese-style joke. Not bad, for a foreigner."

The humor I had aroused was sustained for a few minutes. The men kept repeating the "joke" to themselves as if it were something they should remember to pass on to their friends. Once I finally convinced them of my seriousness, however, their reaction changed radically. Sobered, they questioned why I would choose to examine this particular phenomenon of Japanese life. I was wrong, they said, in thinking that the *mizu shōbai* was significant. Significance rests in cultural traditions such as *ikebana* (flower arrangement), or the *ie* structure of Japanese families and lineages, or even the modern organization of politics. Why not choose one of these subjects to study, they suggested, instead of the *mizu shōbai*, which is "without meaning (*imi ga nai*), has no significance, and matters not at all, or very little, even to those who enter it on a regular basis"?

This reaction to my research topic was common among the Japanese I spoke to. Few laughed as easily as this group of men at Bijo, who initially assumed it was a joke, but most agreed that the *mizu shōbai* was an odd subject for an American female to be examining and one that was somewhat inappropriate and off-putting. Some felt uncomfortable about it and would use the word *kowai* (literally "scary") to describe the thought of a foreigner

145

penetrating this particular aspect of their culture. To look at the tea ceremony or marriage practices would be far more sensible, respectable, and
healthy, they implied.

Others could not comprehend the seriousness with which I approached
this subject. To them the *mizu shōbai* and scholarship were antithetical. This
attitude was shared by the university, which resisted accepting me as a research student, though it eventually gave in. The administrators who read
my proposal assumed that I would need a "sexologist" because of the very
nature of the subject, and they didn't have one on their staff. Later, at a
research gathering, I overheard two of the male professors talking of my
research in Japanese, which they thought I didn't understand: "She is the
one studying the dirty (*kitanai*) side of Japan." At this they both laughed.

Serious consideration of Japanese behavior in the *mizu shōbai* was in part
resisted because, as Tomita of the JASE (Association for Sex Education—
Nihon Seikyōiku Kyōkai) explained to me, there is a bias within academe
against scholarship on sexuality except in its physiological and medical aspects. Tomita, the founder of the first sex education institute in Japan, spoke
from years of experience in trying to gain legitimacy for his own scientific
and scholarly research. Kobayashi, a professor at Tokyo University, made
the same point in a roundtable discussion:

> Since a long time ago, sex has been a topic discussed in literature,
> but apart from such thinkers as Sartre and Marx, it has not been
> readily pursued in other fields such as philosophy. This makes the
> discussion of eros in Japan—what does this mean to Japanese—a
> highly interesting one. (1970:20)

Muramatsu, a doctor and medical commentator, agreed, saying that school
doctors are regularly inept in answering sex-related questions because they
have not received training in such matters: "In Japan, sexology is looked on
as being unseemly (*futō*)" (1970:20).

Recognizing this vacuum regarding sex in all disciplines save literature
and the arts, Morimoto, himself a university professor, sought an explanation:

> Even though my profession is literature, I can't define the meaning of
> "*sei*" [sex] in the Japanese language and this troubles me. I believe
> this word "*sei*" became a translation for the English word "sex" in
> the Meiji Era (1868–1912). But the translation isn't a clean fit. The
> English word "sex," for one, has more the connotation of nature. So I

think many in Japan have adopted this notion of sex being equated with nature instead of culture. (Morimoto 1970:21)[1]

The suggestion is that resistance to sex in scholarship is due to a linguistic lack: the Japanese language is devoid of a lexical meaning for sexuality. Other Japanese offer other explanations. According to Mizuno, an editor, only sex for reproduction is considered an appropriate subject for scholarly research, for permissible discussion between doctors and patients, and for respectable conversation in polite company (Mizuno 1970:22). By contrast, sex for pleasure may lead to talk, but it will be talk that lacks the earnestness and sobriety of scholarship.

Of course, the *mizu shōbai* I set out to study—and in particular the forays into the *mizu shōbai* that were work-related and work-endorsed—was not only or necessarily about sex, as so many of my interviewees, female and male, were eager to make clear. Yet the hesitancy to address this phenomenon in serious discourse seemed consistent with the attitude displayed when the subject was simply and explicitly recreational sex. I realized at the time that my own position as a foreigner, a female, and an academic could also be contributing to the reluctance many Japanese exhibited in discussing any part of the *mizu shōbai* with me. Initially they often seemed uneasy and suspicious of my motives. If I was "serious," why was I studying the *mizu shōbai*, and wouldn't I be likely to get it wrong—seeing it as just sleazy, for example? And was I also sleazy, given my choice of topic and the cultural inclination of Americans to approach such a subject on a serious basis? The men laughed at me. The women said little or changed the subject.

Yet my sources increasingly revealed more once they knew me and became convinced of two facts: my seriousness in wanting to understand this phenomenon from their perspective, and my sincerity—my intention to do academic research, not a muckraking exposé of the underside of Japanese life. What I learned from them can be summarized as follows:

1. What men do in the *mizu shōbai*, at company expense, is not something Japanese sit around talking about at great length. While much talk transpires in a hostess club, little does outside of it.

---

1. Sano (1981) also mentions the word *sei* and how it is variously misused and misunderstood. He notes, as an example, that a party of men returning from a sex tour abroad were given a reentry form at the airport in Tokyo which included a query about *sei*. All that was wanted was an indication of gender, male or female; but the men wondered if it meant "How many times did you have sex while you were gone?" This led to a discussion of how honest they should be.

2. Whatever takes place in the *mizu shōbai* is not what Japanese think of as matters of social importance in a man's life or as anything they would include among the structures, traditions, and practices most significant to and representative of Japan.

3. Whatever meaning the *mizu shōbai* has, it is constructed mainly for men and offers two principal attractions—sexuality and the *mizu shōbai* woman.

4. When the *mizu shōbai* is spoken of as the setting for a corporate entertainment of *sarariiman,* the discussion centers not on what concretely ensues·in the *mizu shōbai* but on the effect it is supposed to have on the men.

The following incident is illustrative. One Saturday evening I was in the company of five Japanese women—all married mothers in their twenties or thirties who met quite regularly to talk and drink beer. Noticing around midnight that the husband of the hostess hadn't returned home, I asked her casually where he was. She looked at the clock and answered with extreme nonchalance, "Is it work or I wonder if it's play?" Returning to her own play, she said nothing more about her husband. I realized later that she hadn't mentioned him at all during the five hours of drinking that had preceded my inquiry.[2]

I later interviewed many of these women and asked them about the late nights their husbands keep. The consensus was that they had no idea what their husbands were actually up to—how much was business and how much was drinking and "playing" with other women. They admitted that they did not question their husbands; they didn't want to know, or feel they had to know, so long as the man was fulfilling his role as provider. Ignorance was preferable, even desirable.

These women were not naive. They assumed that their husbands sometimes philandered or would do so at some point in their marriages and that their husbands' partners in sex would most likely be women from the *mizu shōbai.* Given this possibility, it is significant that these wives also stressed how necessary going into the nightlife was "for business." Work ties needed to be made or maintained. And the men needed to "relax." The *mizu shōbai* provided opportunities for both work and sex, and in the absence of frank discussion with their husbands the wives never knew whether on any particular night the men were engaged in one or the other or both.

---

2. These women liked to drink and had Saturday night drinking sessions on a fairly regular basis, as I later learned. Their children were being taken care of by mothers, mothers-in-law, or husbands.

Part 2 addressed the Japanese tendency to talk vaguely around, rather than directly about, the work-related activities of men in the *mizu shōbai*. There my interest lay in locating the social domains and cultural categories Japanese allude to in speaking of this practice. Arguing that recreation in the hostess club is contextualized in terms of more general behavioral patterns in Tokyo, I took a close look at the societal and cultural structures that support the *mizu shōbai*.

Here my aim is different. I look specifically at the company-sponsored ritual of groups of men entering bars and clubs to drink and flirt with women. My analysis is guided by how the participants and the spouses of participants frame the key elements in the experience. These key elements were not elaborated on by the men and women I spoke with, but they were a defining presence in nearly every discussion:

1. Men become tighter and closer as a result of going out together; the practice strengthens the *ningenkankei* (human relations) of a work force and builds the trust needed for a deal with a client.

2. While out drinking, a man relaxes; the tensions that build up during the workday are eased.

3. The role of the *mizu shōbai* women facilitates the first two effects but may not be limited to them.

4. Sexuality, real and imagined, is what is most liberating and pleasurable about what goes on at night.

How do the last two elements relate to the first two, which, it should be pointed out, were always mentioned first in the accounts I obtained? The outings were expected to accomplish an opening up (*uchitokeru*) between men and a loosening up (*kinchō o toku*) for the individual man. Accordingly, explanations were functionalistic: the end is what counts, and it justifies, interprets, and displaces the means. The means were not only disproportionately discussed but were not clearly connected to the end they were expected to serve. Drinking, talking nonsense, singing, flirting—these help the man relax and open up to other men in ways not possible at work. Often this was the extent to which the mechanism of the hostess club was seen to serve, fitting the man to other men and the man to himself in ways that "function" to sustain the operation of work.

The role of the woman and the place of sexuality were often described or alluded to as important, but precisely how they were important was left vague. One group of married women to whom I lectured asserted almost unanimously that the *mizu shōbai* was only about work and not about sex at all, though one woman ventured to say that the hostess was a pivotal figure because of the "service" (*sa-bisu*) she gave. When I asked her what "service" she was talking about, the woman didn't know but speculated that it probably had something to do with making it easier for the men at the table to pursue what they were really there to do—talk to each other.

Pushing this woman perhaps more than I should have, because of my interest in the subject, I described to her what, minimally and concretely, the "service" of a hostess consists of: lighting cigarettes and pouring drinks. Why, I asked, would this be so significant to a group of men "for their work" and why, come to think of it, couldn't men do these things for themselves? The woman seemed not to know. She admitted that she had never been to a hostess club and that her husband never told her about his experiences there. Her "imagining" of the hostess world had included the hostess, but in what capacity and why, she couldn't say.

My argument in part 3 is that whatever men say they need, think they're doing, and justify as necessary "for work" in the *mizu shōbai* is effected symbolically and ritualistically through women and the sexuality they represent. I am not arguing that all men have sex in the *mizu shōbai* or even that the *mizu shōbai* is mainly or essentially about sexual acts. Rather, I offer that corporate interest sends male workers of the higher echelons off to the *mizu shōbai*, that the interest rests in structuring the subjectivity and desires of workers in a particularly "male" way, and that this form of masculinity is structured chiefly by women and the sexual illusions of the *mizu shōbai*.

My inquiry in this section proceeds at three levels. First I take the functionalist paradigm—what happens in the nightlife serves corporate needs for male bonding and male relaxation. If we accept this functional view of the *mizu shōbai*, how do we define the "opening up" and relaxation, and how is it produced? Second, I challenge the functionalist model at both ends: Why else might the *mizu shōbai* woman and her representation of sexuality be sought out by men, in groups and at company expense, and what else besides male camaraderie and a release of work-related tensions might be the effects of these *mizu shōbai* constructions of gender and sexuality? Third, I contemplate the corporate manipulation and support of these male rituals. Corporation money endorses the institutionalizing of the *mizu shōbai* and, in particular, the male bonding that takes place there. The desires of individual men may be piqued by the *mizu shōbai*, but it is male desire as a particular construct that is managed by corporations.

9

Male Bonding

The two stories that follow describe outings to the *mizu shōbai* in which men seek to build bonds of fellowship or express the bonds they share. Although neither outing was supported by the *kōsaihi* of company funds, both were male rituals, and it is for this ritualism that I relate the stories here.

The first was told me by Narabayashi, the marriage and sex counselor quoted in part 2, who spoke with me at length about the *mizu shōbai* and Japanese male behavior. In this context he gave the following account, passed on to him by a friend.

Mori, a professional man then in his late fifties, one day received a phone call from Takai, with whom he had attended college some twenty or twenty-five years earlier. Contact with classmates is maintained in Japan on a constant if irregular basis. (I recall one man in his sixties who came to Bijo one night after attending a reunion of his kindergarten class.) Mori and Takai kept in touch by phone and saw each other maybe twice a year to reminisce about old times.

Takai, a *sarariiman* well situated in business, offered to treat Mori to a night out on the town. Mori accepted but revealed to his friend that the *mizu shōbai* was a world he did not know very well, since he was a teetotaler whose occupation did not take him to clubs and bars at company expense. Takai enjoyed being in a position to introduce his friend to a realm he was intimate with, and he played the generous host. They went from club to club, visiting places with lovely hostesses and excellent service. Mori felt that he was being luxuriously indulged, and both men were enjoying themselves.

Around midnight, Takai took Mori to what was intended to be the final destination, a love hotel where he had commissioned two prostitutes in advance.[1] He interpreted Mori's surprise as a sign of pleasure and presented

---

1. Love hotels are hotels where rooms are rented by the hour and are used primarily for sexual relations. Typically love hotels offer a wide range of rooms with various "services"—

151

the women as the crowning touch in an evening devoted to satisfying male desires. In truth Mori was disgusted. He refused the woman, finding the action of his friend to be more presumptuous than considerate.

Takai, for his part, was confused and insulted. Not comprehending the psychology of a man who wouldn't sleep with a woman who was already paid for, he conveyed to Mori his assumption that, given the chance, any male would bed down with an attractive woman. Takai had also assumed, according to Narabayashi, that finding sex together would further strengthen their friendship. So he read Mori's refusal far less as a personal statement of his sexual attitudes than as an indictment of the friendship between them. Indeed, the relationship was terminated that night. Takai never called again, and Mori understood that the rupture was too deep to ever mend.

The second story was related to me by Dan, an American anthropologist who spent a year at *Tōdai* (Tokyo University) during the late 1970s. In the course of his studies he participated in a graduate seminar with seven or eight other male students. From early in the school year mention was made of a "group outing," of going outside Tokyo together to have a good time.

Finally a date was picked. Dan was given only a sketchy idea of the plan: they would go by train to a resort three or four hours from Tokyo and spend a night there. Though his female friends at the university warned Dan not to go, saying that the men in the group had a bad reputation, he decided to join the party. The group was convivial and in good spirits when they arrived at the resort. They were all to share one room (a common practice when vacationing in Japan and particularly so for student outings).

They enjoyed a dinner with drinks and *geisha*-like attendants. The mood was lively and relaxed. Next they ventured into the night, going from one club, bar, and strip joint to another and becoming progressively drunk and rowdy. They told jokes and sexual stories, touched or made passes at the hostesses, watched strippers, sang songs. Finally, well after midnight, all the men except one piled into a cab and returned to the resort. Dead drunk, they slept the rest of the night and got up the next morning to return to Tokyo.

---

revolving bed, mirrored ceiling, video camera, video player, stocked refrigerator with beer and food, sex toys and contraptions—where the price depends on the particular package of the room. Often photos of these different rooms are posted outside the hotel. The exterior design of these places used to be intentionally conspicuous—gaudy colors and designs in outlandish but recognizable shapes, like the liner *Queen Mary* in shocking pink. Writing in 1991, however, I hear that there is a trend away from such external ostentation and toward greater subtlety. I thank Miriam Silverberg for this observation.

The man who had left the group had visited a prostitute. Although Dan learned of this fact the next morning, the news generated absolutely no interest. Instead, the "big outing" itself garnered all the attention and continued to be the topic of much talk in the weeks that followed. Referring to what a good time they had had, the men created an impression that they had all indulged in extreme debauchery.

Dan at first found the references amusing, then perplexing; after all, only one of the seminar members had actually engaged in anything more than the usual drinking behavior, yet all (save Dan) claimed such participation.

The Structuring of Groups through Rituals

The French sociologist Emile Durkheim proposed in his book *The Elementary Forms of the Religious Life* (published in 1915) a thesis that has now become axiomatic in anthropology: social relationships are given symbolic expression in totems, which are objects used to symbolically and ritualistically encode social relations. According to the Durkheimian model, a totemic object could be anything—a snake, a lizard, a stone—because its meaning comes from not the thing itself but what it stands for—a clan, a phratry (level of social organization), a tribe. Further, according to Durkheim, the process of symbolization is functionally necessary. Social groups need shared symbols in order to organize a collective identity as well as purpose. The suturing of social links requires, that is, both the production and maintenance of common goals, gods, and routines.

While Durkheim's theory of social symbolism has been highly influential in fields such as anthropology, structuralism, and semiotics, his functionalist perspective—that social rituals and symbols "function" to preserve a group—has been heavily critiqued. That the symbolic behavior of saluting a flag, for example, has social meaning and utility is widely accepted. What is not, however, is the premise that such rituals simply emerge arbitrarily and consensually from a preestablished group of people and that they function to preserve a social unity that is equally agreeable to all members of the group. Problematizing such a concept, contemporary scholars (working in such diverse areas as Marxism, feminism, film theory, cultural studies, and subaltern studies) argue that social symbols are often tied to very specific economic, political, and gendered relations that do not impact equally on all those they affect. Rituals are not necessarily unifying or unresisted and they do not simply reflect social relationships but also construct them. Questions that are asked now about any ritualistic activity such as nighttime recreation by groups of men include these: Who designs and organizes this behavior? Are participants given a voice and choice in their participation? Who is excluded from participating and on what grounds? What relations (social/economic/political/racial/gendered) are enforced by this behavior? What effects does participation as well as nonparticipation have on other aspects of the lives people live?

The two outings described earlier were rituals (defined here as routinized activity that symbolically expresses and constructs social conventions) that shared several structures:

1. The participants knew each other before the event and participated on the basis of their mutual ties.

2. The format of the behavior—drinking, flirting with women, telling jokes—was familiar and acceptable, up to a point, to the participants.

3. The participants perceived a relationship between the first two structures; what they did together on the outing was meant to symbolize their unity as a group.

Structurally similar, these two outings shared a further resemblance; the planners selected the same format—alcohol, women, and sexual play. This format was chosen for its assumed appeal to the male participants and to encourage a heightened sense of maleness that would link them together.

That is, maleness was made to be ritualistic and symbolic. But why? According to Japanese, such outings seek an "opening up" of the participants that is experienced as a personal release and is a means to get closer to the others. But why and how precisely does a format of male drinking and sexualizing produce an effect of opening up? Further, is there a collective understanding that this is the agenda for male bonding? In the outing Takai arranged, Mori rejected this understanding and, in so doing, was perceived to reject Takai's friendship. Mori felt coerced; the members of Dan's seminar group apparently did not.

Thomas Rohlen, in an article about social order as it is taught to children in Japanese nursery schools (1989), points to the potential coerciveness of group membership: "To not attach or to refuse to accept group influence is to place oneself outside, and to eventually justify a different, potentially very coercive kind of treatment" (1989:30). While the subject of Rohlen's research is different from that of male rituals in the nightlife, both what he says and what he neglects to say about the ideology and construction of Japanese groups is nonetheless pertinent. He proposes that the introduction to "group living" (shūdanseikatsu) is the main lesson to be learned at this initial stage of the educational process. Children must learn to cooperate with others, to conform to the rules and routines of the school, and to subordinate personal desires and impulses. These are structures that cannot be taught at home (so he was told by Japanese mothers and teachers) because of the very nature of the mother-child bond (1989:18–29). At home, mothers indulge their children and children depend on their mothers: this relationship is not acceptable at the nursery-school level and so is not reproduced by the teacher.

When children enter school they must adopt a new orientation. Now they will be identified and must behave according to group membership— what school they belong to, what age group, what class, what *han*. According to Rohlen, children assimilate their attachment to specific groups, as well as the ideology of group attachment, primarily through the repetition of everyday routines. The school organizes its academic year systematically through such routines, as do institutions such as commercial companies.

The multiplicity of routines produces an order of precision and cleanliness to which the children are expected to adhere. Naturally, this order and its adjunct, conformism, are produced by and on the authority of the school. Rohlen writes, however, that this institutional authority is made agreeable and acceptable to the child by being disguised in three ways: (1) "intimacy and authority are not separated"—the routines, order, and authority figures of the school are fashioned to be friendly, cozy, and pleasant; (2) the teacher (as prime authority figure for the child on an everyday basis) "steps back at times from the exercise of authority"—instead of being heavy-handed, the teacher may let the group decide on a particular issue, thereby protecting "authority from appearing coercive"; and (3) authority is increasingly displaced from the institutional figure of teacher onto the group of students— the teacher encourages the group to use its collective voice to dictate order and conformity; other children, for example, are encouraged to persuade a misbehaving classmate to behave (Rohlen 1989:28–31).

Though Rohlen's tendency in this article is to view collectivized authority as benign, he has clearly revealed the mechanism by which Japanese who belong to such institutions as school and workforce are organized into groups and how these groups become the enforcers of an order and behavior dictated by the institution acceptable to its members. To conceal authority without losing it, an institution must shift concentration from management or authority figures to the groups within the institutions and the human relations within the groups. Then any "we/they" or "I/you" dichotomy seems to be erased, or, as the Japanese scholars Aida Yuji (1972) and Minami Hiroshi (1978) asserted, "public and private domains are inherently blurred" (Rohlen 1989:34). The conformity demanded by a group feels familiar, not oppressive. Rohlen demonstrates that a key element in this familiarizing process is having groups share "fixed routines" that are experienced as "pleasant and desirable" (30).

One obvious fixed routine of Japanese corporate life is the foray into the nightlife by groups of male workers. Rohlen, who has also written about Japanese corporate life, treats the routine as functionally parallel to the routines shared by nursery school children.[2] It is one type of a series of routines that, once shared, will lead to a bonding between workers. In Rohlen's treatment, the precise content of the routine matters less than the fact that it is mutually engaged in by all members of a group. By sharing "hardships" and "pleasures" and participating equally, groups are both structured and satisfied. "Full participation in the voluntary and informal events of the group is thus a major goal in itself, since participation is the measure of acceptance, openness, and satisfaction. It is part of a reciprocal arrangement, the individual's contribution to the whole" (Rohlen 1989:29).

Like Durkheim before him, Rohlen denies the symbolic importance of specific rituals and fails to point out how such symbolism serves not only to cohere group formation but also to construct it. He also ignores key questions: Who establishes these rituals? Might they be more "pleasant and desirable" to certain parties and less so to others? Are there agendas or interests being served other than that of "group membership"? What precisely does "group membership" mean as an effect or condition of these shared rituals? And why are specific rituals structured in the manner that they are? The rituals and routines indulged in by various groups in Japan are not, to my mind, functional equivalents. They all reflect and encourage group attachment, but there are variations in how they do so, with what construction of "group," and with what implications for the individual members within those groups.

Ritualistic Male Behavior at a Hostess Club

In order to assess the relationship between what men say the nightlife rituals are intended to do and what actually takes place, I return now to the ethnographic material I gathered in the hostess club Bijo.

One evening Ono, the owner and president of a small cosmetics com-

---

2. See particularly *For Harmony and Strength: Japanese White-Collar Organization in Anthropological Perspective* (1974).

pany who visited the club about once a month, came into Bijo with two men he was obviously hosting. One, Kawasaki, was an employee at Ono's firm; the other, Ohtani, had done some work for Ono and was being considered for a full-time position. Ohtani and Kawasaki were both in their late twenties, and Ono was in his mid-fifties.

All three men had obviously been drinking, probably at a restaurant or, more likely, another club. Ono, who liked me, asked the Mama to assign me to their table. When I joined them, Ono immediately complimented me on my dress and related every detail he could remember about me to the two other men—I came from America, I was associated with a university in Tokyo, my subject area was anthropology, and so on. Fussing over me excessively, he told his guests that he'd been so embarrassed the first time we met that he hadn't been able to look at me, but the second time he did look, and found me pretty, and then each time subsequently he had enjoyed me more and had been more comfortable with me.

Kawasaki and Ohtani were amused by Ono's confession. They kept poking fun at him, noting how cool and sophisticated he'd pretend to be around women but how shy and inept he became when having a real encounter. They joked that he was getting old and was losing his memory, that he came to the office late every day and did little work once there, that he thought he was good-looking but really wasn't, and that he thought himself much smarter than he actually was. Ono took all this ribbing in stride, bemoaning to me how tough these youngsters were being on him but never refuting a single point.

In between telling his guests about me and declaring how much he liked me (and, as the night wore on, how much he adored me, was infatuated with me, hoped to marry me), Ono told me about Kawasaki and Ohtani. Both men were hard workers and university graduates, had studied English, enjoyed various hobbies, and were to be married in the near future. He demanded that each pull out of his wallet the picture of his fiancée. When the men complied, Ono admired the pictures, calling the two women beautiful and exclaiming that he just couldn't believe these guys would soon be married men. The pictures of the women were pulled out three or four more times during the night.

Ono insisted that I sit between Kawasaki and Ohtani while he sat alone on the other side of the table. From this distance he kept building me up to the two men and telling me directly how crazy he was about me, in terms more ardent than in the two or three times the two of us had talked together previously. Once, when the piano player was on break, Ono demanded that

Kawasaki get up and play. This was not common policy at Bijo, but Ono was insistent and Kawasaki played. Though Kawasaki was too drunk to perform well, Ono kept ordering one of the waiters to turn up the mike so everyone could hear better. When Ohtani went to the washroom, leaving Ono and me alone, Ono nonchalantly asked me to accompany him the next week to Paris, where he was going to a conference. I was evasive, and never gave him a "final answer."

When the two younger men returned to the table, Ono solicited their advice about a certain matter he would be pursuing at the Paris meeting. For a few minutes Ohtani and Kawasaki gave serious consideration to the issue and answered like colleagues. Ono listened carefully, said it was good advice, and thanked them both. Then the banter started again: jokes about Ono, questions to me about America, stories told about university life, inquiries by Ono about what I wanted in a man and assurances that he had at least one thing I wanted and wouldn't that be enough for a husband? It was getting late, and Kawasaki and Ohtani asked if they couldn't go home. After all, they had to be at the office early, unlike Ono, who wouldn't arrive until noon. They wondered aloud if they could sleep late the next morning. Ono ignored the question and insisted that they stay. He reminded them that they were all having a good time.

Around midnight all three got up to sing. Ono sang the last two songs of the evening, very seriously and dramatically. The two younger men praised his singing to me at the table while also flirting with me and telling me that they hoped they could see me again soon. By 12:30 they were the last guests; Mama and I saw them down in the elevator and waited with them for a cab.

I won't call this a typical encounter in all respects, but it had elements typical of many of the interactions I observed or participated in while hostessing at Bijo. The customers had a relationship outside the club; motivation and payment for the outing were based on this relationship; the men came to the club together and stayed together all evening; activities consisted of telling stories, flirting, drinking, and singing; there were many allusions to women, sex, romance, and male sexual prowess; and there were repeated exclamations about how enjoyable the outing was, reinforced by laughter, pats on the back, and use of the word *"tanoshii"* (enjoyable, pleasant).

Why the night out? What did it accomplish? Because Ono kept complimenting the two young men, I assumed his aim was at least partly to reward his full-time employee for working hard and to either check out the second one or persuade him to work full-time. Ono wanted his guests to have a good time, but how they were to do so, he did not leave entirely to them. In fact, he used tactics as coercive as those Takai had used with Mori, if less extreme. He gave orders that his guests never refused: "Take out the pictures of your fiancées!" "Play the piano!" "Drink more!" "Sing!" And when Ohtani and Kawasaki wanted to leave, he withheld permission.

Rohlen's theory that group events rely primarily on simple participation seems to be contradicted by this example. Participation by all members in a fashion by some measure equal and mutual *was* required, but the participation did not come about spontaneously. Rather, it was directed by one member of the party.

The personal relaxation and group bonding that Japanese men identify as reasons for participating in the nightlife were nonetheless realized by Ono and his party. All the participants would probably agree that they felt relaxed and closer to one another after that evening at Bijo. Note, however, that they unwound in a set way and that the two employees participated in activities they couldn't refuse. Even the way they opened up (*uchitokeru*) to each other had its rules and limitations. The stories they told of and to each other, for example, were part personal, part manufactured. Personal stories could go only so far and never become too personal: the fiancées' names were repeated and their pictures looked at often, but who they were, from what backgrounds, and what kinds of relationships they had with their boyfriends were never mentioned. The manufactured stories, about me in particular, were easier to share and for this reason, perhaps, were elaborated on and prolonged.

Ono knew, of course, that I would play along with his stories; after all, hostesses are expected to accept all that the customer says and does.[3] Ono would never have discussed me the way that he did if we had actually been involved romantically or sexually. Then the relationship would have been private; I would have been in a category something like that of wife, and wives are referred to only jokingly and infrequently at clubs. By playing a game that was not "real," Ono could in a sense share me. He spoke of me as if he desired me for himself, but in the speaking I came to serve as a sort of collective, stand-in mistress for them all, someone they could talk to and about together. Although I had joined their group, I did not become part of it, and when they left, of course, I stayed behind.

---

3. If a man's lechery gets out of hand, we were told to subtly let the manager or a waiter know so that they could switch us to another table. To handle the problem on one's own would be very disagreeable for the customer, the club, and the hostess herself.

The boundaries by which this play with a hostess are bracketed, I would argue, are as important as its content. A woman's flirtations can loosen up a group, but were she to become attached to any one of the men personally, this contribution could well be canceled out. Ono considered sexuality and womanhood to be useful in the context of this one night out with Ohtani and Kawasaki. Had I pursued his seeming attraction outside the club, his reaction would have been quite different.

My encounter with Ono's party had lasted a little over two hours, substantially longer than most parties at Bijo (the norm was about an hour) and far exceeding the time a hostess usually remains at one table (about half an hour). So, in this sense, it was not a typical encounter between hostess and customers. Here, more briefly, are some other encounters that suggest the variety of interactions I observed at Bijo:

One evening, about 8 P.M., I was seated with a party of three for about twenty minutes. The host, Hashimoto, told me that he had once worked for the American Army and the French Foreign Legion, but he didn't identify his present occupation. He was accompanied by two colleagues—Sasaki, who was quiet and soft-spoken, and Katsura, whom one of the hostesses had told me she strongly disliked. Eri, the veteran hostess who had years of experience in the *mizu shōbai* and seemed unflappable, was also seated at the table and quickly engaged Katsura in conversation. I spoke mainly with Hashimoto. He was a big talker and didn't seem to mind that Sasaki remained rather quiet. All three men were in their fifties and sixties.

Hashimoto told me that he was a linguistics buff and proceeded to instruct me on various points in the etymology of the Japanese language. Using a big black pen, he wrote words and characters on the paper coasters and acted very much like a professor. Our conversation centered on this subject. I would ask him questions, and he would very happily and earnestly answer them.

In the midst of the conversation I was having with Hashimoto, Katsura would occasionally turn to me and direct a question or remark my way. Once he prompted Eri to ask me when I had lost my virginity. He also asked me questions directly: "How many boyfriends do you have?" "How many do you sleep with?" Since I had been told by the manager to conceal all details about my personal life, I usually answered such questions, which were asked repeatedly, in an evasive or outrageous manner. This time I replied that I had many boyfriends and that I slept with them all. The men laughed much more heartily at the questions posed by Katsura than at my answers.

After a while, I was moved to another table.

One busy evening I was seated with a party of five. The members of the party mentioned that they were all from the same iron and steel company. Ushijima, who remembered me, asked me to sit between him and another man, Toshishima, who announced immediately that he hated foreigners (*gaijin*) and pushed me as I passed by him to take my designated place. Ushijima started telling me a story about the Suntory Company, and at one point he mentioned the port city of Kobe. Upon hearing that I'd never been there, he said to Toshishima: "She's never been to Kobe. Why don't you take her?"

Toshishima shuddered visibly at the suggestion, and everyone at the table laughed loudly. Ushijima and the others continued to tease Toshishima about me.

After a while another hostess, Keiko, was assigned the table. When it turned out that she came from Kobe, Toshishima declared that Keiko should be the one to take me to Kobe. At this the other men started taunting Toshishima again—about how he really should act better toward women, and so on. Keeping a grumpy look on his face, he muttered that he actually preferred men, that even a woman with large breasts, like Keiko, couldn't attract him. This last comment he repeated a few times—Keiko had big breasts but still he wouldn't be able to stand spending time with her.

I was sitting at a table of four, all men in their early forties, who spoke quietly and interestingly about relations between the United States and Japan, universities, travel, and so on. At one point the Mama came up, asked them how they all were doing, and told one of the men that he looked more handsome every time he came to the club. She smiled intimately, told them to enjoy themselves, and then went to the next table.

One of the men spoke about singing in a club like this, saying it wasn't a matter of enjoying it but of having to do it. "It's inevitable" (*shō ga nai*), he said. Someone asked me how tall I was, and they in turn told me how big their penises were. One said that his was 50 centimeters long. Another motioned with his arms to indicate that his was two feet long. Another said his was so big that he could jump rope with it, which made walking a big inconvenience.

Another hostess was called over, and I was assigned to a different table.

The first guests to enter the party were Komukai and Terada, men in their 40's. Because there were at this time no other customers, all the hostesses joined the men at their table. One hostess immediately called Komukai cute (*kawaii*) because his face was chubby and he had dimples. Another said she could just imagine what he had looked like as a boy—probably exactly the same. The rest agreed.

The two men said that they had seen Mayumi in the elevator to Bijo and couldn't believe that she was a hostess here. She looked so young and fresh, so un-*mizu shōbai*-like. They asked her to sing, encouraged her in spite of her protests that she really had no voice at all, and then analyzed her appearance while she stood at the microphone. Her legs were pretty, she looked slender, she had no breasts whatsoever. . . . When Mayumi returned to the table, they told her she had been incredibly "cute" (*kawaii*). Periodically they'd return to talking about her body. They knew she was still young, but did she realize that she had no breasts at all? Would they grow maybe in a few years? Mayumi went along with the men, saying that her breasts probably wouldn't grow and she'd be stuck with small ones her whole life.

After this the men started discussing foreheads and asked us all to pull the hair off our faces so they could see how we'd look that way. Keiko's admission that her forehead was marred by an ugly layer of baby fat drew instant disagreement from the men; she looked far better that way, they suggested.

Mama came over and flattered Komukai and Terada by saying that everyone who came to Bijo was very nice. The men laughed and pointed out that Mama said that about all her customers. She then put her arm lightly around Keiko and Haruka and told the men that they were very good hostesses, always nice to the customers and pretty too. Two of the hostesses she called *menkui*—people who are quick to judge others by appearance.

Keiko sang a song when the men asked her to, and Machiko followed, though she first mimicked Mayumi's embarrassment and protests. The other hostesses started talking about chest hair, figuring the hair on the piano player's chest went down to mid-chest, which was okay for a man. Komukai and Terada preferred not to talk about their own bodies but wanted to speak about ours. One said I was tall and had long legs. He mentioned that my hair was all wrong, however, and was really very unbecoming, flopping over my forehead as it did.

They next assessed the breast size of all the hostesses. One was told that hers were just right; another, that hers were big; a third, that hers were nonexistent; two others that, though they might have breasts, this wasn't apparent to a viewer. Then they asked the hostess they had judged as the best-endowed to tell them her bust size in centimeters. She apologized profusely for not knowing this. She promised to take the measurement and tell them next time.

As other guests entered the club, we all were eventually moved to other tables, and the two men left.

The first party one evening was a man named Hasemi; his daughter Sumiko, a fourth year college student; and Takuma, who had just hired Sumiko. Referred to as the *ojōsan* (young lady), Sumiko was at first very embarrassed to be seated with so many hostesses (all of us). Two of the hostesses kept complimenting the *ojōsan*—how sophisticated she seemed, how poised, how pretty; and Mama echoed the hostesses' honeyed words when she came to the table.

Hasemi quickly became interested in Haruka and told Kiyomi, the hostess who was sitting next to him, to switch places with her. He then lavished praise and attention on Haruka, who at one point turned to Sumiko to say that her father was good at flattery (*oseji*). The daughter replied that it wasn't flattery because her father only told the truth.[4]

Hasemi did most of the talking at the table. He loved his wife and daughter and regarded them as the most important people in his life, he said, but this didn't prevent him from falling for a woman like Haruka. While holding Haruka's hand and sitting close to her, he spoke of how indebted he was to Takuma and always would be for giving his daughter a job. Takuma said no, no, it was *he* who was getting the good end of the deal with this hard-working young woman. At this point the two men asked the table of hostesses what impression the *ojōsan* made. I commented that she looked like a hard worker and they all laughed loudly, saying yes, yes, that was right. I also said the *ojōsan* was pretty, but Sumiko disagreed, saying that the novice hostess Mayumi was a beauty but she herself was not.

Hasemi announced that my hair was very unattractive, tried to rearrange it, scowled, and said that it still wasn't right. Haruka explained that Hasemi preferred women with a certain pulled-back hairstyle and that this was one of the reasons "father" liked her so much. Hasemi added that he liked all of Haruka, everything about her, and touched her breasts and thighs. Haruka smiled, didn't pull away, commenting again to me that "papa" was very kind.

4. I found the daughter's casualness regarding her father's flirtations with Haruka to be strange, but according to an interviewee—a woman in her twenties—Japanese families may know in a general way and accept what a man does in the nightlife. In the experience of a friend of mine, Takano, her father would occasionally discuss a hostess or describe a particular evening in a hostess club as part of his Saturday evening dinner conservation. (Most other nights except Sunday he was at work or in the clubs). As a teenager, Takano also helped him practice his singing, assuming the part a hostess would in a duet.

There still being no other parties at Bijo, Hasemi got up to sing a few songs. His daughter complained, saying that she loved her father but his voice was intolerable and this singing of his was the most embarrassing aspect of his behavior. She kept mumbling *"mō ii"* (that's enough), but her father kept singing. Haruka asked Sumiko how old she was, and upon learning that the *ojōsan* was twenty-one, she revealed that by that age she had already seen much of the "dirty" (*kitanai*) side of life. Mama came up to the table again and resumed complimenting the daughter's youth and beauty. Takuma said he couldn't see why Mama was fussing so much, considering that there surely couldn't be more than a year's difference in their ages. Mama smiled sweetly, but when I laughed, she poked me and said, "Why, you understood that?"

In the middle of the evening Takashi, who received special treatment from Mama because he spent so much at Bijo, entered the club with three other men. From his behavior I assumed that they were clients or potential clients. I was seated with them for their entire stay, nearly two hours. They asked me perfunctory questions about my status in Japan and my country of origin, commented on the club (only Takashi had been there before), and remarked on how young and beautiful the Mama was. At one point the conversation became serious, and for perhaps forty-five minutes I simply sat at the table, lighting cigarettes and pouring drinks. No one said a word to me; my presence was totally ignored.

Woman Servicing the Group

As these seven portraits reveal, certain patterns surface in the gendered (male-male, female-male) interactions between customers and hostesses. Men like to be in charge or have the appearance of being in charge; to be the focus of attention or the ones deciding to whom the attention will be directed; to have their words listened to and accepted; and to be generally fussed over, pumped up, complimented, flattered, and indulged. Men structure these behaviors mainly with women. With other men they agree on things, share jokes, praise one another or playfully put each other down, and engage in parallel or joint behavior (flirting with different hostesses, for example, or flirting together with a single hostess).

In all this the woman is obviously a useful device: she livens things up for all who enter.

The worst party is one in which people say little, drink nothing, and refuse to sing. To avoid such dreary failure, the host is happy to hand the responsibility for the party's success to the hostess. If she accomplishes her objective—a warm, pleasant atmosphere, a lively discussion—she will be a successful hostess. Just as men will say that purchased sex is pleasurable, so too is the social intercourse facilitated by a paid-for woman—in both cases, however, the debt to the woman and the obligation of the relationship are easily wiped out.

In this male ritual about work but also play, the female is important but she can also be insulted, ignored, and walked away from. As is repeatedly enacted in the scenes described above, the *mizu shōbai* woman is continually "put in her place" by the men for whom she's lighting cigarettes, pouring drinks, and instigating conversation. She is lectured, her appearance is evaluated and criticized, her body is ogled and pawed, and she is required to do as the customer asks, whether it be to sing or play the part of potential mistress. That in performing in this subservient manner, the woman is also putting the men in a particular position—a position in which they can commune with one another in a way that confirms, enhances, or sometimes creates work relations—is either ignored or denied.

Consider Hegel's analysis of the master-slave relationship. A master dominates a slave and from a position of authority extracts the slave's labor. Yet the master himself is unskilled in the arts of subsistence and relies on the slave for both the production of his food and the affirmation of his identity as master. That is, the master is only master in the eyes of the slave, and the master is only fed when the slave, as slave, provides the master's food. If the true nature of this relationship is recognized—that, in some sense, the master is far more dependent on the slave than the slave on the master—the master and slave will each have a greater awareness of both self and other (Hegel 1977:111–19).

The men entering a club like Bijo to bond for the benefit of business or work often are as unskilled in the procedure as the master who can't produce his own food. They frequently come through the doors straight from work, tired, uptight, and insecure. The success of a business contract may rest on this night; or the evening may be seen as a reward for overtime work, extreme devotion, or incentive. The men understand the evening's agenda (work) and the principle of the ritual (to make work seem like nonwork).

The drinking, singing, talking dirty, discussing irrelevant things, and other fixed routines that are expected of men in a *mizu shōbai* setting promote relaxation. Some men are able to initiate or maintain these routines on their own; for others, however, the start-up is wearying. There will always be men who wipe their brows and shift nervously in their seats in miserable anticipation of singing in front of their coworkers. The hostess helps such men, insisting that they drink and sing, if they're not doing so already; pestering them with questions if they're quiet, or giving them an opening for a lewd remark; and with her *mizu shōbai* identity and body, moving them into talk that is strictly "men's talk" with no overtones of work.

In a figurative sense the hostess produces the food a group of men will consume as their evening of male recreation. Yet like the master who cannot recognize his dependence on the slave if he wishes to maintain his own identity as a master, the men cannot recognize the debt they owe the hostess if they wish to maintain that their night out is more about fun than it is about work and that they, as men, are more important than the women. So a woman is paid; the relationship of domination is assured; and no matter how much the men flatter and romance her at the table, they will leave her behind as readily as they welcomed and depended on her when they entered the club. In order to remain dependent on the woman, the men must mask their dependence.

No one, of course, is actually deluded. Companies are paying hostess club bills on expense accounts that customers sign for in the company's name, yet in order for this "humanization" of work to have effect, the work agenda must be concealed or disguised. Work on the premises of work is one thing; work on the premises of a hostess club is another; and if the difference weren't significant or valuable, companies wouldn't pay hundreds of thousands of dollars a year to make the difference. The principle of what Roland Barthes calls the "alibi" is engaged. There is a "constantly moving turnstyle" between two orders of meaning—a meaning of work concealed behind one of play, a meaning of play fashioned to accommodate one of work (1972:123).[5]

The "work" that a night in hostess clubs is expected to accomplish— everyone getting along, opening up, engaging in smooth and easy palaver— must therefore not feel like work. It must feel, in fact, like "nonwork"—a

5. As Barthes uses the concept, the relationship is actually between form and meaning: between a first (denotative) order of language ("language-object") with its relationship between signifier and signified combining into a sign (filled with meaning) which is emptied to become an empty form. This form is then borrowed by a second order ("metalanguage") which refills it with a different, added meaning. This second order is also what Barthes refers to as myth, and it is the signifier in myth that "exactly reproduces the physique of the *alibi*" (1972:123). Important to Barthes is the manner in which myth is a "double system" moving back and forth between two levels and orders of signification: for example, a rose can be a flower, but also a sign of or for passion, and also a sign of or for a sensitive male.

concept difficult to comprehend and accept in a culture where hard work is valued and where time off has a negative connotation. Keeping a group of men relaxed and engaged in a hostess club is hard work, as I learned from experience and heard verified by the other hostesses as they discussed their jobs at the club. Yet to recognize the night out as work and the woman's role in it as work is to remove the alibi and reduce the evening to one term (work) when the effectiveness of the ritual depends on its shifting between two terms (play and work).

So the men, among themselves, laugh, joke, pat each other on the back, keep exclaiming about what a good time they're having. With the women, however, their behavior differs. They flirt, talk, lap up the hostesses' attentions, and feel indulged, but ultimately keep these women distanced—by judging their looks, leaving them at the door of the club, and keeping them assigned to a different and secondary order of being: the mizu shōbai women.

Totemically and ritualistically, women working in the nightlife serve the men's groups and the bonding they entail. In the process, the woman becomes a construct, a type, a symbol. This construction of femaleness in the mizu shōbai will be discussed in the next chapter.

10

The *Mizu Shōbai* Woman
Constructing Dirtiness and Sex

American Fraternities: "Men" Constructed out of Abuse to Women

In *Gang Rape: Sex, Brotherhood, and Privilege on Campus*, the anthropologist Peggy Sanday examines a ritual called "train" or "training," in which a group of American college men serially or collectively rape a woman. Typically, the woman is incapacitated by drugs or alcohol during the incident and not likely to try to escape while the rape is happening or to report it afterward.

While there are vast dissimilarities between this ritual and those I've described involving men and women in hostess clubs in Japan, there is a structural similarity in the manner that the men symbolically and ritualistically enact their manliness and their male bonds through a woman. In the case of the gang rape, as interpreted by Sanday, it is the extreme version of a more general and constant fraternity ethos (not necessarily operative at all fraternities, she points out). This ethos is first experienced by frat "brothers" when they join the group. One of the major symbolisms during initiation is for the new men to be feminized—splattered with blood, taunted as weak, called "pussy," "bitch," and so on. This feminine portion of a man must then be symbolically removed in the company of the all-male brotherhood (Sanday 1990: 135–55).

Once accepted into the fold, the new brother must now display his "manliness," the symbol of membership and shared identity. Sanday writes that manliness in fraternities is based on two components: the penis and heterosexual sex. Penis size is discussed, sketched, caricatured, and written about in fraternity memos. It identifies the man as a man and links him to the other men in his group. Hence, the more active a man is with his penis, the greater status he can achieve in the fraternal order. But there is a condition: sex with another man doesn't count. Even though the bonding and orientation in a fraternity is what Linda Williams (1989) calls "homosocial" (relations between members of the same gender even if that doesn't include acts of sex), homosexual acts are considered polluting and debilitating to a male.

Women are therefore central to the construction of manliness as the means to an end, if you will. A woman's value to the brothers is strictly sexual. If she enters the fraternity's premises for a party, she is fair game. If a brother succeeds in "scoring," her name is written on a posted "score-board," and, particularly in the case of a gang rape, she is insulted, her morals are questioned, and her reputation is demeaned. The woman has provided a service to a group of men. Woman as a construct is fashioned as desirable and necessary, but after the sexual fact is looked on as dirty and expendable.

In the hostess club, too, though the cultural and institutional dynamics differ, ritual dramas involving gender and sexuality are similarly enacted. Here the men share a common bond of work, much like the bonds of the fraternity membership. And they interact with women in order to build and secure the ties of manliness. Differences certainly exist between the fraternity and the hostess club. In the club, the men are older, the women are paid, the place is not the men's own, and sexual intercourse occurs infrequently, voluntarily, and privately, off the premises. Nonetheless, Sanday's work on American fraternities bears a notable relation to the conditions present in the hostess bars of Japan, and I will refer to it as I question the symbolic and ideological role of "Woman" in hostess club outings by white-collar men.

A Class Club Makes for a Class Man

Bijo is considered a second-class club (in a hierarchy of perhaps eight classes) not because of its furnishings (exquisite) or its Mama (*bijin*—beautiful) but because its hostesses are generally judged to be average or mediocre in appearance. I once asked Abe, the manager, why the Mama didn't upgrade her hostesses if this was the only factor lowering Bijo's ranking. He said that it was a matter of economics; the Mama didn't have to pay her hostesses what higher-class hostesses would demand and could therefore charge her guests a more "reasonable" rate (at that time between $75 and $150 per guest for a stay of perhaps an hour or an hour and a half). With some, if not all, of the attributes of a first-class club, Mama was able to attract customers who wanted the classiness of the top-rated clubs but appreciated Bijo's moderate prices—about one-third that of clubs in the first class.

Kao ga kiku—showing one's face—is the phrase Yoda uses to describe the structure and experience of visiting a first-class club. This activity translates to an expression and display of social status in the presence of others (1981:29). For men who use a hostess club to entertain clients or employees, the classiness of a club becomes a sign of social prestige. It reflects the importance of both the company and the man doing the entertaining as well as the regard the host has for the party being entertained (Tabe 1986). Bijo's Mama, with her freshly coiffed hair, expensive kimono, perfectly matched accessories, and air of elegance and refinement, symbolizes the wealth and status—real or imagined—of the club's clientele.

Mama makes only token appearances—flitting from table to table, singing one or two "special songs," and joining a departing group to wish them farewell—yet her presence impresses the customers. By contrast, hostesses, who stay at individual tables, relate to men in ways that may be central to the interactions of the group, and are flirted with openly and explicitly, are easily dismissed or disregarded.

Why is there a difference in the treatment of the Mama and the hostesses, the subcategories of the *mizu shōbai* woman? I'd like to consider first the reason why hostesses, depended upon so constantly at a table with many men, are degraded and devalued by the customers they serve.

Mother Substitutes Who Are Not Mothers

One theory advanced by various Japanese and non-Japanese thinkers is provocative as it relates to this subject, if not entirely convincing on its own. This is that hostesses act as mother substitutes, coddling men, as would a mother, and indulging them with a maternal-like acceptance and understanding of behaviors that, to a Westerner, seem insulting or invasive. Ian Buruma, a journalist and scholar of Japanese literature, subscribes to this theory. Writing of the pervasiveness of the mother image in the religion, literature, cinema, art, and popular culture of Japan, he says, "It is often hard to avoid feeling that in male-female relationships in Japan every woman is a mother and every man a son" (1984:19).

Buruma uses a multitude of examples to illustrate how deeply rooted in the Japanese culture this mother fixation is and how gender relations are premised as well as modeled on the mother-child bond. He also distills the behavioral coding of the relationship: mothers sacrifice themselves for their children, children depend on and presume upon the sacrifices made by mothers. Accordingly, a mother has two options for correcting a child's misbehavior—to induce guilt in the child for accepting her sacrifices or to withhold affection (1984:19). Buruma writes of a mother's firm control over children and interprets the preponderance of a rape motif in film, literature, and comic books today in the following terms.

According to Buruma, fear of female power produces male masochism and male aggression; the latter is responsible for a long tradition of male sadism against women (1984:53). Beginning, he argues, with the *Nihonshōki*, a legendary Japanese history text, written in the eighth century, that is believed to contain the first recorded stories of men slitting the bellies of pregnant women (54), violence against women is common in Japanese literature, film, and other cultural media. The structure of many of the tales is similar. A man rapes a female, the female is transformed into a lascivious woman, the male admits that this is the only way he can be satisfied, and the woman comforts him. Though she has been violated in a forceful and violent fashion, the victim forgives her attacker, Buruma stresses, just as a mother would forgive her child. He adds that at the time of being attacked, the woman frequently mutters that at least this male is better than her weak, impotent husband—who is usually depicted as a *sarariiman* (58–63).

Others writing on gender and sexuality in Japan often agree with Buruma that the mother-child relationship has a primary impact on the social and sexual construction of adult heterosexual relations. (See, for example, Narabayashi 1982; Wagatsuma 1982; Fukuda 1982; Mizuno 1982; Sano 1991; Yuzawa 1982). Though the process by which elements in a mother-child relationship become sexualized or organized into patterns of adult erotic desire is not often made clear, the tendency is to concentrate on male sexuality, particularly the sexual behavior of men in the public realm (for example, with women who are paid for) and to trace this to two structures formed within the mother-child bond—the female being in charge (parentally) and the male being indulged (childishly).

These structures can be spoken of quite differently. The Japanese anthropologist Wagatsuma Hiroshi, for example, related to me an interpretation resembling Buruma's for a common motif in pornography that he considered unique to Japan—a man sucking or suckling the breasts of a woman he then violates sexually. The two-step scene constitutes the two sides of a psychological relationship, Wagatsuma argued: the dependence of the male on his mother, and the resentment, hostility, and aggression such dependence breeds. Men *need* maternal women and hate them *because* of their need; so went Wagatsuma's theory.

Narabayashi has argued a similar position. A feeling of violence (*hageshisa mitai na mono*) simmers in Japanese males as a result of "Mama Godzillas"—mothers who "meddle" (*ijiru*) in their children's lives and cause particular harm to their sons (1982:21). Narabayashi does not try to tie overbearing mothers to violence and violent sex. Rather, he argues that the degree of nurturing that mothers extend to their male children produces men who are sexually weak, with problems of primary impotence (can't perform with wives), diminished sex drives, or sexual appetites that can only be expressed and engaged with prostitutes. The simmering violence in males, he implies, emerges in a stance of dominance, which is what a man pays for with women in the *mizu shōbai*. Looked at the other way around, this makes for men who can't perform sexually unless the structure of dominance is in place (21–22).

John David Morley has written a novel about the *mizu shōbai*, *Pictures from the Water Trade: Adventures of a Westerner in Japan*, based on his own experiences. Using the mother-son relationship to describe male behavior with women who are paid, he focuses on a gesture he saw made repeatedly by men sitting in clubs and with a hostess whom they had never seen before. They would speak about her breasts or touch them as boldly and presumptively as they would fruit on the table. The breasts in these dramas, Morley suggests, are a sign and symbol of something maternal, and the meaning and pleasure in handling them rests mainly in being allowed to do it at all. It is "reassuring and comforting" to him that the hostess, like the mother, is there *for* him. That he mentions her breasts or touches them without asking becomes, therefore, a privilege he's allowed as well as a mark, as Narabayashi might suggest, of dominance.

These writers imply that Japanese males desire—at some level and with some women—a relationship with two elements: being nurtured, taken care of, and indulged; and being regarded or treated as important, as the one in charge. They also stress three points that I doubt many observers of Japan or Japanese would seriously contest: (1) this male desire is inspired by an ideology of motherhood in Japan that structures mothers to be sacrificing caregivers and children to be care receivers often well into adulthood; (2) the model of mother-child relations becomes the culturally dominant model for gender—male as care receiver and female as caregiver; and (3) these two positions can become sexualized—sexually, males desire to receive from and to be taken care of by females.

Although these observations are valid and useful, they fail to answer
other questions about the *mizu shōbai* and the behavior of men, specifically
with hostesses in a hostess club. For example, when a man talks about the
breasts of a hostess he doesn't know, perhaps will never see again, and probably won't have sexual intercourse with, is he acting only like a child, specifically like a male, explicitly as a sexual desirer, or a combination of all
three? Or, as I asked myself and many of my interviewees, no matter how
this question is answered, why aren't men going home and talking to their
wives about *their* breasts? Or are they? Stated differently, what makes this
talk of breasts and this behavior between men and women specific to the
location and conditions of the hostess bar?

Certainly the service women provide and the indulgent stance they assume in the nightlife, often with aggressive and expectant men, contributes
to this behavior. But most men have a wife or mother or both to indulge
them at home and need not depend on a *mizu shōbai* woman to provide the
sole bit of "mothering" in their lives. I suggest that women in the nightlife
appeal *because* they are not the real mother or wife in a man's life. With a
mother or wife, a man has continuous bonds; with a *mizu shōbai* woman, a
man is free to come and go.

These heterosexual and heterosocial relations, unlike those a man has
privately at home, are bounded and limited. A Japanese man's relationship
with his mother tends to be the most intimate and emotionally deep-seated
attachment in his life. It goes on and on, as one man in his fifties said one
night at Bijo in praise of his relationship with his own mother. Although his
mother was so old she could barely walk, she got on a bus three times a
week to come to her son's house to do his laundry because, now divorced,
he had no woman at home to take care of his needs. He enjoyed the hostesses because whatever he owed them could be paid for at the door. His
debt to his mother, by contrast, would never end.

Both the value and devaluing of a *mizu shōbai* woman rest in this particular construct, I argue. She is not a "real" mother, even though she acts in
many ways mother-like, and the difference she poses is partly expressed
through the sexualization of her body. The hostess is a mother, by definition,
whose breasts can be commented on, laughed at, perhaps even touched.
Because she is paid to be treated this way, there is something dirty about her,
the sexuality she evokes, and the world of the *mizu shōbai* she represents. All
of this sexual dirtiness, in turn, makes the woman who works in this world
ineligible for respectable marriage, ineligible therefore to become a respectable mother with legitimate children. She disavows motherhood by becom-

ing a *mizu shōbai* woman. Thus in a culture where motherhood is considered "natural" for women (Yuzawa 1982), the *mizu shōbai* woman is constructed as a female who transgresses her very nature. For this she is degraded; for this, however, she is also enjoyed.

This double-sideness of being a woman who takes care of a man in some ways but does not take care of him continuously in the status of mother or wife was confirmed to me by many of the people I spoke to and through my observations of the services provided by hostesses and expected by customers at Bijo.

Taking Care of Men

A man named Nambu told me that without fail he visits a prostitute at least twice a month, although the fee is high (between 20,000 and 30,000 yen at that time—from $100 to $150 for perhaps an hour) and that if he had more money he'd go more often. The appeal is that prostitutes are experts at taking care of men. It is for this expertise, the woman's skill in managing him sexually, that Nambu visited the soaplands so often.[1]

Asked in a different context whether he ever used condoms to protect himself, Nambu answered in a way that elaborated on this "taking care of" position. The short answer was no (this was 1982 and pre-AIDS), and the reason was that for him to bring up the matter would be to destroy the relationship. The prostitute was in charge, he wanted her to be in charge, and he paid for this service. When asked about his wife, Nambu described her as beautiful, with big breasts and a vigorous sexual appetite. With him, he said, she was sexually frustrated because he rarely "took care of" her and therefore was, perhaps, a bad husband. But he added that males need variety in their sexual lives, so rather than have an active sex life with his desiring wife at home, Nambu had occasional sex at home and semiweekly sessions with an expert, in-charge prostitute—rarely the same woman.

In Nambu's case, a prostitute was valued not simply because the relationship with her was or could be terminated immediately but also because she

1. Nambu was willing to be interviewed, along with a friend and coworker, about his sexual behavior inside and outside the home. The openness of the informants during this interview was facilitated by the fact that I had known them for over a year in a different capacity (as teacher of an English class they both attended) and the fact that I was obviously pregnant. Because to them I was already almost in the category of mother, it seemed easy for them to speak to me about sexuality.

could be relied upon to take care of him in a very precise and complete way while he was with her.

This same attitude toward a *mizu shōbai* woman's value and place was expressed one evening by a group of Japanese workers who asked my husband and me to join them for a night out on the town. Coworkers, in fact, of Nambu, their party consisted of two women (both unmarried and in their twenties) and five men (three were married, and all were in their early forties or older). Most of the evening was spent in a series of small clubs, the type of pocket-size establishments with a Mama, no more than one or two hostesses, and seats to handle about ten guests that fill certain streets and buildings in Shibuya and other sections of Tokyo. At each place we'd drink, eat an assortment of food on small plates, sing to the *karaoke*, and joke in a bawdy style. The two female workers were flirted with mildly by the men in the party and the men were flirted with more boldly by the hostesses, who held their hands, caressed their shoulders, told them they looked handsome and sang well.

After the two female workers had gone home, one of the males suggested we go to a disco. Once there, the behavior of the men changed remarkably. Whereas they had acted confident and cocky around the hostesses, here they became reticent and shy. They giggled about one woman whom they all wanted to dance with because she had the biggest breasts in the room, but they wouldn't ask her (she was dancing without a partner) or any other woman to dance for the entire time we were there. Instead, they sat together or danced together as a group.

Later I asked one of the men why he hadn't asked any woman to dance. He answered that it was out of embarrassment—if he had asked someone, she might have refused. The possibility of being rejected is partly what Japanese men pay to avoid in the *mizu shōbai*; their money assures that the woman will say yes to the figurative dance, taking care of the male ego.

Women in the nightlife flatter men, but how much else they do in the way of taking care of the male and how extensive and constant the flattering can become was demonstrated to me every night I worked at Bijo. On the surface the job looked easy; but as the following story shows, it could require amazing presence and management.

One night Eri and I were assigned to a table with two guests. The men, an Indian and a Japanese, both worked for Air India and had been to the club before. First shaking Raj's hand, Eri asked when they had been in last, thereby initiating a substantial conversation. Raj thought it was two months, Eri thought it was three, Ono thought it was four.

Ono wanted to know where I had learned Japanese, and Raj began to discuss his own history in studying the language. Eri kept trying to change the subject. She asked if she could order beer and when it came she drank it, announcing, "*Biru o nonde nemukute nemukute*"—I'm really getting sleepy from drinking this beer. Next she asked Raj what the symbol on his cuff links stood for. He answered that it was a centaur and stood for the company where he was employed. Eri said that she had a symbol too, a hairpiece that stood for health, happiness, and prosperity. Scanning both Raj and Ono for additional symbols of the centaur, she found one on Ono's tie, one on Raj's handkerchief, one on a pen stuck in one of his pockets. Touching their clothes and pulling out various objects, Eri seemed as invasive of these men as many men seem invasive of the hostesses when they comment on their bodies, rearrange their hair, and tell them they should lose weight. Eri also managed to disrupt the conversation about language learning that had been initiated by the customers themselves. In this case she had not simply taken care of the men; she had taken over. But if the men were disturbed or annoyed about this, they gave no indication.

Another evening, when Eri and I were again seated together with a party of three men from the same company, all in their late forties to early fifties, Eri's behavior was again very assertive and controlling. She insisted that each customer get up and sing, chided one of them for not drinking enough quickly enough, "suggested" that one was hungry and then "suggested" what he should have to eat, and directed the conversation. She was moved to another table before I was, and after she left the customers commented on her hostessing. Explaining to me, the interested foreign anthropologist, the principles of hostess clubs, the men assessed Eri as the best type of hostess. "She understands and takes care of men well and she makes things easy for them when they come into a club like Bijo." In fact, Eri had single-handedly orchestrated the dynamics and order of what took place at the table.

This posture of actively "taking care of things" was assumed much more by experienced than by inexperienced hostesses, I noticed, and each experienced hostess had her own style. Both Machiko and Haruka (women in their late twenties who had worked at least seven years in the *mizu shōbai*) had standard ploys for initiating and reinitiating conversation. Machiko would say something outrageous; Haruka would announce how unintelligent or how oversexed she was. By contrast, Mayumi (the nineteen-year-old university student) was passive, waiting to be spoken to. Although some men liked her style, she obviously made others uncomfortable and silent.

Tables with Mayumi sitting at them, particularly if the evening was young and the men were not yet drunk, were likely to be duller than those attended to by a veteran hostess.

No matter how proficient the hostess was at organizing and leading the various activities at the table, all hostesses, even novices like Mayumi and myself, quickly learned three skills that fall under the rubric of "taking care of ": servicing the cigarettes and drinks of customers, servicing male egos with compliments and flattery, and servicing male authority by never contradicting what the man says. As quickly as the hostess learns to manage the pack of matches and the ice tongs, she learns to praise men and accept what they say. The complimenting, however stylized and formulaic it may seem to an outsider, constitutes a running commentary on whatever the man does and however he chooses to present himself.

If the man tells a joke, the hostess comments that he's a good teller of jokes. If the man announces he went to England the week before on business, the hostess says that he must be smart enough to speak fluent English. If the man sings a song, the hostess proclaims him one of the finest singers she's ever heard. If the man says he golfs, the hostess pulls up his shirt sleeve and says no wonder his arm is so muscular and tanned. The skill, as I learned, is to accept, reflect, and augment the man as he has chosen to reveal himself. Whether he talks about his thirty-foot penis or his joy in collecting stamps, the hostess is supposed to hear him out, comment on what he says, and swear that the qualities he has revealed are exactly what a woman like herself finds irresistibly attractive. The hostess is not supposed to challenge the man's presentation of himself, and she is never to coopt his authority by reversing their roles. I became aware of both these rules when I transgressed them at Bijo.

On one occasion, when I was seated with Haruka and a party of three men, one of them immediately charged that I had lines on my forehead and called me "Grandma" (*Obaasan*). This man, named Sada, sat next to Haruka and told me repeatedly how much he preferred her and how fond he was of young girls—really young girls. He interrupted my conversation about Japanese customs with another man at the table to tell me about a young woman he had met in California who adored him. At this I said "Congratulations" (*omedetō*), which infuriated him. He accused me of being sarcastic, and when one of his friends tried to help me out by saying that actually I was very impressed, Sada asked if that was true. I said it was, but he remained hostile. When the men got up to leave and Mama asked me to accompany them down the elevator, Sada pushed me to the far side of the elevator and told me to stay away from him. Still scowling, he told Mama that I was a very argumentative (*rikutsuppoi*) person. Later I asked Mama if she was upset with me for angering this customer. She said no, some men just were like that. But I was more cautious thereafter.

Taking care of men in these various ways is the service women as hostesses provide. The degree to which the gendered interactions that result depend on a woman's being in control stands in stark contrast to the rituals of fraternity gang rape described by Sanday (1990), in which men typically encourage, force, or wait for a woman to lose control through drugs or alcohol. In hostess clubs it is the men who are supposed to lose control, and they are led, inspired, and allowed to do so by the women precisely because these women remain in control of themselves and, to some degree, of the men as well. The geometry of sexuality and masculinity is organized very differently, then, in these two settings.

To be a male in the fraternities of Sanday's descriptions is to make a female vulnerable and to presume upon her vulnerability to consummate sexual acts. A male takes control and establishes his masculinity by first rendering the female out of control. Weak women make for strong men. And this is best dramatized in rituals of violent and unequal sex. By contrast, in the hostess club, it is women who can and do stay in control that make men feel masculine. This is the process Yoda refers to as "recognizing" a man (*mitomeru*) and making him feel appreciated and approved (1981: 28). A hostess, he says, is best equipped to effect this feeling because she doesn't know the man in any other setting and because she's received "training" (*kunren*) to guarantee the man stays happy by accepting the "surface expression" of anything he says (28). The more competent the female performance, the more manly the man is made to feel. Skilled and clever women make for men who are assured of their manliness, and the drama takes place around not violent and coercive acts of consummated sex but around rituals of sexual interest and pretend sex that the women are as willing to stage as the men.

Profane Non-Mothers Who Act Maternally

The logical question to ask at this point is, Why are such dramas of staged sex(uality) in the hostess club so effective in making men feel like men? If this book were about American culture, as is Sanday's, the question would be, Why must real acts of unequal and violent sex take place in fraternity settings to produce the particular construction of masculinity demanded there? In this context, it is interesting to note that while Americans are inclined to view American culture as far less chauvinistic than Japan's, Japanese such as Wagatsuma and Ishikawa find a culture of machismo in America rather than in Japan. Wagatsuma, an anthropologist who has studied American society and culture, points out that in the United States "there is a long tradition of respecting violent men. The male-leaning America is also a violent country" (1982: 25). Ishikawa Hiroyoshi, a professor of sociology, has similarly written about a tendency toward masculinization in American society that is expressed through violence, including songs, films (particularly John Wayne movies), and political leaders like Ronald Reagan (25).

Both Wagatsuma and Ishikawa believe that Japanese men are weak and emasculated. I would put it differently. Japanese men, I argue, probably fantasize about taking women violently, against their will, in acts of unequal sex, in a manner similar to the ritual enactment of masculinity in the fraternity rituals that Sanday describes.[2] Yet in Japan there is a more pronounced need—encouraged, prolonged, and institutionalized by various social practices—for males to depend on females in a number of ways, thus building a degree of dependence into their construction of masculinity. For an American male, displaying a dependence on a mother beyond a relatively young age impinges on his masculinity. In Japan, this is not the case. There is no enforced ideological break from the mother in late adolescence and often no physical break.[3]

When Sanday writes, therefore, of the initiation rites at fraternities, where one of the symbolic transformations is extricating boys from attachment to their mothers (1990: 156–73), one can postulate that subsequent acts of coercive and unequal sex are being engaged in to express a new manliness based on "independence." The woman is needed for these displays, but she can be dead drunk or not even conscious. This is hardly the case in the hostess club. Here the success of the interaction and how masculine the man is made to feel often depend on how conscious and in control the woman actually is. In this sense, writers like Buruma and Morley are

2. As is the repeated trope in *ero manga*, the erotic comic books that are so popular in Japan. For analyses of this phenomenon, see Buckley 1991; Kusamori 1981; Sato 1981; Schodt 1986.

3. I have been told stories of mothers who accompany their sons to university entrance examinations, to the boards where results are posted, and to job interviews. I have also heard from female sources that the attentiveness their husbands display to their mothers is in no way duplicated in their attention to spouses. One woman pointed out that her husband always remembered his mother's birthday with a gift and a dinner invitation to a restaurant, but he never remembered her own birthday, and if she reminded him, he'd give her money and tell her to buy something for herself.

right when they suggest that in such places men depend on women who, in taking care of and indulging them, act like mothers. Yet Buruma's reference to "sacred mothers" in Japan overlooks the category of Japanese women whose construction is based precisely on their being neither sacred nor real mothers. And this is the *mizu shōbai* woman.

This type of woman can be aptly described as a profane non-mother who acts, in some ways, maternally. That she can coddle the man and stroke his ego is crucial; that she can also be dominated, considered "dirty," and easily abandoned at the end of the night is crucial as well. And there is a direct relationship between these two parts of the hostess's package. She is needed as a mother is, but the need can be masked, denied, and paid off because she is in a category different from and socially far below that of a mother. In my perception, the meaning of much of the staged sexuality, particularly the rituals surrounding breasts, comes from the latter part of this construction—reminding and reestablishing for the man the devalued and disavowed status of the woman. The message seems to be that the female's body is there merely to serve and please the male. That her services also far exceed her bodily presence is thus made easier for the male to bear along with his already overloaded set of dependencies on real mothers, wives, bosses, companies, and coworkers.

In this sense, the interest devoted to a hostess's breasts is perfunctory; it is the least, rather than the most, maternal-like service the woman is expected to provide. A comment like "Your breasts are as flat as a board" is intended to be crude; it verifies the man's right to be crude at the expense of, and through the vehicle of, the *mizu shōbai* woman. The gesture is symbolic and typically brief; over as soon as it is begun, it is less an overture to something heterosexual with a woman than it is a homosocial statement about being a man. A man asks a woman where her breasts are hanging out for the night and the other men laugh; a man tells the woman her breasts are like melons and the other men giggle; a man is led by a hostess to check out the size of her left breast and the other men guffaw. The gesture is standard; so is the male response.

I would thus argue that much of what is fashioned as sexual play and body-part talk at the hostess club is neither about sex per se nor about women acting as mothers. It is something in between, and this makes it difficult to speak productively about "mothers" as well as "sex" in this context.[4] The suggestion has been made to me (usually by Japanese women

4. For the purposes of this discussion I am following Rosalind Coward's definitions of sex, sexuality, and sexual identity. *Sexuality* may be defined as the representation of activities involv-

who have never been in a hostess club or by Western academics or businessmen who have anticipated sexual affairs with hostesses and not found them)
that what takes place in hostess clubs has nothing whatsoever to do with
sex. Certainly no acts of sexual intercourse are consummated on the premises, and from what Bijo's management and customers confirmed, few sexual liaisons between staff members and customers transpire outside the
club.

Yet the language and behavior at the tables are sexually charged. Why
conversation so often hovers around sexual matters—and why sex is confined to conversation—can be explained by two conditions operating in
men's use of the hostess club. First, most customers enter in groups with
the purpose of nurturing male bonds. Thus while a conversation or flirtation
with a hostess may be personally pleasing to a man, he must keep his focus
and attention on the other men. A woman may be present, but the night out
is with and for the guys. A message is encoded each time a man interrupts a
conversation another man at his table is having with a hostess about food,
Paris, or clothing to ask the woman when she lost her virginity, how many
boyfriends she sleeps with, or why she doesn't have breasts.

Second, the sexual talk maintains the *mizu shōbai* woman's currency as a
construct of and for men. Referring to the woman's body as sexual is done
so with a definition and construction of "sexual" that not only accommodates male relations but maintains their priority. Reduced to the topic of
breasts, the woman becomes something the men can talk about, agree on,
and share. This type of sexuality—talked-about sexuality, and sexuality that
is only and all talk—structures gender: females are objects to serve males,
males are subjects who can designate and dominate females.[5] When
speaking about a woman's breasts, men assume an identity far more
unifying and uniform than the one they are assigned through work during
the day. Ranks of difference and possible discord are dissolved when all
men become *sukebei* (desiring, lecherous males) in a club. In the process
of discursive transformation, however, it should not be forgotten that men
are created as a construct of Man as much as women are created as a
construct of Woman.

Besides providing an agreed-on language in which speakers can become

---

ing sensual aims and gratifications, *sex* as the act where sensual aims and gratifications are
achieved, and *sexual identity* as the public representations of sensual aims and objectives as
integrated into the personality (1983).

   5. Here the word *designate* refers to the stance men often assume in a hostess club of
judging the hostess in terms of her appearance, and advising her on how she should conduct
herself. See Chapter 3 for descriptions of this behavior.

agreeably "men," sexuality and womanhood in the hostess club are fixated on such standard and repeating tropes as breasts for another reason. These breasts are not approached as would be the breasts of nursing mothers—snuggled up to and lingered over as the sources of nurturance, affection, and an enduring bond. Rather, they seem called up in order to be dismissed. Many times I remember conversing comfortably and productively with customers about a variety of issues, none sex-related. If there was intimacy, it was one formed socially as if between equals or friends. Then, seemingly out of nowhere, would come the breast comment or joke.

The conversation would stop for a moment, halted by the man's need to look at the other men so that they could laugh together as the "men" such a remark or gesture confirmed them to be. The gesture was intended to be not for me but *about* me, not toward but away from greater intimacy of a heterosocial or heterosexual nature. This move cut me off, kept me away, put me in my place; it established a distance between the woman and the man, and by doing so it created the impression and illusion of a man in charge, a man not close to this woman, a man not dependent on women at all. In a sense, then, an abrupt touch or reference to a woman's breasts is truncated as a sexual gesture. It doesn't lead to an act of sex and isn't an invitation to intertwine bodies later that night.

This doesn't mean, however, that even such breast talk has nothing to do with sex or a man's sexuality. My sense is that what Japanese men seek in hostess clubs is to be made to feel good about themselves. The turn-on, which may or may not lead them to actively seek out sexual release after leaving the hostess club at some other establishment or at home with a wife, is the buildup to their ego. This is not the service the hostess provides by fielding the occasional, if annoying, breast barb. It is the service for which her skills, control, and aptitude as a savvy *mizu shōbai* woman are most needed—telling each and every man that he looks good, sings well, tells funny jokes, has beautiful brown eyes, and appears sexy.

From what I've observed and been told by male informants, Japanese men can listen to this ego boosting endlessly. The fact that they can sit next to one hostess at one club for an hour, a second hostess at a second club for an hour, and a third hostess at a third club for an hour and never negotiate actual sex with them thus becomes less curious. The women may use a sexually flirtatious style, but what is produced has less to do with a heterosexual relationship than with a man's relationship with himself or other men. In this sense, the sexuality is masturbatory; the erotic object is not the woman but the man, and the female is just a device to enhance the male's self-image. Other clubs in the *mizu shōbai* provide the service of masturbating a man to ejaculation.[6] In the hostess club, by contrast, the masturbatory ejaculation is of the ego only.

Certainly some, perhaps most, men in hostess clubs fantasize about sexually consummated relations with the hostesses whose breasts they're saying are big. My concern is not whether they have such sexual desires but why they spend so much time (and somebody else's money) talking about desires in the presence of women with whom they are very unlikely to consummate them. I don't agree with those who say that the talk and behavior at hostess clubs are not about sex at all. I would argue rather that such activities reflect and contribute significantly to constructions of male sexuality. The hostess makes a man feel good about himself and his male colleagues. This is the real pleasure of the hostess club. And, if after hours of expensive buildup he wants sexual release, he can easily make a cheap stop at a *pinku saron* on the way home.

Women Made Dirty by the Dirtiness of Men

Lacan (1977) has written that persons first realize their "self" as a totality by seeing themselves in a mirror. In the hostess club a man relies on the hostess to reflect a self-image that flatters him. For this dynamic two qualities are needed in the woman assuming the mirror/slave position: the ability or willingness to produce a good reflection of the other (being a good mirror), and willingness to accept the role of subordinate party in a relationship with the man (being a slave). Women assume the position of hostess in hostess clubs based on these two qualities, which are assigned and attributed to their femaleness and which, in this sense, they "naturally" share with all women—like mothers, they can build up and indulge others (particularly children), and as females, they rank lower than men in social status.

Because of universal attributes they're assumed to possess, women are most culturally and ideologically appropriate to play the role of servicer of male needs and egos in the hostess club. Once they become a part of the *mizu shōbai* world, however, they no longer stand for Woman in general but become instead a very specific kind and category of woman. The *mizu shōbai* woman is denoted, most specifically, by her sexiness. Yet the sexiness or sexuality of the *mizu shōbai* woman is not really hers as much as it is that of

6. *Gendai no Me* 1980:173.

the men whom she serves. So in this sense the *mizu shōbai* woman stands for something considered more male than female. She represents men in a sexual desire that even in this realm is perceived to be far more a male impulse than a female's. While *mizu shōbai* women provide a service judged to be socially legitimate, the legitimacy of the service extends only to the men seeking the service, not to the women servicing the men, who are seen as somehow transgressing their very nature by being sexualized, even in talk, by males. The woman's position then becomes one of degradation—she is the slave. From that position she can reflect a flattering image to the man, who receives it as master. By sexualizing and degrading the female through his own sexuality, the male is situated in a relationship where the inequality of gender is exaggerated and made pleasurable in ways not normally operative.

What I'm suggesting is that some of the sexual talk in hostess clubs is a strategy for constructing gender rather than a sexuality or heterosexual interest per se. Because sex talk degrades the woman but not the man, it emphasizes a gender imbalance that gives a man the pleasure of dominating. Putting the woman down is merely another means for structuring this relationship. After sufficient inflation of his ego, the man may in fact proceed to a sexual encounter with a woman, probably a different and less expensive woman than the one or ones who made him feel so confident. So hostess club sexuality constructs gender, but hostess club gender also constructs male sexuality.

At Bijo, the interactions customers had with one hostess in particular illustrate this operation. Machiko, a woman about twenty-five, had worked in the *mizu shōbai* since graduating from high school and was immediately recognizable by customers as a professional *mizu shōbai* woman. She had the hostess skills and style—introducing herself with bawdy comments, keeping customers laughing and talking with unseemly stories, remembering men's names and encouraging them to sing, singing herself—when asked—with a beautiful and appealing voice, and holding men's hands or falling over their laps when everyone was laughing. Machiko was an effective and popular hostess. She was also gay—a fact that most of the regular customers seemed to know and one Machiko would announce periodically at tables by referring to herself as *kama* (a rude term for homosexual).

Significantly, Machiko's homosexuality seemed to change nothing of the flavor or tenor of either her "feminine" behavior or the gendered interactions she engaged in with men. Acting as if she were sexually interested, she'd tell men they were handsome and talented, touch their shoulders and hands, and whisper intimately into their ears. This she would do with new customers, who were unaware of her sexual preference, as well as with old customers, some of whom would ask me if I "knew." What mattered then, as far as Machiko's hostessing went, was not what kind of sexual desires she had but simply what persona she was willing to assume and projected in the club. The "sexuality" of *mizu shōbai* women, particularly those in first- or second-class hostess clubs, rests primarily in this—not what they sexually are but the sexual role they assume for men. When a man tells a hostess she has no breasts, for example, the hostess nods in agreement. And when the hostess is a veteran hostess like Machiko, she is as likely to call attention to the size of her breasts as are the men.

That a hostess is expected to empty herself in a sense—strip herself of a personal identity and subjectivity to become the image and construct of Woman desired by men in hostess clubs—is common knowledge. The manager demanded this as the first condition to my becoming a hostess. Ordering me to remove my wedding ring, he said that I must never reveal my marital status and must answer with jokes or lies if questioned as to whether I had boyfriends or a husband.[7] Many customers told me that while the hostesses pretended to lack any attachment, they assumed that outside the club most hostesses were attached to men in a relationship of romance or marriage. One interviewee spoke specifically of the Mama, noting that one of her great appeals was the illusion she projected of having no patron. While he assumed that the Mama was in fact involved, not knowing definitively made it possible for him to enjoy flirtatious play with her. If the existence of a patron were made known, flirtation would no longer be satisfying, and Mama's business, he predicted, would sharply decrease.

This construction of the *mizu shōbai* woman—erasing the realities of her personal life in order to assume a formulaic identity in the nightlife—is also pointed out by the *Gendai no Me* editors of the book *Hikisakareta Sei* (Sex that Is Torn to Pieces):

These women [prostitutes] make three, four times what the average OL [office lady] does. But why is it that they don't talk to either cus-

---

7. As a reviewer of this manuscript pointed out, Bijo policy seems inconsistent on this issue—demanding that hostesses conceal certain facts of their identities outside of the club (marriage) but not others (homosexuality). The difference, I suggest, rests in the nature of these two identities—married women are wives and possibly mothers, whereas lesbians presumably are not. To the customer this distinction is significant, given that, as I have already argued, a hostess is valued for her willingness to simultaneously act like a mother and accept a social status as *mizu shōbai* woman who is not a mother. That a heterosexual marriage is a far greater threat to the role played by hostesses than homosexuality is a fact very revealing as to the construction of a hostess and her sexuality.

tomers nor the women they work with about personal matters such as their motivation in entering this business, their family lives, their future plans . . . ?

Most of these women who work in clubs, snack shops, restaurants or other establishments in the *mizu shōbai* display a deceptive attitude about their husbands, lovers, men. And this attitude is displayed to customers as well as fellow workers. (1980: 175)

The authors suggest that Japanese men, particularly when receiving a sexual service such as fellatio, don't want to know about the woman's life; they simply want the service. This distancing between sexual servicer and sexual recipient is also observed by Sano Shinichi (1981) among groups of Japanese sex tourists who visit the brothels of such countries as Thailand and the Philippines. What is desired is simply the flesh that is purchased with money, unaccompanied by a personality or any social commitment. This depersonalization of a female whom a male sexualizes keeps men more concentrated on themselves and each other, on being a male and being men together.

Again, as the *Gendai no Me* editors put it, the desire is not so much for a woman whose desires are sexual and female as for the type of woman who, for money, is willing to indulge the man in the expression of *his* desires (constructed therefore as being manly). To allow men the expression of these desires, which while legitimate are still socially constructed as dirty, animalistic, and base, a woman is degraded.[8] Men at Bijo told me that *mizu-shōbai* women are dirty (*kitanai*), not respectable, a different breed, a type apart, not the kind of woman a man would marry. Such comments were often made immediately before or after a man would talk to a hostess and ask about her breasts.

Many of the women I spoke to confirmed this assessment. One woman,

---

8. Traditionally, sexuality has not been conceptualized this way; it has been treated as a matter of nature rather than morality or sin (Buruma 1984; Kawai 1988; Schodt 1986). Contemporary attitudes regarding the *mizu shōbai* and its dimensions of sexuality seem to be both consistent and inconsistent with these traditional notions. Though there is something inherently seedy or dirty about the *mizu shōbai,* a man can still visit it openly and frequently without these visits being considered in any sense a social wrong. In terms of how the *mizu-shōbai* woman is affected by this somewhat contradictory ideology, my sense is that she is regarded in somewhat the same light: dirty, but a dirtiness that men occasionally enjoy. Men seemed to emphasize the role of money—that these women are not only sexualized but take money for it and in fact would do anything for money. The money part seems to contribute as much as, if not more than, the sex part to lowering her status.

married and a mother, explained that men have two sides: a human side that is expressed when they go out to work and maintain their responsibilities to home and family; and an animalistic side that comes out when they drink, exchange lewd jokes, and carouse with women. Men's carousing partners at such times are women who, by definition, are "animals" (*dōbutsu*), unlike the type of female who marries and becomes a mother. In this view females are categorized according to what use they're willing to put their bodies to (procreative or sexually recreational). Males, by contrast, subsume two natures, one lofty, the other seedy. The seedy one is expressed in a domain that men can both enter and leave behind. When they walk out the door of a hostess club or *pinku saron*, they go home. But when women work in a hostess club or *pinku saron*, they are forever marked by this association.

Once one is experienced in the *mizu shōbai*, the experience remains. In questionnaires I passed out to women as well as men, respondents wrote that a woman who "knew" the *mizu shōbai* from having spent time working there would be permanently affected. A *mizu shōbai* woman immediately acquires a record and a blemish that may prevent her from becoming a wife or a mother in the future (*Gendai no Me* 1980). She thus comes to stand for the *mizu shōbai*—a symbol of what this realm is and what it does for men. Her body, her flesh, her breasts are appropriated to serve men in a way they can later dismiss and leave behind. And for all the work she does to make each and every man feel good, the *mizu shōbai* woman then is degraded, put in a place of subordination, and emptied of any identity other than that of reflecting a man in his.

11

Impotence as a Sign and Symbol of the *Sarariiman*

Comic *Sarariiman*

Shoji Sadao draws a comic strip called Special Course *Sarariiman* (*Sararii-man Senkyō*), which is serialized in the weekly magazine *Shūkan-Gendai*. In the first frame of a strip that appears in a collection of his works, the protagonist, "Yamada Ichiro, 29 years old," is introduced. In the following frames Yamada sits alone while his friends romance young women. The caption reads: "Not once in 29 years has he had sex" (*tada no ichido mo moteta kotowa nakatta*).[1] Yamada, looking desperate, repeats: "Not once in 29 years have I had sex!!" A caption adds that he's coughing up blood produced by sexual desire. Then Yamada decides on a plan: he'll ask his friend Tetsuya to take him to a cabaret. When approached, Tetsuya agrees, but he warns Yamada that it will cost a lot of money.

In the ninth frame Yamada slaps down a pile of 10,000 yen notes on Tetsuya's desk, saying that this money represents "half the life of a man moistened by blood, sweat, and tears" (*chi to ase to namida ni nureta otoko no hatsunen*).[2] The two men walk into a cabaret and sit down. Tetsuya whispers to the waiter that his friend is a man who has not had sex once in twenty-nine years and hands over the money to him. Three hostesses come running to the table, sit next to Yamada, and tell him "You're great" (*suteki*), "You're handsome" (*hansamu*), "You're a sexy man" (*iro otoko*). In the last frame Ya-

---

1. While *moteru* (from which *moteta* is derived) generally means to be popular with the opposite sex, in this context it seems to refer also to sex itself. Whether it refers to sex with any female or only the type one pays for or pursues for an extramarital affair is unclear. We do not know, therefore, whether Yamada is married. At Bijo *moteru* was used only in reference to having girlfriends or mistresses.

2. Ten thousand yen equals one man—about 50 dollars.

mada is surrounded by the women, two of whom have exposed their breasts and are telling him that it's okay for him to touch them (*sawatte mo ii*). Yamada is sweating and obviously immobilized. The waiter, observing the scene from afar, comments, "I wonder if he can't respond because the change in his environment has been too rapid?!" and Tetsuya, sitting across the table from Yamada ponders too: "In his case, I wonder if the void (*kūhaku*) he had for 29 years was just too great?!" (Shoji 1980:122–23).

Yamada, the *sarariiman,* is a pathetic figure. Hardworking and diligent as he is supposed to be, his performance at work has been achieved at a price. He has had no time to satisfy other desires, and when he finally takes the time, he is unable to function sexually. Portrayed with sympathy and humor, this *sarariiman* is like many others who appear in the popular culture—television, film, literature, and comics. In fact, the *sarariiman* constitutes a separate genre in both literature (*sarariiman bungaku*) and comics (*sarariiman manga*) (see Schodt 1986). Representing the ideal status and career of middle-class society, the *sarariiman* is commonly represented, nonetheless, in terms of the frustrations, weaknesses, and disappointments he suffers as a result of achieving what he was supposed to as a Japanese man. The *sarariiman* as a stereotype is depicted as the man whose wife won't give him sex (Shoji 1980), whose boss changes his rank every five minutes by remote control, who urinates on his desk because no one pays him any attention, and who is rejected by a female worker when he asks for the loan of both her body and cash (Schodt 1986:112–13).

In Shoji's Special Course *Sarariiman,* cited above, the topic is a *sarariiman's* masculinity. Pursuing the middle-class ideal, Yamada has become a hardworking *sarariiman.* Once he has found his place in society, he is ready for what is represented to be both part of his nature and his reward for working so hard—sexual satisfaction. Yamada's money symbolizes both parts of his masculinity: the work he has been committed to for years and the desire he now has for sex. Who he is and what he wants to become are mediated through money. The joke is that in achieving success in his career, Yamada has lost the ability to enjoy sex, which should be the easy and natural part of being a man. By one construction of masculinity, Yamada is a man; by another construction, he is not. His failed manhood, expressed through sexual impotence, is intended to be a humorous commentary on the realities of being a *sarariiman* in Japan.

Sexuality, as a metaphor, is often used to represent the identity, power, and status of manhood in Japan. The genre of comic books (*manga*) called *ero manga* (erotic comic books) are filled with images of tough men who take what they want sexually from women, to whom they display huge penises. Sexual potency is used as a sign of masculine power, and as Buruma (1984) and Wagatsuma (personal communication) have pointed out for other media, the scenario of rape is predominant. But my own analyses of *ero manga* have revealed that when women are seized, sexual penetration may not ensue. The emphasis is on the act of seizure itself rather than on seizure as a step toward penetration and ejaculation. Like the pat delivered to women's breasts in a hostess club, the seizing of women in *ero manga* signifies that the actor is a dominant male; it encodes a desired construction of masculinity. The move is less toward the female and a heterosexual relationship than back on the male as an expression and confirmation of his maleness. Though the woman is used to express and confirm (autoerotically, homosocially) the male, her role and utility are without significance. The female is used and needed, but disavowed.

A drawing adorns the cover of Shoji's book about men in their role as workers. The image is small and cartoonish—a female with a bouffant hairdo, a wide grin, a skimpy chemise that barely covers big breasts, and high heels. There is little doubt that this woman is intended to be from the *mizu shōbai*. With elbows bent and one leg raised, the woman is drawn as if in action. But what is she doing? Luring a man to dance? Chasing him around the table? Running away so as not to get caught? Whatever the movement, the action indicates that this woman is not passive, and her full smile and wide-open eyes give the impression that she is confident and in control.

This image on the book's cover is intended to represent and comment on the material presented in the book. Yet what is the relationship between this female, with fleshy body and big grin, and the males on the inside pages, who appear to be from the white-collar ranks of Japan's middle-class corporate society? In part, this woman stands for the anticipation, pursuit, and purchase of encounters with women in the nightlife after a hard day's work. The desire men have for these women is presented as very sexual and very male; in fact, contact with such a woman is associated with a man's feeling like a real man. The women are always pictured as young, voluptuous, and smiling; and the men look flattered and pleased to be around them. By contrast, the wives depicted on these pages are typically old and ugly, with sagging breasts and permanent scowls. Although they may be shown in bed with their husbands, they are usually giving the man a hard time. And the perky young female is contracted for with money, signaling the difference between a man who must pay for sexual play and a woman who gets paid for it. When the male pays, the woman, as commodity, is a sign of his measure and worth as a hardworking man. Yet when the woman receives pay for her services, she is what he himself is—a worker who earns money for putting up with one's job.

As representation, then, the female on the cover of Special Course *Sarariiman* stands for many things, some of which are contradictory. She stands for what the male wants (an object of sexual desire), for what he wants to be himself (a male who is powerful enough to get what he wants), and for what he actually is (a worker whose earnings must be sufficient to pay for what he wants).[3] As a woman whose very womanliness is exaggerated and caricatured, she is presented as a device that can both inflate and deflate a male ego, confirm and negate a man in his masculinity, and both empower a man symbolically and symbolize his weakness.[4]

Yamada Ichiro, the twenty-nine-year-old cartoon *sarariiman* who has worked hard all of his working years, is told that he's "handsome," "great," a "sexy man" by the women he has paid. In the next frame, however, he's portrayed as sexually imcompetent in the hands of these women, a mockery of a man, though the comments about his unmanliness are coming from other men. The joke concerns the disjuncture of his masculinity: doing what he's supposed to in one context (work), he has failed in another (sexuality). The cartoon itself, however, is not only making a joke at the expense of men, but revealing a contradiction in the system that men as *sarariiman* must face. Though he is told to work hard as a man, the image is also floated of the male who is tough, in control, and entitled to have his pleasures and desires satisfied by a woman who is not his wife. This image is the one companies and bosses of male workers pay hostesses to create and sustain. Yet not only does this image cost money—what a man must continue to work hard to earn—but the man is kept so busy working that his ability to enjoy the sexual fruits of his success may easily become impaired.

Impotence is a common symbol of the industrious male worker in Japan, representing his insecurities, his frustrations, and his fears. It is a sign of what corporate Japan takes from a man and a charge that corporate careers leave even the most successful white-collar workers crippled and incom-

---

3. The woman in the cartoon is what I call a symbol in contradiction: her depiction is contradictory and what she stands for (the referent, in this case the man) is also contradictory. Much has been written about the role contradiction plays in the symbolization or identification of subjects. See, for example, Althusser 1971 (81–128); Freud 1965 (311–84); Metz 1982; Miller 1987; Marx 1978 (148–63).

4. On the notion of femininity as an exaggerated construct and construct of exaggeration, see Joan Riviere (1986).

plete as men. This is the theme of a cartoon entitled "Just a Man," created by the cartoon artist Tatsumi Yoshihiro.[5] The protagonist, Manayana, is nearing retirement. He has worked hard for years and achieved the rank of personnel director, but now all the work he used to perform is being handled by his successor. He sits all day with nothing to do, with no one speaking to him and no one calling him "boss." In terms of his work, Manayana is made to feel that he no longer exists.

At home, too, this man feels greatly unappreciated. He lives with his wife, his married daughter, and her husband. The two women are always talking about his retirement money and how they plan to spend it. Disgusted that his value has been reduced to this, Manayana complains that his wife is a heartless creature—she has had an affair with her son-in-law and hasn't slept with her own husband for ten years. Incensed by all this injustice, Manayana withdraws from the bank 300,000 yen ($1,500) that he's kept from his wife, and sets out to enjoy himself in the month remaining before his retirement.

This pursuit of personal pleasure consists entirely of seeking sex with women other than his wife. First he goes to a club where a woman tells him he's sexy and performs fellatio on him, but Manayana decides that he should really fall in love with a woman in order to enjoy himself fully at his wife's expense. He registers with an agency to take a woman out on a date. After he takes this "nonprofessional" woman to a restaurant, they go to a love hotel, but in the midst of caresses she asks for more food. Manayana decides it's difficult to "find a woman one can fall in love with" (Tatsumi 1987:22).

Finally at work one day he is approached by Miss Okawa, an O.L. who serves him tea and about whom he's fantasized having sex with "just once" for years. Bereft over losing her fiancé to a wealthy heiress, she asks Manayana to console her by taking her out to dinner. They go to one of the most expensive restaurants in Tokyo and then, at Miss Okawa's suggestion, proceed to a love hotel. The woman of his dreams, the sex he's been envisioning for years, is finally in his grasp, but Manayana can't perform. Though he is desirous, his penis "stayed soft."

Totally disheartened, Manayana considers suicide. He visits Yasukuni Jinja, a shrine where comrades who fought during the war are buried, and there decides against taking his own life. Walking over to a cannon, he urinates on it. His last words are: "I may not be good for much, but you're impotent too, old cannon. . . . Ha, Ha, Ha" (Tatsumi 1987:28).

5. This comic, translated into English, has been included with several other comics by Tatsumi Yoshihiro, in *Good-Bye and Other Stories* (1987).

Though Tatsumi's comic, drawn as part of a genre called *gekiga* (drama pictures), is intended to be far more serious than Shoji's cartoons, both portray the *sarariiman* as a fragmented and fragile human being. In both a man who has worked hard and saved money decides to use his earnings to achieve desires left unfulfilled in a personal life long dominated by the demands of work. But in both cases he fails. His attempt to buy fulfillment with a woman is defeated, and he is left frustrated, failed by both the money he labored for and the body he has too long ignored. Impotence is a sign that something has gone wrong, and with it comes an implied question: For what has this man been working when even the fruits of his labor can't guarantee what should be, and perhaps once was, a matter of mere "nature"?

Money, Work, and Masculinity

Marx's ideas about estranged labor are relevant in this context. As he argued, when humans produce subsistence through labor they also produce themselves. That is, the products of our labor stand as an expression and objectification of who and what we are. In itself, this process is positive, but when the politics and economics of a system are such that workers lose control over the products of their own labor, labor is estranged or alienated. People still work, but what they produce is managed by someone or something else. Instead of seeing themselves positively reflected in the products of their labor, workers see only a thing, and that thing is in someone else's control (Marx 1978:71–79).

Marx attributed the reification of species-being primarily to capitalism, which established money as the medium of exchange for labor and in social relations. In a money economy, everyone works for the same thing and everyone's work is measured by the same medium. The universality of money imposes a uniformity on persons and the products of their labor. Now what we all produce is mediated through money, and money is the mediator we share. Differences, identities, subjectivities are structured no longer on the basis of the products of individual labor but through the universal language and currency of money. We become known and objectified not through what we produce but through what we buy with the money that establishes the value of our labor. It is as consumers rather than producers, then, that we come to differentiate and identify who and what we are (Marx 1978:101–5).

Money, as Marx pointed out, is a curious medium. In and of itself, it has no use value, so its meaning is merely symbolic, imposed from outside. But in a capitalist society where money becomes the symbol and measure of

labor, its power is such that it not only defines meaning but also trans-
forms it.

> That which is for me through the medium of money—that for which
> I can pay . . . that am I, the possessor of the money. The extent of the
> power of money is the extent of my power. Money's properties are my
> properties and essential powers. . . . Thus, what I *am* and *am capable*
> of is by no means determined by my individuality. I am ugly, but I
> can buy for myself the most *beautiful* of women. Therefore, I am not
> *ugly,* for the effect of *ugliness*—its deterrent power—is nullified by
> money. (Marx 1978:103)

In effect, people can buy an identity, given, of course, that they have enough
money. This identity too becomes a commodity—thinking of the self as a
thing that can be negotiated, constructed, and altered. But the process has
two pitfalls. First, as with most commodities, the more one has, the more
one wants. Marx argued that one of the fundamental components and conditions of capitalism is the constant creation of new needs; hence, the consumer is never totally or ultimately satisfied (156). The unsettling feeling of
insecurity and dissatisfaction, in fact, is what compels consumers to consume more. Without the production in people of new desires whose realization is never complete, capitalism would founder.

Second, in a money-based economy where a person buys objects to satisfy needs or wants, money is the constant mediator—what Marx has called
the "pimp between man's need and the object, between his life and his
means of life" (1978:102). What is set into motion then is a vicious cycle.
Looking to confirm and satisfy ourselves in the things that we buy, we buy
more and more, yet the satisfaction and confirmation of the self we are seeking constantly eludes us. Money mediates and constructs who we are, but
the currency itself, no matter how much we individually have of it, is never
in our own control.[6]

---

6. Many scholars have written on the increasing commodification of pleasure, leisure,
and self under capitalist and late-capitalist societies. As an anonymous reviewer of this book
pointed out, Lukacs (1971) situated this discussion in terms of the dominance of the commodity form of which money is only the most generalized instance. This is also the approach taken
by Habermas (1989), Horkheimer and Adorno (1991), and Marcuse (1966), all members of
the Frankfurt School who have traced the emergence of a culture industry—the production of
culture/leisure/self as a commodity that is bought and sold in a consumer market. Habermas
emphasized the increasing split between the private and public spheres of society in this process and the increasing deprivatization of the private sphere (family, home, marriage)
(1989:151). Horkheimer and Adorno focused on the manipulation of the consumer, who is

In its perpetual frustration, the quest to recreate and confirm oneself is Manayana's story in the cartoon "Just a Man." This is a man who wants, more than anything, recognition, but it is denied him on all fronts: by a wife and daughter who think of him only in terms of a pension, and by a company and fellow workers who view his utility and worth as already ended. His employers identify Manayana, the archetypical *sarariiman,* by the work he has done and the wage this work has earned. But reduced to this one identity, itself conditional and evanescent, Manayana feels that he is only a partial man—a fragment of a being that ought to be whole.

Up to this point in the narrative the only frame in which Manayana looks pleased is the one that shows him being served tea in his office by the woman of his dreams, Miss Okawa. This simple act of servicing, performed by a young and subordinate female, reassures Manayana. It is at this juncture that, realizing his alienation, he seeks a corrective. He will purchase reassurance and self-confirmation (*jikokenjiyoku* in Yoda's [1981] term) in order to receive recognition as someone more than, or other than, a worker with earnings. He wants to be "loved," as he puts it, but of the two women he pays to make him feel important, the first performs a sex act on him in a booth in front of others (for money) and the second wants endless quantities of food (purchased with money) before she'll proceed to sex.[7] What the man hoped money would purchase and disguise (his own commodification as a thing) is only magnified and reproduced.

---

promised self-realization and escape by commodified leisure but is perpetually denied both. They conclude that "the paradise offered by the culture industry is the same old drudgery. Both escape and elopement are predesigned to lead back to the starting point. Pleasure promotes the resignation which it ought to help forget" (1991:142). In opposition, Marcuse (1966) argued that the form sexual pleasure takes in an economy of alienated labor is one of alienation as well. By deferring satisfaction, a sexuality of repression ensures that the performance level of workers remains high. Sex is produced in a form that sustains work relations and can therefore only change, Marcuse emphasized, when the economy changes as well.

Haug (1986) addressed these issues from the perspective of the mechanics of the commodity form in late capitalism. Inherent in any commodity is a contradiction between its use value (what it can do) and its exchange value (what it can be exchanged for) which becomes progressively more pronounced as capitalism develops. At later stages, profits depend on producing commodities with so little use value that their faddishness and utility quickly wear out. Emphasis is thus increasingly placed, Haug argued, on a product's image, which advertisers construct to be as desirable as possible. For this role of projecting a desire at the level of image, sexuality is borrowed and itself becomes transformed into a commodity (with an increasingly emptied content).

7. Haug writes similarly of the commodification of sexual pleasure where consumers are driven to purchase sexualized images to fill in the gaps in their everyday lives: "An innumerable series of images are forced upon the individual, like mirrors, seemingly empathetic and totally

Here is one of the main principles and contradictions of the hostess club as well: customers pay money to be reconfirmed in some other way than as salaried workers and breadwinners but can receive this service only if they pay money. There is another part to this operation, however, which both cartoon *sarariiman* I've discussed in this chapter failed to confirm: performance. Men want to appear "functional"; the failed penis, the penis that doesn't stand up and therefore cannot stand for a man who has power, is a fate men fear. It is also a fate hostesses are trained to cushion the man against. Not only do hostesses build the men up by flattering them, agreeing with everything they say, restraining themselves from countering even a stupid or insulting remark; they rarely allude to a man's penis except in extremely flattering, hyperbolic terms.

Claims of penises so long they could be used for jumping rope were often made by customers at Bijo. Like other men's boasts about their bodies—one customer told me about having to cover up his groin when entering the public baths because the size of his penis would embarrass the other men—these fantasize an anatomy that is superendowed. Yet hostesses tend to keep silent about the bodies under men's clothes. At Bijo they often discussed or fingered wearing apparel—shoes, ties, handkerchiefs, suits, shirts, socks—and offered comments on the estimated cost of each article, but they encouraged the male preference for restricting all discussion of bodies to those of women. Women were figuratively stripped of their clothes to allow discussion of the bodies under them; men were not. Their penises, in Lacan's words, could remain phalluses, symbols of and for male power that were not dependent on nor weakened by actual penile size.

That Japanese males are often worried about the size of their penises was revealed to me by Wagatsuma Takeshi (the brother of the anthropologist Wagatsuma Hiroshi, much cited in this book), a gynecologist who runs one of the only fertility clinics in Japan. Boys often come to his office, usually brought by mothers who fear that their sons' penises are abnormally small. Wagatsuma has been so deluged by such queries that he shows the boys—who are mostly age fourteen to nineteen—a chart with "average" penile size charted by year of growth. When I interviewed him in 1981, he had never been confronted by a shockingly small penis, but he found the fear and concern (fed, as he pointed out, by mothers) to be culturally significant.

---

credible, which bring their secrets to the surface and display them there. In these images, people are continually shown the unfulfilled aspects of their existence. The illusion ingratiates itself, promising satisfaction: it reads desires in one's eyes, and brings them to the surface of the commodity" (1986:52).

As adults, sarariiman can have their insecurities about their penises assuaged by professional hostesses. These women will build up the male ego in other terms and won't judge a man's performance—singing, telling a joke, recounting a past adventure—as anything but superlative. And if sex should perchance take place, their job is partly to support, encourage, and praise a man no matter how he performs. It is because of this service that Narabayashi's patients who suffer impotence with a wife can be sexually functional with a prostitute.

The contradiction is always there, though. To assure his recognition as a powerful and competent male, he must pay a female to perform this service. Take away the female, the service, and the money to pay for both, however, and the male is deprived of his maleness. It is not surprising, then, that the research of such scholars as Yuzawa Yasuhiro shows that the sarariiman at the end of his working career is often a weakened and isolated individual. Disengaged from the company where he may well have spent most, even all, of his working years and which has encouraged him to establish an existence separate from his wife and family members, the man, aged fifty-five to sixty-five, is very much alone.[8]

Women who have endured affairs and long absences, with little companionship from their husbands, have often learned how to live and manage on their own. With children raised and money perhaps saved, they are less dependent on husbands than husbands are on them. A man at the age of retirement, by contrast, has been taken care of for long years by the company to which he's been attached, by women in the nightlife who have coddled and flattered him at night, and by a wife who has raised the children and managed the home largely by herself. For this he has obviously paid the price of his labor, but once he is no longer working and making the money to exchange for and justify these various dependencies, he is in a weakened and socially vulnerable position.[9] Manayana, in the cartoon "Just a Man," is one month away from this situation. Impotence for him is a prefiguring: a manhood that in its most manly part can only function now to eliminate wastes. But the case of Yamada Ichiro in Special Course Sararii-

---

8. Yuzawa related the results of his research to me personally.

9. Lifetime employment, named as if it were for life, actually stops about ten years before men are willing to retire. Retirement, that is, is usually mandatory at about age fifty-five. The man receives a hefty retirement package but then must find some other kind of employment for about ten years, when retirement becomes more feasible financially. Sometimes men remain in the same company at a lower status; sometimes they must find employment elsewhere. Whatever course they pursue, this period of time is considered to be one of the most stressful for adult males.

man is even more unsettling. It is as a young worker with money to spare that his male potency vanishes. The stack of cash, a sign of his years devoted to work, becomes symbolically worthless when it won't help him satisfy his sexual needs. The money is shown to be only money. And the man, after years of hard work, is shown to be not even a man.

The Hostess Club and Corporate Masculinity

These two cartoons exaggerate, of course. Corporations that use hostess clubs intend the practice to keep workers content, not provoked into such self-examination about the meaning of work, the money earned, and the sacrifices made in terms of personal life. The purpose, quite simply, is to make workers feel good in a manner that is productive for the company— to encourage workers to remain with the company and to work hard.

The corporations view nighttime recreation first as a perk of the job—a way to reward diligent workers and to maintain their diligence, and, second, as a means to make workers relate positively to the company by bonding them with fellow workers and dissolving any interpersonal on-the-job frustrations and tensions that may be simmering. Both management and workers recognize that company-paid nights at hostess clubs have the double objective of benefiting the *sarariiman* and benefiting the corporation. The fact that a company's objective is not only double in the above sense, but, in fact, *to double*—doubling the worker and corporation together as a unit and merging their identities, subjectivities, and interests—is also more or less known and accepted. Japanese theorists such as Aida Yuji and Minami Hiroshi have referred to this intention as a social fact; Japanese merge their personal and public identities together easily (Aida 1972:67) and think of themselves as workers twenty-four hours a day (Minami 1978:206). But what these scholars regard as behavior innate and traditional in the culture is being actively and ideologically produced to benefit very modern structures of business and economics. And the levels at which the process works, or doesn't work, are not all as consciously recognized or explicitly discussed as that of bringing worker and corporation closer together. I will discuss six of these levels.

First, by the practice of sending workers into clubs at night, corporations literally extend the working day and the workplace into another place. Of course, the meaning of nighttime fun shifts back and forth from an objective designed as "play" (*asobi*) to one designed as "work," and it is by keeping the "play" objective alive that an extension of work can be accomplished.

Second, not only can a worker be kept at his desk late by a promise to take him out for drinks even later, but by this practice the meaning of work, for the worker, is expanded, broadened, and made difficult to pin down. Work now incorporates a realm of pleasure, social relaxation, personal fun, even sexuality. It extends to activities paid for by the company, pursued with one's coworkers, and performed in a public realm which, unlike the private realm of home, family, and wife, is the domain where one also works. Increasingly, work and the dimensions of friendship, play, and relaxation into which it is expanded become familiar. This is where a man spends most of his time and expresses himself in most of the ways he's allowed. Here he comes to recognize himself and establish his subjectivity.

Third, as the public realm of work and work-related play becomes more familiar, the private realm of family and home becomes more estranged. As a man in his late fifties told me one night at Bijo, the idea of relaxation doesn't jibe with the associations framed by family and home. After long years spent away from his household, he found the hostess club more homelike than his real home.

Of course, if home is kept separate and even alien to a man, he will work harder at his job. Not eager to rush from the office to join his family for dinner at six, he is likely to work longer hours at his job. When a family is not pulling him home, the demands a company can make on his time and energies become greater and are more easily accepted.

Fourth, when used as a corporate-paid location for male workers, hostess clubs imbue work with a gender construction. Serving primarily middle- to upper-ranked *sarariiman* in large corporations, the nightlife ideologizes these activities as appropriate only to males. While female executives may occasionally be entertained in a hostess club, this realm is less accessible to them because its structure of play and service is so heavily oriented toward men. Not only is work expanded into the *mizu shōbai* then, it is also masculinized; work as a full-time career becomes something males do, and the full-time, career, *sarariiman* worker is most suitably and comfortably a male.

Fifth, by maintaining the male nightlife as an adjunct to the male workplace, the *mizu shōbai* feminizes the home. All of the females with whom I discussed the *mizu shōbai* thought of it as masculine. If work required participation in the *mizu shōbai*, work was not meant for a woman—that was the implication. They found their more appropriate "place" to be at home. Such a feminization of home means that female labor at home is also naturalized and encouraged.

If making dinner and taking care of children are a woman's work and responsibility, women are more likely to manage a home on their own and less likely to expect a husband to share in these domestic duties. This gendered division of labor is a worldview confirmed by Yuzawa Yasuhiro's research on social roles: Japanese women, he discovered, expect men to bring home a paycheck and little else (1982). Willing to work hard at home, women free men from this duty. Men, so freed, are thus able to work longer at a job.

Sixth, when men are encouraged to seek and express their male desires in the *mizu shōbai*, they are placed in a public realm where the control, management, and commercializing of their desires is possible. To pay a hostess for flirtation and a prostitute for sexual engagement requires money. In order to produce that money, a man must continue to work.

If, by contrast, a man were to be most sexually aroused and engaged by a wife, satisfaction of his sexual urges would cost nothing. No business or industry of sexual servicing could be generated if men preferred going home. Further, men desiring more romance or companionship with a wife might be increasingly willing to leave work earlier and more often, and even to pursue it during allocated vacation time.

By adding nighttime recreation as an extracurricular routine, companies routinize workers in manners that are beneficial and complementary to those that structure *sarariiman* during the day. Workers are oriented away from home and toward a public domain where they learn to construct and express themselves as workers as well as men. Being drawn for more hours into an arena negotiated through money, worker relations, and stylized masculinity fashions an identity more appropriate to the company. The offices and clubs that serve the *sarariiman* become more comfortable and familiar as the home becomes less so; public space feels personal, and domestic space feels alien and strange.

The objective of nightlife recreation sponsored by corporations is ultimately this: to fashion a construction less of work than worker—a worker whose subjectivity is such that work is his prime orientation. Others speak of such extracurricular fraternizing as the "humanization" of work in Japan, the *ningenkankei* or human relations that, as Aida put it, stand as the warm and "true" underside (*ura bunka* = back culture) to a front culture composed of a necessary, but "false," cold structure of ranks and social responsibilities (1972:57–58). Restated, the humanization of work is, most importantly, the humanization of the worker, making worker and a certain definition of "human" synonymous. And the definition of "human" is that of "male"—a male human who, by the constructions of maleness, works hard, doesn't leave the office before his boss, rises in rank, brings a good paycheck home to his family and wife, goes out to drink with men he works with, plays golf on weekends with coworkers and clients, minimizes family vacations and doesn't take all the vacation time allocated him, doesn't spend much time at home or with his children, leaves the management of the family to his wife, and considers himself first and foremost a worker whose commitments are first and foremost to his job.

As in any system of ideology, the intention here is to make a subject not feel subjected. The structure of the group models and molds the person in terms of a self that is acceptable and recognizable. As is often described for work practices in Japan, the alignment and suturing of worker to workplace is highly visible. Most Western researchers, however, fail to note that this coupling of worker and workplace is not a defining characteristic of all workplaces for all workers in Japan. Its operation is most noticeable and consistent for full-time, white-collar male workers in middle- to large-size firms.

A worker's attachment to work is meant to be cemented, (over)determined, and symbolized—making it not only lifelong but contiguous with other parts of a man's life. A *sarariiman* may find that his neighbors, golf mates, Saturday baseball team players, drinking buddies, matchmaker for marriage, wedding guests, coconspirators in sexual escapades, and counselors for marital problems are basically drawn from the same group of coworkers. As John Nathan says in a movie about the commercialization of Kentucky Fried Chicken in Japan (*The Colonel Goes to Japan*), Japanese workers conceptualize their attachment to work in terms not so much of working for a company as belonging to it.

This sense of belongingness is structured by another work pattern, that of job rotation. Specific duties, work tasks, and even company or branch assignments are rotated so as to make workers less specialized. Trained to have general skills and value to the company, workers are no longer identified by a specific occupation or craft; the "bodyframe specialist" of old has been replaced with a "worker for Toyota."

Marx believed job rotation to be less alienating than the traditional specialized structure of work, which becomes enslaving in its exclusivity. If, by contrast, workers can do many kinds of work, no one task limits the manner in which workers identify and express themselves. The ideal, as Marx put it, is to be able to hunt, fish, herd sheep, and criticize without being either constrained by one of these activities or labeled as exclusively a hunter, fisherman, shepherd, or critic. If we labor variously, our work experience is extended and our identity is expanded to being more "human being" than worker of a single narrow specialization (1978:160).

Despite the logic of this argument and others used to prove that Japanese workers feel more valued and less alienated in their work situations than do workers in other industrialized nations, the role of the workplace in formulating, demanding, and managing the attachments workers must make to their company constrains the worker in other ways. As I've already described, those workers most privileged and successful in landing *sarariiman* positions in large corporations are generally bound for more years and in more ways than other categories of workers in other places of work. Possibly liberated from a lifetime at only one task and granted the security of a lifetime job (which makes being fired unlikely, no matter how one performs, at least until age fifty-five), a *sarariiman* receives these benefits only by agreeing to remain working at one company. And this attachment to one company imposes its own forms of homogenization. Those who stay are conditioned to be like-minded subjects. Jobs, tasks, and routines may, to some extent, be individualized; but attachment to company collectivizes other forms of behavior as well as identity.

I believe this subjectivization to be the main agenda of the *mizu shōbai* as used by major corporations. The *mizu shōbai* is not for or about sex; companies are not paying for their workers to go out and find sexual partners. Rather, they are paying for their workers to be and become men with a particular construct and utility—the type of men who will make good and committed workers. For this, a certain kind of sexuality is useful, a sexuality of play that services men, bolsters the male ego, and makes them feel confident and assured. This play, formulated as heterosexual, keeps men together in a work-related context, in relationships that are work-based, and in a public and institutionalized setting that shares these frames with work far more than with home. Men are being treated similarly, in ways that develop a manhood that is uniform and can be shared. Thus, though hostess clubs are sexually charged, the rituals of hostess club sexuality are, as a practice that is supported and endorsed by corporations, much more about gender than they are about sex.

Although I would argue that the agenda of Japanese businesses is to use nighttime recreation as a means of homogenizing male workers, this is not to say that the system necessarily works this way for all workers all the time. Though hostess bars may be manipulative and coercive, they are rarely considered oppressive. Some of the men I spoke to found the routine tedious, but many more said that it was a welcome opportunity for relaxation and fun. Of course, as the manager of Bijo put it, using the hostess club for relaxation and fun becomes a matter of routine at an early age for many *sarariiman*. This is what is familiar and known, what he called "the *sarariiman's* bad habit" (*warui kuse*). As a union organizer was quoted as saying in *Hikisakareta Sei* (*Gendai no Me* 1980), carousing in bars and clubs with paid-for women is what powerful men do in Japan.

From what I understand, however, there is often more to it than simple relaxation. Some men *do* arrange sexual encounters with hostesses for later in the evening. Some men also manipulate the system for pleasures that are more personal than corporate. Whenever he wanted to go golfing or to visit a fancy hostess club, one client of an informant would simply call and demand that his "client" status be activated. Others, Bijo's manager told me, alter their bills and claim to be entertaining on business when in fact they are out with friends. The *Gendai no Me* authors also record instances of men using *kōsaihi* (company funds) to visit soaplands; one famous brothel, they report, has fancy cars hired by companies lined up outside every night. These bills too are laundered and altered (1980:165).

More common, however, is the use of a hostess club and a hostess simply to make a man feel good—to express himself before an audience he may not be guaranteed anywhere else. Men talk, usually in snatches interrupted by other speakers, conversations, and activities (like singing) at the table, but they talk, and the talk is sometimes of themselves. They speak of themselves through stories: memories of childhood ambitions, accounts of past adventures, descriptions of recent trips, facts from hobbies like history or linguistics or stamp collecting, jokes that have been perfected, and tales of sexual performances or romances. In this sense, Dorinne Kondo (1990) is right when she argues that there is not just one subjectivity of and for Japanese but multiple subjectivities. Japanese craft who they are, she says, and their craftings take place in different social settings and with different constructions of the self.

Where I disagree, however, with Kondo's portrayal of multicentered postmodern Japan is that not all the subjectivities Japanese craft are equally encouraged or rewarded. As the Comaroffs (1990) argue about postmodernists who speak of the multiplicity of stories that can be told about people, history, culture, and society, not all stories are similarly valued. Men, even *sarariiman* at big companies, represent themselves in ways that are distinct and that distinguish them from the man sitting next to them. This is more pleasurable for some men than for others, and as with one customer in particular at Bijo—a man in his late forties with a limp, who taught company accounting and came to Bijo on his own and with his own money—it may be his sole reason for coming. He came to speak about himself to women who would listen.[10] I assumed that he was not married; he told me he worked very hard all the time. Bijo was his only diversion, and for this chance to create and recreate himself he probably spent most of the money he earned. In paying the female to service him as a male, however, this customer was no different than any other. He could express himself personally, but the personal expression was a commodity he bought with his labor as a worker and a male.

Of all subjectivities that can be crafted in a hostess club—*sukebei*, joker, womanizer, singer, stamp collector, linguistic authority—there is one that is preeminently staged: that of being a male who can pay a female to service him. This is the subjectivity institutionalized by the *settai* practice and institutionally supported by big business in Japan (and until the 1982 tax revisions, by the government). Thus, the explanation for why men drink with women in bars and clubs on company expense cannot be found in factors of nature or even culture (as these explanations are most commonly placed in Japan). It is not mere male biology, the mothering instincts of a female, or a long tradition of a male demimonde that alone causes such gendered patterns of behavior. Rather, mothers who stay at home with children and men who stay at work in clubs, away from home, are rewarded in these patterns by major Japanese institutions.[11]

On the surface, men may seem to have gotten the better of the deal. But, as I often wondered, who will they talk to and who will pour their drinks when the money for hostess clubs dries up? As the days of work and nights in the *mizu shōbai* end, the men will go home. But home has been managed by a woman who has controlled it as her own space for a long time. For this moment, the long years of having one's ego stroked by young hostesses who get paid for that service is hardly the best preparation. And after the decades he has spent almost entirely in the company of other men, the *sarariiman*, on his retirement, may be faced with the possibility of a dyadic, long-term heterosexual relationship for, in some sense, the first time.

10. Called *sensei* as an appellation of respect because he was a teacher, this man would come into Bijo at least once a week, sit with one hostess, and talk about himself. Often assigned to be his partner, I learned that "*sensei*" was a very passive conversationalist, responding to questions about himself but never asking a question in return. Talking to him was hard work, but he obviously enjoyed his discussions of religion, childhood days, and travel.

11. Women are encouraged and rewarded for good mothering, particularly by the institution of education. If a child passes entrance examinations into a prestigious high school or university, for example, the mother will be praised as much as the child.

References

Aida, Yuji. 1972. *Nihonjin no Ishiki Kōzō* (The Structure of Japanese Consciousness). Tokyo: *Kodansha Gendaishinsho*.

Allison, Anne. 1991. Japanese Mothers and *Obentōs*: The Lunch-Box as Ideological State Apparatus. *Anthropological Quarterly* 64(4): 195–208.

Althusser, Louis. 1969. *For Marx*. Ben Brewster, trans. London: Verso.

——. 1971. Ideology and Ideological State Apparatuses. In *Lenin and Philosophy and Other Essays*. New York: Monthly Review Press.

Amanuma, Kaoru. 1987. *"Ganbari" no Kōzō* (The Structure of "Ganbari"). Tokyo: *Kikkawa Kōbunkan*.

Asahi Journal. 1992. *Kodomo o Umanai Onnatachi* (Women Who Don't Bear Children), 17 January, 22–26.

Barthes, Roland. [1957] 1972. *Mythologies*. Annette Lavers, trans. New York: Noonday Press.

——. 1982. *Empire of Signs*. Richard Howard, trans. New York: Hill and Wang.

Benedict, Ruth. 1946. *The Chrysanthemum and the Sword*. Boston: Houghton Mifflin.

Bernstein, Gail Lee. 1983. *Haruko's World: A Japanese Farm Woman and Her Community*. Stanford: Stanford University Press.

Bestor, Theodore C. 1989. *Neighborhood Tokyo*. Stanford: Stanford University Press.

Buckley, Sandra. 1991. "Penguin in Bondage": A Graphic Tale of Japanese Comic Books. In *Technoculture*, ed. Constance Penley and Andrew Ross. Minneapolis: University of Minnesota Press.

Buruma, Ian. 1984. *Behind the Mask: On Sexual Demons, Sacred Mothers, Transvestites, Gangsters, and Other Japanese Cultural Heroes*. New York: Pantheon Books.

Butler, Judith. 1990. *Gender Trouble: Feminism and the Subversion of Identity*. New York: Routledge.

Clark, Rodney. 1988. Industrial Groups. In *Inside the Japanese System: Readings on Contemporary Society and Political Economy*. Stanford: Stanford University Press.

Clifford, James, and George E. Marcus, eds. 1986. *Writing Culture: The Poetics and Politics of Ethnography*. Berkeley: University of California Press.

Comaroff, Jean, and John L. Comaroff. 1991. *Of Revelation and Revolution: Christianity, Colonialism, and Consciousness in South Africa*. Vol. 1. Chicago: University of Chicago Press.

Coward, Rosalind. 1983. *Patriarchal Precedents: Sexuality and Social Relations*. London: Routledge and Kegan Paul.

Coward, Rosalind, and John Ellis. 1977. *Language and Materialism: Developments in Semiology and the Theory of the Subject*. Boston: Routledge and Kegan Paul.

Creighton, Millie. 1992. The *Depāto:* Merchandising the West while Selling Japaneseness. In *Re-Made In Japan: Everyday Life and Consumer Taste in a Changing Society,* ed. Joseph Tobin. New Haven: Yale University Press.

Dalby, Liza Critchfield. 1985. *Geisha.* New York: Vintage Books.

Doi, Takeo. 1973. *The Anatomy of Dependence: The Key Analysis of Japanese Behavior.* John Bester, trans. Tokyo: Kodansha International.

Dore, Ronald P. 1973. *British Factory, Japanese Factory: The Origins of National Diversity in Industrial Relations.* Berkeley: University of California Press.

Dworkin, Andrea. 1981. *Pornography: Men Possessing Women.* New York: Putnam.

Embree, John F. 1939. *Suye Mura: A Japanese Village.* Chicago: University of Chicago Press.

Freud, Sigmund. [1925] 1962. *Three Essays on the Theory of Sexuality.* James Strachey, trans. New York: Avon Books.

———. 1965. *The Interpretation of Dreams.* James Strachey, trans. New York: Avon Books.

Foucault, Michel. [1976] 1980. *The History of Sexuality,* Vol. 1: *An Introduction.* Robert Hurley, trans. New York: Vintage Books.

Fujimura-Fanselow, Kumiko. 1985. Women's Participation in Higher Education in Japan. *Comparative Education Review* 29.

Fujita, Mariko. 1989. "It's All Mother's Fault": Childcare and the Socialization of Working Mothers in Japan. *Journal of Japanese Studies* 15(1): 67–91.

Fukuda, Yoshiya. 1982. *Zadankai* (Roundtable). *Juristo* 25: 8–26.

Gendai no Me. 1980. *Hikisakareta Sei* (Sex Which Has Been Torn to Pieces). Tokyo: Gendai Hyōronsha.

Habermas, Jürgen. 1989. *The Structural Transformation of the Public Sphere: An Inquiry into a Category of Bourgeois Society.* Thomas Burger, trans. Cambridge: MIT Press.

Hall, Stuart, Dorothy Hobson, Andrew Lowe, and Paul Willis, eds. 1980. *Culture, Media, Language: Working Papers in Cultural Studies, 1972–79.* London: Unwin Hyman.

Harvey, David. 1989. *The Condition of Postmodernity: An Enquiry into the Origins of Cultural Change.* Cambridge, Mass.: Basil Blackwell Press.

Haug, Wolfgang Fritz. [1983] 1986. *Critique of Commodity Aesthetics: Appearance, Sexuality and Advertising in Capitalist Society.* Robert Bock, trans. Minneapolis: University of Minnesota Press.

Heibonsha Karucha—Today. 1980. No. 10. *Asobu* (play), ed. Tomioka Taketo.

Hegel, Georg Wilhelm Friedrich. [1977] 1980. *Phenomenology of Spirit.* A. V. Miller, trans. Oxford: Oxford University Press.

Hendry, Joy. 1987. *Understanding Japanese Society.* London: Croom Helm.

Horio, Teruhisa. 1988. *Educational Thought and Ideology in Modern Japan: State Authority and Intellectual Freedom.* Steven Platzer, trans. Tokyo: University of Tokyo Press.

Horkheimer, Max, and Theodor W. Adorno. [1944] 1991. *Dialectic of Enlightenment.* John Cumming, trans. New York: Continuum.

Imamura, Anne E. 1987. *Urban Japanese Housewives: At Home and in the Community.* Honolulu: University of Hawaii Press.

Ishida, Eiichiro. 1974. *A Study of Origins and Characters.* Honolulu: University of Hawaii Press.

Ishikawa, Hiroyoshi. 1982. *Po-nogurafi* (Pornography). *Juristo* 25: 228–33.

Kakinuma, Chisato. 1992. *Nanimo Kangaenai Hitobito* (People Who Don't Think about Anything). In *Bessatsu Takarajima* no. 107 *Sekkusu toiu Oshigoto* (Sex Work).

Kano, Mikiyo. 1985. *Shufu towa Nanika* (What Is a Housewife?) *Juristo* 39: 184–89.

Kawai, Hayao. 1988. *The Japanese Psyche: Major Motifs in the Fairy Tales of Japan.* Dallas, Texas: Spring Publications.

Kobayashi, Naoki. 1970. *Zadankai* (Roundtable). *Juristo Zōkan: Sei: Shisō, Seido, Hō* (Sex: Thought, System, Law), no. 1372 (December): 19–42.

Kondo, Dorinne. 1990. *Crafting Selves: Power, Gender, Discourses of Identity in a Japanese Workplace.* Chicago: University of Chicago Press.

Kusamori, Shinichi. 1981. *Mizu no Ranpi* (The Dissipation of Water). *Juristo* 25: 234–41.

Kyutoku, Shigemori. 1981. *Bogenbyō* (Disease Rooted in Motherhood). Tokyo: Sanma Kushuppan.

Lacan, Jacques. [1966] 1977. The Mirror Stage as a Formative of the Function of the I. In *Ecrits: A Selection.* Alan Sheridan, trans. New York: Norton.

Lewis, Catherine C. 1989. From Indulgence to Internalization: Social Control in the Early School Years. *Journal of Japanese Studies* 15(1): 93–123.

Lukács, Georg. [1968] 1971. *History of Class Consciousness: Studies in Marxist Debates.* Rodney Livingstone, trans., Cambridge: MIT Press.

Marcuse, Herbert. [1955] 1966. *Eros and Civilization: A Philosophical Inquiry into Freud.* Boston: Beacon Press.

Marx, Karl. [1844] 1978. *Economic and Philosophic Manuscripts of 1844.* In *The Marx-Engels Reader,* ed. Robert Tucker. New York: Norton.

Marx, Karl, and Frederick Engels. [1947] 1978. *Economic and Philosophic Manuscripts,* ed. C. J. Arthur. New York: International Publishers.

Metz, Christian. 1982. *The Imaginary Signifier: Psychoanalysis and the Cinema.* Bloomington: Indiana University Press.

Miller, Daniel. 1987. *Material Culture and Mass Consumption.* Oxford: Basil Blackwell.

Minami, Hiroshi. [1953] 1978. *Nihonjin no Shinri* (The Psychology of the Japanese). Tokyo: *Iwanami Shincho.*

Mizuno, Rieh. 1982. *Zadankai* (Roundtable). *Onna no Me de Mita Otoko no Sekushuariti* (Women Look at Male Sexuality). In *JASE Sex Education Today.* Tokyo: Nihon Seikyōiku Kyōkai.

Morimoto, Kazuo. 1970. *Zadankai* (Roundtable). *Juristo Zōkan* no. 1372 (December): 19–42.

Morley, John David. 1985. *Pictures from the Water Trade: Adventures of a Westerner in Japan.* New York: Harper and Row.

Mouer, Ross, and Yoshio Sugimoto. 1986. *Images of Japanese Society: A Study in the Social Construction of Reality.* London: Routledge and Kegan Paul.

Nada, Inada. 1992. *Shigoto no Naka ni Kumikomareta Yoka Kyūjitsu no "Gorone futei" Minaosu toki* (The time I looked back on the "irregular napping" of weekends: the construction of time off within work). *Asahi Shimbum,* 19 August, p. 24.

Nakane, Chie. 1970. *Japanese Society.* Berkeley: University of California Press.

Narabayashi, Yoshi. 1982. *Zadankai* (Roundtable). *Juristo* 25: 8–26.

Oshima, Nagisa. 1970. *Zadankai* (Roundtable). *Juristo* no. 1372 (December): 19–42.

Peak, Lois. 1989. Learning to Become Part of the Group: The Japanese Child's Transition to Preschool Life. *Journal of Japanese Studies* 15(1): 93–123.

Richie, Donald. 1987. *A Lateral View: Essays on Contemporary Japan.* Tokyo: The Japan Times, Ltd.

Riviere, Joan. 1986. Womanliness as a Masquerade. In *Formations of Fantasy,* ed. Victor Burgin, James Donald, and Cora Kaplan. London: Methuen.

Robertson, Jennifer. 1991. Theatrical Resistance, Theatres of Restraint: The Takarazuka Revue and the "State Theatre" Movement in Japan. *Anthropological Quarterly* 64(1): 165–77.

———. 1992. Doing and Undoing "Female" and "Male" in Japan: The Takarazuka Revue. In *Japanese Social Organization,* ed. Takie Sugiyama Lebra. Honolulu: University of Hawaii Press.

Rohlen, Thomas P. 1974. *For Harmony and Strength: Japanese White-Collar Organization in Anthropological Perspective.* Berkeley: University of California Press.

———. 1983. *Japan's High Schools.* Berkeley: University of California Press.

———. 1989. Order in Japanese Society: Attachment, Authority, and Routine. *Journal of Japanese Studies* 15(1): 5–40.

Rosenberger, Nancy. 1991. Gender and the Japanese State: Pension Benefits Creating Difference. In *Anthropological Quarterly* 64(1): 178–93.

———. 1992. Images of the West: Home Style in Japanese Magazines. In *Re-Made in Japan: Everyday Life and Consumer Taste in a Changing Society,* ed. Joseph Tobin. New Haven: Yale University Press.

Sakaiya, Taichi. 1991. Japan's Scandalous Expense Accounts. *Sankei Shinbun,* 7 October.

Sanday, Peggy Reeves. 1990. *Fraternity Gang Rape: Sex, Brotherhood, and Privilege on Campus.* New York: New York University Press.

Sano, Shinichi. 1981. *Sei no Ōkoku* (Empire of Sex). Tokyo: *Bungeishunju.*

Sano, Yoko. 1991. Freud to Kleenix (Freud and Kleenix). In *Hon no Zasshi* 94 (April): 94–95.

Sato, Ikuya. 1991. *Kamikaze Biker: Parody and Anomy in Affluent Japan.* Chicago: University of Chicago Press.

Sato, Tadao. 1981. *Teizoku Bunka towa Nanika?* (What is Low Culture?) *Bessatsu Takarajima: Manga Ronsō* no. 13: 62–77.

Schneider, David. [1968] 1980. *American Kinship: A Cultural Account.* Chicago: University of Chicago Press.

Schodt, Frederick L. 1986. *Manga! Manga! The World of Japanese Comics.* New York: Harper and Row.

Shoji, Sadao. 1980. *Sarariiman Senkyō* (Special Course *Sarariiman*). Tokyo: *Rippu Manga Bungo.*

Silverberg, Miriam. 1991. The Modern Girl as Militant. In *Recreating Japanese Women, 1600–1945,* ed. Gail Bernstein. Berkeley: University of California Press.

———. 1992. Constructing the Japanese Ethnography of Modernity. In *Journal of Asian Studies* 51(1): 30–54.

Silverman, Kaja. 1992. *Male Subjectivity at the Margins.* New York: Routledge.

Smith, Robert. 1982. *The Women of Suye Mura.* Chicago: University of Chicago Press.

Tabe, Shiro. 1986. *Kigyō kōsaihi to Zeijitsumu Jōhō* (Practical Information about Taxes and Enterprise Company Expense). Tokyo: *Zeimu Keirikyōkai.*

Tada, Michitaro. 1974. *Asobi to Nihonjin* (Play and the Japanese). Tokyo: *Chikuki sōsho.*

Takei, S., and K. Teraoka. 1985. *Tokei* (Time). Tokyo: *Kaiseisha.*

Tamanoi, Mariko. 1991. Songs as Weapons: The Culture and History of Komori (Nursemaids). In *Journal of Asian Studies* 50(4): 793–817.

Tatsumi, Yoshihiro. 1987. *"Good-Bye" and Other Stories,* trans. David Rosenthal. New York: Catalan Communications.

Tobin, Joseph J., David Y. H. Wu, and Dana H. Davidson. 1989. *Preschool in Three Cultures.* New Haven: Yale University Press.

Tomioka, Takeko, ed. 1980. *Asobu* (Play). Tokyo: *Heibonsha Karucha—Today,* no. 10.

Tsuda, Masumi. 1987. *Shinsedai Sarariiman no Seikatsu to Iken* (The Lives and Opinions of Modern Generation *Sarariiman*). Tokyo: *Tōkyō keizai shinpo.*

Vogel, Ezra F. 1963. *Japan's New Middle Class.* Berkeley: University of California Press.

Wagatsuma, Hiroshi. 1982. *Zadankai* (Roundtable). *Juristo* 25: 8–26. *Zōkan SōgōTokushu* (*extra edition, collective issue*): *Ningen no Sei: Kōdō, Bunka, Shakai* (Human Sexuality: Behavior, Culture, Society).

Williams, Linda. 1989. *Hard Core: Power, Pleasure, and the Frenzy of the Visible.* Berkeley: University of California Press.

Yamamura, Yoshiaki. 1971. *Nihonjin to Haha. Bunka toshite no Haha Kannen ni Tsuite no Kenkyū* (The Japanese and Mother: Research on the Conceptualization of Mother as Culture). Tokyo: *Tōyō Shuppansha.*

Yoda, Akira. 1981. *Otoko ni Totte Onna towa Nanika?* (What Are Women to Men?) Tokyo: *Nihon Jitsugyō Shuppan.*

Yuzawa, Yasuhiko. 1982. *Katei ni okeru Otto no Yakuwari* (The Role of the Husband in the Family). In *Gendai Seikyōiku Kenkyū* (Sex Education Today). Tokyo: *Nihon Seikyōiku Kyōkai-Henshū.*

Zizek, Slavoj. 1989. *The Sublime Object of Ideology.* London: Verso.

Index

Aida, Yuji, 23, 79–80, 88–90, 114–116
alibi, 81, 166–167
amae. *See* hierarchy
approval, 118
Asanuma, Kaoru, 119–120
asobi. *See* play

ba. *See* group orientation
baby-sitting, 125 n. 2
back culture, 87–90, 114–116; definition of,
    88; "outlaw" conception of, 114–115
Barthes, Roland, 13, 81, 100 n. 8, 166–167
Bijo: Mama of, 38–39; membership in,
    42–44; routines of, 42–56; space of,
    36–41; spatial/visual appeal of, 37–41;
    waiters of, 39, 44–45
breasts. *See* breast talk; conversation; "pat,
    the"; symbolism
breast talk, 47–49; conventions of, 48, 180;
    hostesses involved in, 62
bureiko, 35
Buruma, Ian, 170–171, 190
business cards, 87

Comaroff, Jean and John, 14, 100 n. 8,
    203
comic strips, 188–193, 195; erotic, 189–193
commodity form, 17; pleasure as, 194–196
    nn. 6–7; sex as, 137
communitas, 35
company expense. *See kōsaihi*
conversation, 46–54; breast talk in, 47–49;
    honne in, 48; insults, jokes, and pretense
    of, 51–54; *tatemae* in, 48
corporate tax laws, 9, 126 n. 3
Coward, Rosalind, 180–181 n. 4
cultural essentialism, 80; example of, 123;
    Japaneseness in, 79–83

Doi, Takeo, 84, 90
drinking, 45–46; alcoholism from, 46 n. 3;
    as language, 100–101; drunkenness
    from, 45–46
Durkheim, Emile, 153, 156

economic growth, 9
economic slump, 9
English language, 51
ero manga. *See* comic strips, erotic
estranged labor, 193
examinations, 92–94; role of mother in,
    111–112

fantasy, 22
fetish, 21
flirtation, 60
Frankfurt School, 23, 194 n. 6. *See also*
    Haug, Wolfgang; Lukács, Georg
front culture, 87–90, 114–116; definition of,
    88
functionalistic explanation, 15 n. 13

ganbaru, 119–120
gang rape, 168
gender: division of labor, 91–94; education,
    93–94; exclusion from "clubbing,"
    24–25
gossiping, 115–116
group orientation, 84–87; frame as a, 86;
    racial homogeneity as a, 85; verticality as
    a, 86

Haug, Wolfgang, 17, 194–196 nn. 6–7. *See
    also* Frankfurt School
Hegel, Georg, 165
hegemony, 14, 29, 100 n. 8
heritage, 53

211

hostess club
- to make work non work

- Commodity exchange
        role of $

            hostess doesn't owe men
            men don't owe hostess

        hostess reinforces masculinity

        men on men = equality
                         put downs

        men w/ ♀ = superiority
                         physical body

school v home
   tidy   untidy
home v. work